Playing Hopscotch in Heaven

Lectionary Liturgies
for
RCL Year A

Thom M. Shuman

Bearers of Hope and Wonder

ISBN: 1490970827
ISBN-13: 978-1490970820

DEDICATION

For over 25 years I have been fortunate
enough to share my life and faith
with colleagues-in-ministry
on a regular basis at breakfasts and lunches.
This book is dedicated to the members of
the Winchester breakfast gang,
the LPB lunch group,
and the Urban Pastors of Cincinnati Presbytery.

As groups, and as individuals, these folks have
challenged and comforted me,
prodded and praised me,
encouraged me to be faithful and foolish,

and I am forever grateful!

Table of Contents

Additional Liturgies

Since becoming an ordained minister in the Presbyterian Church (U.S.A.) I have been a lectionary preacher. I have chosen to let the appointed texts for each Sunday (from the Revised Common Lectionary) guide me in sermon preparation, hymn selections, and prayers. Some years ago, finding myself dissatisfied with options when it came to worship resources based on the lectionary readings, I began the discipline of writing a liturgy for each Sunday. Like any discipline, it serves as both an incredible challenge, as well as a burden at times. But in taking on this discipline, I have learned to view the texts with fresh eyes, seeking to speak of our God with language and images which might resonate, not just in me, but in the souls of others.

Isaiah 2:1-5; Psalm 122
Romans 13:11-14; Matthew 24:36-44

Call to Worship
We don't always know that time it is,
but according to Jesus, it is time to watch.
We're not always sure what we should wear,
but according to the Spirit, we should wear garments of Light.
We're not always sure what we should do,
but according to God, we should always seek good
for those around us.

Prayer of the Day
Architect of the Kingdom's streets:
you teach us all
we need to know,
    if we will but open our hearts,
    and listen to yours.
You challenge us
to quit working the night shift
in sin's sweat shops,
    and to dance in the Light
        of Advent joy.

Seeker of our Good:
you sneak in
    and steal our lives
    out of death's tight grasp.
You wander the streets
of our world,
    sweeping up our sins,
    casting them into
        the dustbins of our past.

Holy Spirit,
you are as close to us
as the breath in our lungs:
helping us to treat everyone
    with honor and respect;
healing us with serenity
    in these days of stress;
taking us by the hand
    to walk us home
    to the kingdom.

God in Community, Holy in One,
help us to be faithful watchers,
as we pray as Jesus has taught us, saying,
Our Father . . .

Call to Reconciliation

We don't know when Jesus will return, and we are not to worry about it. But we do know when we do wrong, when we hurt people, when we disappoint God. But God will change our sins into acts of mercy, and our failures into faith. Join me as we pray to our God.

Unison Prayer of Confession

In this season of sales, shopping, and stress, God of Light, we confess how easy it is to slip off your paths. We can become so focused on having good times, we forget to take the time to do good for your people. We slip easily into Santa suits, but find Jesus Christ an uncomfortable fit for our lives. We find ourselves strangely jealous over the gifts others receive, yet have trouble accepting those gifts of peace and serenity you hand out so freely.

Forgive us, Breath of Salvation. By your mercy, we can once again walk the streets of your kingdom, being alert for the signs of your grace and hope in our midst. Teach us your ways of peace and reconciliation, that we may truly live as the disciples of our Lord and Savior, Jesus Christ.

Silence is kept

Assurance of Pardon

This is the good news: you will be swept away in the waters of mercy, salvation carrying you home to God's heart.
Peace, serenity, healing, hope - these gifts, and more, are ours in this Advent season of watching and waiting. Thanks be to God. Amen.

Great Prayer of Thanksgiving

May the Lord of Advent be with you.
And also with you.
People of God, lift up your waiting hearts.
We lift them to the One whose heart longs for us.
People of God, give thanks to the One who draws near to us.
Let us go to God's Table to offer our thanks and praise

It is always good and right
to stand in your house of peace

6

with thanksgiving on our lips, Holy God.
When chaos threatened to rule,
you raised up creation,
    validating it with your Word.
Standing within the gates of Eden,
we were bound firmly together with you,
    your love and grace as close
    as the breath of the Spirit.
If we had known that sin and death
would come to steal us away from you,
    we could have been prepared.
But they swept us away
in the flood of their temptations,
    and we didn't know how to resist.
Your prophets were sent forth
to teach us your ways,
    but we clung to the fading shadows
    of our rebellious lives.
Finally, you sent Jesus to remind us
that it was time to become
your children once again.

Therefore, we come to you,
our songs of thanksgiving
and our prayers for peace
mingling with those of every time and place:

Holy, holy, holy are you, Peace of Jerusalem.
All creation flows towards to you.
Hosanna in the Highest!

Blessed is the One who will teach us to turn
    our weapons into instruments of healing and hope.
Hosanna in the highest!

Holy are you, God who comes to us,
and blessed is Jesus Christ, your Son, our Salvation.
When we seek evil
for those around us,
    he takes the time
    to teach us to do good.
When we went as far away
from you as we could,
    he came to bring redemption
    close to our hearts.

When we did not realize
how sin and death
were coming to rob us
of our relationship with you,
    he knew it was time
    to go to the cross,
        to place our feet back on
        the streets of the kingdom.

As we remember Immanuel coming to us,
we would keep awake, preparing ourselves
to live out that mystery we call faith:

Christ died, walking in God's path;
Christ rose, walking in the light of God;
Christ will return for the sake of the house of God.

In this time of anticipation,
send your Spirit upon the gifts
of the bread and of the cup,
and on those who gather
around the Table of Joy.
Besides this, send your gifts
when we least expect them:
    the gift of peace,
        that we might turn humvees
        into harvesters of reconciliation;
    the gift of hope,
        that we might transform weapons
        into harps and guitars;
    the gift of time,
        that we might be prepared
        to serve all who come to us
            in their brokenness and despair.

Then, when that day and hour come,
and we are gathered with
our sisters and our brothers,
our enemies and our friends,
around the Feast in Heaven,
we will be bound firmly together
for all eternity with you,
walking in your Light,
as we sing forever of
God in Community, Holy in One. Amen.

Second Sunday of Advent
Isaiah 11:1-10; Psalm 72:1-7, 18-19
Romans 15:4-13; Matthew 3:1-12

Call to Worship
We gather in this comfortable place, to prepare for a new day:
a day when the wolf and the lamb will get an apartment together.
So prepare your hearts for the day when peace will rule the earth:
when the leopard and the kid will share a mat at naptime.
Prepare the way, the way where old notions are overturned:
when the cow and bear will have coffee,
their children playing in the backyard.
Get ready! Prepare the way!

Prayer of the Day
God of wonders,
you continually stun us
with your gifts of Advent:
your welcoming heart
    with room for every single person;
your ancient words of hope
    which remain as fresh
    as the breeze through the trees;
your passion for justice,
    so all might be set free.

Root of Jesse,
Branch of righteousness:
you do not judge
    by what your eyes see
    or your ears might hear.
You look at the poor,
    and see your mother and sisters,
you open your heart to the lost,
    and welcome your brothers and father.

Wisdom from on high:
as we stand in silence,
    pour the transforming waters
    of grace and peace over us.
Whisper your Word to us,
    lest we rely on ours too much.
Place the shawl of compassion around our shoulders
    that we might be your servants.

God in Community, Holy in One,
listen to our words and to our hearts,
as we pray as Jesus has taught us,
Our Father . . .

Call to Reconciliation
We, who have stood in the refreshing waters of baptism, often forget our
need to be cleansed. We, who have heard the voice of love, often speak
with anger and meanness to others. God calls us to be wise enough to
change our ways, so let us answer with our confessions, as we pray
together saying,

Unison Prayer of Confession
**We long for you to come to us, Creator of Goodness. But too
often, we do not seem to share your vision of how the world should
be, or we are to live. You dream of resentful enemies sitting down
together, but we feast on bitterness. You would have us sing with
one voice, but we prefer to be soloists. You would have us serve
others, but we sit quietly, expecting you to come and fill our every
need.**

**Forgive us, Approaching God, and help us to turn to welcome
you with open arms. May we prepare for your coming by opening
our hearts to that healing hope and surprising mercy which is ours
in Christ Jesus, our Lord and Savior.**

Silence is kept

Assurance of Pardon
This is God's word of acceptance and affirmation: we are forgiven, we
are loved, we are called to be servants to all creation.
**Forgiveness falls like a gentle shower upon us, sinking deep into
our hearts and souls, so we might be nourished and nurtured as
God's children. Thanks be to God. Amen.**

Great Prayer of Thanksgiving
May the God of Advent wonder be with you.
And also with you.
People of God, lift up your hopeful hearts.
We lift them to the One who fills us with all joy and peace.
Blessed be the One who comes to speak for the poor,
to set free those imprisoned by despair.
**May the glory of the One who welcomes all to this Table
fill our sisters and brothers throughout creation.**

10

God of Wonder:
your Spirit did not rest,
but transformed chaos into creation,
    the mountains crying 'Glory!' with one voice,
    the hills echoing the glad refrain.
You welcomed us into
your garden of peace and hope,
    but we flocked to sin and death,
        those entertainers who seduce us
        with their temptations and tricks.
The prophets were sent
to help us understand our brokenness,
    but we turned our backs
        when they sang of your hopes for us.
And so, you prepared Jesus
to come to us, so we might know
the very nearness of your kingdom.

Therefore, we would join our voices
with those of every time and place,
who sing of your glory:

Blessed be the God of Advent,
who alone showers us with grace!

O come, people of God,
let us walk in the Hope
which paves the paths to the kingdom!

Holy are you, God of all creation,
and blessed is Jesus Christ, your Child,
who became our servant to save us.
He came,
    so that those who could only speak
    in anger to one another,
        might sing songs of peace at your Table.
He came,
    to shower the living waters of grace
        upon our hope-parched souls.
He came,
    to sweep death from
    the bottoms of our hearts,
so we might dance
in your life forever.

Even now, as we prepare to celebrate
his birth, and ache for his return,
we sing of that mystery we call faith:

**In rejection's stable, Hope was born;
on death's cruel tree, Hope cried out;
in our hearts, we long for Hope to return.**

Come to us in these moments,
God of Advent,
pouring your Spirit
upon the bread and the cup
    that we might be drenched
    by your grace and peace.
Then, when we are filled
with your justice and righteousness,
    send us forth into the wilderness
    of despair and loneliness,
        to bring joy and hope;
        to be servants to the poor;
        to be voices for those silenced by oppression;
        to become a bumper crop of reconciliation
in a world strewn with the stumps
from the violence of war and fear.

Then, when all time has ended,
all pain and hurt is gone,
you will welcome everyone to your Table,
where we can sing 'Glory!' with one voice
to Father, Son, and Holy Spirit,
God in Community, Holy in One. Amen.

Third Sunday of Advent
Isaiah 35:1-10; Luke 1:47-55
James 5:7-10; Matthew 11:2-11

Call to Worship
Be patient! God is coming to us!
**The One who teaches joyous songs to all of creation,
comes to open our ears to life.**
Be strong! God is coming to be with us!
**The One who paves a path to Bethlehem
will walk with us every step of the way.**
Do not fear! Here is your God!
We worship the One who comes to save us.

Prayer of the Day

Now, there is a road
    where the blind will see
    the signposts leading home.
Now, the burning sand of sin
    will become an ice rink
    for your children.
Now, the voiceless
    become the soloists
    in the chorus of hallelujahs.
Now that you have built
a holy way to our hearts,
Advent's Creator,
    we no longer need
    to wander off your paths.

Now, the crippled
    will dance with the stars.
Now, your precious crop
    of justice and reconciliation
    planted in oppression's desert
        will burst forth in glory.
Now, the pockets of the fatcats
    will be turned inside out
    so pocket change can loosen
        the chains of despair and grief.
Now that you have come,
Advent's Grace,
    we no longer need
    to put hope on hold.

Now, those who refuse
to listen to their enemy
    will hear your sweet whispers
    of peace for all.
Now, those we have offended
    will be blessed by
    your healing touch.
Now, those who mutter
about the unfairness of it all,
    will offer all they have
    to the poor.
Now that you are incarnate
in our hearts,
Advent's Joy,

we no longer need
to be afraid.

God in Community, Holy in One,
now, we will call ourselves blessed,
as we pray as Jesus has taught us,
Our Father . . .

Call to Reconciliation

It would be easy to grumble that the world has kidnapped this holy
season, emptying us of hope and joy. But we must admit how often
we fail to tell the true story of Christmas, by how we live our lives. Let us
confess our reluctance to be storytellers, as well as to live out the story,
as we pray to God, saying,

Unison Prayer of Confession

**Ever Present Peace, you came to save us, but that is so hard to
remember in this hectic season. Our impatience for Christmas to
arrive gets in the way of listening to our children singing in their
rooms. We let the blinking lights blind us to your quiet presence in
a noisy world. We get so caught up in the stories of violence, we
cannot hear your voice reminding us not to be afraid.**

**As you poured out your mercy on all who have gone before us,
Gardener of deserts, shower us with grace and forgiveness. Then,
our eyes will be opened to all your wonders, our ears will echo with
the anthems of the angels, and our emptiness will be filled with the
life gifted to us through Jesus Christ, our Lord and Savior.**

Silence is kept

Assurance of Pardon

Dear ones of God, this is the good news: God comes to us to bring the
healing of hope, to put the joy of justice into our hearts.
**We need wait no longer. We will go and tell everyone what we have
seen and heard! Thanks be to God. Amen.**

Great Prayer of Thanksgiving

The God who is coming to us be with you!
And also with you!
Lift your hearts to the One who turns barren deserts into seas of grace.
We lift them to the God who fills our longings for peace and hope.
Beloved of God, let us lift our praise and thanksgiving to our Lord.
We come to God's Table with glad songs of joy on our lips.

In that first moment of all time,
you crafted creation out of chaos,
ever-surprising God.
Beauty blossomed abundantly
    in every corner of your gift,
everlasting joy and goodness
        were the playmates you gave to us
        as we strolled through your Garden.
But we became too nearsighted
to see the grace awaiting us
in your infinite heart.
Hamstrung by arrogance,
    we walked the burning sands of sin,
    limping down that dusty road
        to death's prison.
You sent Isaiah and Miriam,
Hannah and Amos,
to call us home,
    but our ears were stuffed
    with the world's empty promises.
Then, you asked Jesus
to walk the holy way,
leaving glory to be born
in a stable.

Therefore, with those who have been raised,
and those who long for your coming,
we join the choirs of angels
who forever sing of your glory:

**Holy, holy, holy, God who fills the hungry!
All creation sees the glory of the LORD.
Hosanna in the highest!**

**Blessed is the One who comes saying,
'Be strong, do not fear!'**

Holy are you, Hope-full Heart,
and all creation calls your Child,
our Savior, Jesus Christ, blessed.
Listening to you weeping
in the night for your lost children,
he set aside eternity's riches to come:
    to fill the shallows of our souls
    with your grace;

to snatch us away
    from those wild beasts called sin and despair;
to pay the ransom
    for those kidnapped by death.

And so, as we prepare to celebrate his birth,
as we journey once again the holy ways,
seeking to hear and proclaim
his life, death and resurrection,
we whisper of that mystery we call faith:

Christ died, scattering sin from our hearts' imagination;
Christ arose, knocking death off its throne;
Christ will come again, according to the promise
    made to our ancestors.

May the gift of your Spirit,
Advent's Hope and Peace,
be poured out on the simple gifts
of the bread and the cup,
and on those who come
simply to find healing and hope.
And when we have been fed
by your surprising grace
and filled with your peace,
may we go forth to the world,
    where our weak hands
        will become calloused by compassion;
    where we will bend
        our feeble knees, reaching down
            to lift up the fallen;
    where we will become fountains
        of living water for those
            parched by the wilderness
            of their lives.

Then, when sorrow and sighing
have been chased away from us,
and we gather with all generations
around your Table in heaven,
everlasting joy will be our song,
and gracious hope will be our refrain,
as we sing to you through all eternity,
God in Community, Holy in One. Amen.

Fourth Sunday of Advent
Isaiah 7:10-16; Psalm 80:1-7, 17-19
Romans 1:1-7; Matthew 1:18-25

Call to Worship
We gather, for it is time to prepare:
angels are about to burst forth into song,
singing of the peace and hope we need.
We gather, with expectation our guest:
for joy is inviting us to join in the dance
of the shepherds around the night fire.
We gather, eager to begin the celebration:
people, longing to reach Bethlehem;
people, eager to kneel at the manger;
people, ready to cradle the Babe;
people, hoping to be made whole.

Prayer of the Day
If you came to us,
we would not be afraid
    to take grace
    as our life's partner;
we would not fear
    adopting peace and hope
    into our family.
So come to us,
God-who-takes-away-our-fears.

If you came to us,
we would not be afraid
    to serve the broken of the world,
    for that is how
        you bring healing and restoration;
we would not fear
    to choose the good,
    knowing we receive the grace
        to be your beloved disciples.
So come to us,
God-who-is-our-sign.

If you came to us,
we would not be afraid
    to reach to the heavens
        to embrace your dreams;

17

we would not fear
> to journey into the future,
> for there we will find you
> > waiting to welcome us home.

So come to us,
God-who-dwells-with-us.

Come to us,
God in Community, Holy in One,
as we pray as you have taught us, saying,
Our Father . . .

Call to Reconciliation

In our brokenness, we will find no healing until we turn to the Peace who comes to us. In our emptiness, we will find no hope until we turn to the Grace who comes to feed us with forgiveness. Let us speak those words which are so hard to say, so we may hear the whispers of God's mercy.

Unison Prayer of Confession

With the songs of the angels in our ears, we cannot hear the way we speak words of hurt and anger to others; looking for the shepherds to arrive, we do not see the homeless family by the side of the road; waiting to sit down at a fine feast, we ignore those whose bread is their fear, whose cup is filled with their lost dreams.

Come to us, Promised Sign of restoration:
> **come to open our eyes;**

come to us, Child of compassion:
> **come to melt our hearts with your tears;**

come to us, Servant of the poor,
> **come to lead us to serve the lost.**

O come, o come, Immanuel:
> **to forgive us, to heal us, so all that was promised might be fulfilled for us.**

Silence is kept

Assurance of Pardon

Dear children of God: do not be afraid. The promise given long ago has been kept once and for all in the birth at Bethlehem. Rejoice, rejoice, for Christ has come for you.

Grace and peace are the gifts God has given to us, not only on this day, not only in this season, but in all the moments to come. Thanks be to God! Amen.

Great Prayer of Thanksgiving
May Immanuel be with you this day!
And also with you!
Beloved of God, lift up your hearts.
We lift them to the One whose face shines with love for us.
Household of God, let your voices ring with joy and gladness.
We sing of the One who has come, come to save us and give us life.

When chaos was empty and barren,
you created the stars of the night,
    to light the way for grace;
you filled the hollows of the sea
    with the waters of life.
Lord God of creation,
you shaped us in your image,
        so we might feast on the bounty
            of the garden you gave us,
        so we could drink deeply
            from the fountains of goodness.
But we belittled your gifts,
thinking that those jewels
    called sin and death
        were priceless beyond compare.
We filled our minds
    with the empty dreams of temptation,
    and wearied you with our rebellion.
As you sent the prophets
with hope in their hands
and reconciliation on their lips,
    we turned our backs,
        laughing among ourselves
        at their faithful obedience.
Finally, you sent Jesus,
the One who, by refusing evil,
could help us to choose the good.

Therefore, with the faithful of every time and place,
we lift our songs to thanksgiving to you:

Holy, holy, holy, Lord God of hosts.
All creation calls on your name.
Hosanna in the highest!

Blessed is the One who comes, God-with-us.
Hosanna in the highest!

Holy are you, Shepherd of all creation,
and blessed is Jesus Christ, your Servant, our Savior.
When you could not wait
for the world to conceive of peace,
    you sent him to show us how
    to end our violent ways;
when you could not wait
for us to find hope,
    you sent him to speak
    your promises to us;
when you could not wait
for us to stumble upon love,
    you sent him to walk the earth,
    so we would know how
        to treat our friends and enemies;
when you could not wait
for us to return to you,
    he went to the cross
    to bring us home.

As we prepare to celebrate his birth once again,
as we sing of our longing for him to return,
we proclaim that faith which is often a mystery:

Christ died, refusing to choose evil;
Christ is risen, that we might choose good;
Christ will come again, his face shining in glory.

Send your Spirit to come quickly
upon the gifts of the bread and the cup,
and upon your beloved gathered here.
Fill our empty and barren lives
with the rich harvest of joy,
    so we may take your sheaves of blessings to the world;
heal our weary and wounded souls,
    so we may go to minister to the broken-hearted around us;
enlarge our vision,
    so we might see that kingdom of peace, reconciliation and hope
      you prepare for all your people,
    so we might go forth
        to embrace our sisters and brothers.
And when all time has come to an end,
we will no longer need to dream,
but will sit with you at your Table,
surrounded by family and friends,

by strangers and enemies,
    feasting on the bread of life
    and drinking deeply of grace's vineyard,
    joining our voices as one to praise you:
God in Community, Holy in One. Amen.

Blessing
As you go to walk the streets of the kingdom, take a Light to guide you:
we take the light of faith,
to share it with everyone we meet.
As you go to walk the streets of the world, take a Light to guide you:
we take the light of hope,
to carry it to those we are blessed to serve.
As you seek to walk God's holy way, take a Light to guide you:
we take the light of patience,
believing we will find God with us.
As you open your hearts to God's dreams, take a Light to guide you:
we take the light of promise,
knowing that God has come to save us.
As you go forth to reach Bethlehem,
travel with faith and hope into God's future:
with joy and gratitude,
we go forth into God's vision of peace.

Christmas Eve
Isaiah 9:2-7; Psalm 96
Titus 2:11-14; Luke 2:1-14, (15-20)

Greeting
The people walking in darkness have seen a great light;
on those living in the shadows of death a light has dawned.
Jesus Christ is our Life and Light. In Christ's name, welcome!
In Christ's grace, let us worship God!

Call to Worship
Let us go, just as we are, to see what has happened.
Let us go with the shepherds:
let us go and find the One
of whom the angels sang.
Let us go with those who are wise:
let us go and find the One
who brings God's truth to us.
Let us go with the poor in spirit, and in flesh;
let us go with those who are humbled by life:

21

**let us find the Glory of God
born in a stable, and placed in a feeding trough.**
Let us go with our friends and family,
let us go with our neighbors and with strangers,
let us go with all the children of God:
**let us go to find the One who comes
to lead us home to God's kingdom.**
O come, let us go to the Babe of Bethlehem!
**O come, let us adore him!
Christ our Lord!**

Call to Reconciliation
We begin with such great hopes, such great dreams. We are going to be better, to treat others more fairly, to love more deeply. But we come to the manger once again, knowing our failings, and aware of our brokenness. Let us confess to the One who comes, that our lives might be made new.

Unison Prayer of Confession
**God who comes to us, forgive us . . .
when our shadowed lives dim your Light;
when the tinsel of Christmas means more
to us than your truth;
when our hearts of stone resist the pain
and brokenness around us;
when we care more about what is under
the tree, than the damage we do
to your creation and to your children.**

**Have mercy on us, Healing God,
so we might
tear down the walls we have built
to keep your love away;
so we could
seek your justice for our sisters and brothers;
so our hearts
would become cradles for your Son,
our Lord and Savior, Jesus Christ.**

Silence is kept

Assurance of Pardon (based on Is. 62:10-12)
Go, go through the city, preparing for the people;
repair, repair all the roads, filling in the holes,

raising a banner for all to see.
God has spoken to all people,
saying to sons and daughters:
    'See, your Savior comes;
    to make good on my promises,
    to bring redemption to all people.'
And we will be called God's Beloved,
the Redeemed of the Lord;
God will seek us out to live
in the New Jerusalem,
where no one is left behind. Amen.

Great Prayer of Thanksgiving
On this silent night, God is with you.
God is also with you.
On this holy night, God's Grace comes to us.
Our hearts rejoice in his becoming one of us,
that we might become one with God.
On this Night of nights, the shadows of the world
melt away before God's Light.
We join the choirs of angels in singing to the universe
the good news of the birth of Jesus.

This is the night your heart bursts open with Joy,
this is the evening Grace pours out of heaven,
this is the moment when you come
to make all things new,
ever-creating God.
You shaped light out of the shadows of chaos,
and molded your children from the earth,
    looking in the mirror as you formed us,
    breathing your Spirit into our empty lungs.
Made for life with you
in the Garden you designed for us,
    we ran away into the wilds of the world,
    believing we were wiser than you,
        that we could make our own way.
Yet your love never failed us,
your compassion was never taken from us,
you would not abandon us in our foolishness.
You brought us out of slavery
into that land of promise and hope.
You sent your prophets to speak to us
of your disappointment in us,

and to remind us of your dreams for us.
Your love for us was so passionate,
that you sent your only Son
to become one of us
that we might be one with you again.

So on this night when heaven reaches down
to caress creation with healing,
we join the angel choirs who sang your glory,
and with your people in every time and place,
caroling the good news which is ours:

Gloria! Gloria! In excelsis deo!
Creation joins in the angelic chorus of joy.
Hosanna in the highest!

Blessed is the One born this night for us.
Hosanna in the highest!

Holiness is who you are, God of Christmas,
and blessings come in Jesus Christ, your Child of Grace.
Finding no warm welcome at his birth,
    he knew the cold shoulder of friends at his death;
born in the rude confines of a barn,
    he knew the suffering of your children;
sent to be your Word made flesh,
    he calls us to follow him into your Kingdom;
proclaimed by the prophet as our Prince of Peace,
    he died in the quagmire of human violence.
By his death and resurrection,
you have given new life to all creation.

So, as we gather on this holiest of nights,
we proclaim that mystery we call faith:

Born in the shadows of night,
    Christ is our light;
dying on a rough cross,
    Christ is our life;
rising from a cold tomb,
    Christ is our hope;
returning to us once more,
    Christ is our promise.

Pour out your Spirit upon us,
Wonderful Counselor,
and on the gifts you have given us.
We lift the broken bread,
    praying we would be made whole,
    at peace with one another,
        and reconciled to you.
As we drink from the vineyard of grace,
    we believe that our salvation has come,
    and we are one with Christ,
        our flesh filled with his spirit of sacrifice,
        our spirits refreshed by his compassionate heart.
As your joy flows into us,
may we become a river
    carrying your justice to the poor;
as your hope sings in our hearts,
    may we carry your righteousness to all who suffer.

And as we taste the promise
of the feast you prepare for us in your kingdom,
may we live for you and serve your children,
as we have been served by the Child of Christmas,
Jesus Christ, our blessed Savior. Amen.

Christmas Day
Isaiah 52:7-10; Psalm 98
Hebrews 1:1-4, (5-12); John 1:1-14

Call to Worship
Wonder of wonders, God has come to us!
Not as a judge, but a Savior,
not in power, but as a servant.
Wonder of wonders, God comes to us!
Not in silence, but in the Word made flesh;
not in the shadows, but bringing Light.
Wonder of wonders!
God is with us!

Prayer of the Day
Angels sang their anthems
at the midnight hour
    to awaken a sleeping creation;
shepherds came to worship you,
    and went away rejoicing;

wise ones gave their hearts to you,
     so they could dwell in yours.
O Immanuel,
we adore you!

You came to us as a baby,
     to hold us in your grace;
you came to us in a stable,
     so we would have no trouble finding you;
you came to us in poverty,
     to enrich our lives.
O Beautiful Messenger of Peace,
we adore you!

You play with us
     in the streets of the kingdom;
you build your home
     deep within our souls;
you walk with us
     in the winter of life.
O Wisdom from on high,
we adore you!

God in Community, Holy in One,
all the faithful lift their songs of joy to you,
even as we pray as Jesus has taught us, saying,
Our Father . . .

Call to Reconciliation
God became one of us, so that we could see the face of love, hear the
voice of peace, be touched by the hand of grace, know the heart of
mercy. God comes to us, offering us forgiveness and peace. Please
join with me as we pray together, saying,

Unison Prayer of Confession
You came in weakness, Mighty God:
     forgive our grasping for power.
You came in humility, Prince of Peace:
     forgive us for wanting more than others.
You came in poverty, Everlasting One:
     forgive us when we do not see your family
          sleeping on our streets.
You came in gentleness, Wonderful Counselor:

forgive us for the anger we speak
and the pain we cause.

Child of Bethlehem, be born in us today:
forgive us,
heal us,
make us new;
then we will join the angels
in singing your praises
this Christmas Day
and all the days to come.

Silence is kept

Assurance of Pardon
Break forth into singing, children of God: for the Babe comes to comfort
us, like a mother rocking her son to sleep, like a father wiping away the
tears of his daughter.
(sung) ***Joy to the world! the Lord is come:***
Let earth receive her King.
Let every heart prepare him room,
And heaven and nature sing,
And heaven and nature sing,
And heaven, and heaven and nature sing.

Great Prayer of Thanksgiving
May the Child of Bethlehem be born in you.
And in your heart as well.
Children of God, lift up your hearts.
We lift them to the One who came to us
that first Christmas morning.
People of God, give thanks to the One who is always with us.
O come, O come, Immanuel, to feed us at your Table.

When you were weary
of chaos as your companion,
Everlasting God,
you whispered to the Word
who sang Creation's song:
mountains sprang to attention,
rivers and oceans splashed your feet,
and the dust from the Carpenter's table
was gathered up and shaped in your image.
Spirit breathed life into us,
that we might dance with you forever.

27

But when we looked beyond your glory,
and saw the decorative temptations
the world dangled before our eyes,
    we rushed to embrace sin and death.
Yet you looked past our rebellion,
seeing the people we could become,
and so sent Isaiah and Hannah,
Simeon and Anna as your faithful witnesses.
When we continued to turn up
the world's volume to drown out your pleas,
you sent the Word of hope
in the silence of a stable.

Therefore, we join with the angels of Bethlehem's skies,
and all those who sing of your steadfast love,
in every time and place:

Holy are you, God of Christ-filled mornings.
All creation remembers your steadfast love and faithfulness,
    breaking out in joyous song:
'Hosanna in the highest!'

Blessed is the One who brings us the victory of God.
Hosanna in the highest!

Holy are you, Mighty God,
and blessed is the One who comes in your name,
our Lord and Savior, your Gift to all the world.
You would not keep the Word to yourself,
    but sent him to tell us
    of your hopes for us.
You did not cling to the Prince of Peace,
    but poured him out to end
    our enmity and violence with one another.
You could not hold your Heart in your hands,
    but allowed him to be broken
    on the tree of Calvary
        that we might be made whole forever.

So, as we celebrate his birth, his life, his death and his resurrection,
we remember the faith which he models for us,
and gives to us as our inheritance:

In the beginning, Christ was with you, creating life;
on the cross, Christ died with you, defeating death;

28

**from the empty tomb, Christ rose with you, bringing salvation;
from glory, Christ will come again with you,
   the Light which could not be overcome.**

As we gather at your Table,
send your Spirit upon the bread and the cup,
and upon us, your children.
As you sent Jesus to be born of Mary,
   may we bear the burdens of others;
as you became One with us in the Child,
   may we live at peace with all people;
as you have brought us out
of the shadows of our sin,
      may we carry the Light of the world
         to all who live in the shadows
            of oppression and injustice.

Then, when we gather at your Table
prepared for all people in your kingdom,
we will sing that new song first caroled at creation
and echoed through Bethlehem's hills:
"Glory to God in the highest,
and on earth, peace, goodwill to all." Amen.

First Sunday after Christmas
Isaiah 63:7-9; Psalm 148
Hebrews 2:10-18; Matthew 2:13-23

Call to Worship
All God's people - boys and girls, men and women:
come and worship!
Shepherds, wise ones, saints, and angels:
come and worship! Come and worship!
All who need the Savior, all who long for comfort:
come and worship! Come and worship Christ, the newborn King!

Prayer of the Day
In your love, which never ends,
Steadfast Grace,
you hear the cries
   of all the two-year-olds
      cast aside by the world,
and the weeping of their mothers
   who cannot feed them
      because there is no hope.

29

Wrapped in an old blanket
to keep you warm in a cold stable,
and smuggled into Egypt to keep you safe,
Marginalized Messiah,
you know the searching of refugees
    for a place they can call home,
    for a life they can call safe.

Cradling the innocents killed in war,
remembering those driven from their homes
    by fear, greed, or power;
singing laments with all the parents
    who cannot give their children
    the lives they should have,
you proclaim God's name for us,
Spirit of Sanctuary.

God in Community, Holy in One,
you fill our hearts with yourself,
for you continue to come into this world.
Give us the peace, the joy, the hope to carry
to all who cry out to you this day,
even as we pray as Jesus has taught us, saying,
Our Father . . .

Call to Reconciliation
Born of Mary, in a child called Jesus, God knew life as we know it: our
pain, our doubts, our temptations, our hopes. Without sin, Jesus could
choose to judge us; instead, he redeems us and is the midwife of our
birth into new life. Let us confess our sins, so we might be filled with
God's grace and joy in this season of holiness and hope.

Unison Prayer of Confession
**Dweller in eternity, you became a little baby for us. We chase
down the corridors of power, while you enter the hallways where
weakness and suffering reside. We grab for more and more, while
you let go of glory to become one of us. We reduce our Savior's
birth to tinsel, toys, and trash to be placed by the curb, while you
widen your embrace to welcome all thrown out by the world.**

**Forgive us, Joyous Love. Come among us, filling our hearts with
your grace and truth. Open our lips, so we might sing with the
angels. Send us forth with the shepherds, to tell everyone we meet
of the good news of the birth of the One who brings us life, Jesus
Christ, our Lord and Savior.**

30

Silence is kept

Assurance of Pardon
The news we have hungered for fills our lives;
the news we have been searching for has found us;
the news that is for all people is proclaimed:
a Savior has been born - for us!
The One who is our hope has arrived;
the One who is our life has come to us;
the One who is our joy is in our midst:
Jesus Christ the Lord! Thanks be to God! Amen.

Great Prayer of Thanksgiving
May the God of all innocents be with you.
And also with you.
Celebrate the One who comes to be with God's people.
We lift our hearts to God our Savior.
Sing of the steadfast love of the Lord.
We praise God along with angels, shepherds, and little children.

All creation recounts your gracious deeds,
God of Christmas and beyond:
    all the angels praise you from heaven's heights,
    sea creatures in the deeps sing your carols;
    shining stars twinkle your glory,
    flying birds and creeping things echo your songs.
You alone are exalted, shaping all
for the children created in your image.
But temptation spoke to us in dreams,
    and we fled into the embrace of death.
You sent prophets to search for us,
so that your hopes might be fulfilled,
    but we refused to listen to the
    brokenness of your heart.
So Jesus came into our lives
to lift us up and carry us home.

So with the politicians and the powerless,
with the immigrants, as well as the insiders,
we sing our praises to you:

Holy, holy, holy, God of glory above earth and heaven.
All creation praises you forever and ever.
Hosanna in the highest!

Blessed is the One who comes to fulfill the words of the prophets. Hosanna in the highest!

You alone are holy, God of steadfast love,
and blessed is Jesus Christ, your Child, our Savior.
Putting aside the robes of glory,
    he came to be wrapped in diapers.
Experiencing every single thing as we do,
    he is able to strengthen us in every part of life.
Seeing how sin tricks us, he came
    to lead us out of its slavery.
Knowing that it would be infuriated,
he went to the cross,
    reducing death to a lump of a word,
        as he strode out of it's useless grasp.

As we celebrate the birth of the Child,
as we remember the death and resurrection of Christ,
we recount that mystery we call faith:

Christ died, setting us free from the fear of death;
Christ rose, filling us with the hope of life;
Christ will come, to lift us up and carry us to God.

Pour out your Holy Spirit
upon the gifts of the bread and cup
and on your children gathered here.
As we eat of this bread
which restores us to life,
    may we hear the mothers
    weeping for their sons
        held captive by poverty;
    may we listen to the fathers
        who lie awake in the night
        worrying about their daughters.
As we drink from the Cup
which is your Spirit for us,
    may our sophistications
    be washed away, so we
        can hear the cries of all the
            innocents.

And when your gracious deeds have ended,
and we are gathered in your glory

with our sisters and brothers,
we will fill all time with songs of praise to you,
God in Community, Holy in One. Amen.

Holy Name of Jesus
Numbers 6:22-27; Psalm 8
Philippians 2:5-11; Luke 2:15-21

Call to Worship
We come, in need of blessings;
we come, seeking closeness with God.
Let us go, to find our God.
We come, from the shadows of our lives,
seeking light and hope.
Hurry, let us go to find the One we have heard about.
We come to God, seeking peace
for our lives, for our world.
Come, let us go, believing the Word we have seen.

Prayer of the Day
Majestic God,
we cannot begin to imagine you,
    yet you have made us in your image;
we wonder why you notice us,
    when we are surrounded by creation's glory;
we have been made stewards of life,
    and you choose to share your own with us.

Name above all names:
you call us 'sister' and 'brother'
    claiming us to share in your work;
exalted above all creation,
    you humbled yourself for our sake;
able to do all things,
    you choose to work through us.

Spirit of Grace:
when we look for majesty,
    you bring us to a manger;
when we yearn for glory,
    you hand us a mop;
when we want to exalt ourselves,
    you point us to the Cross.

God in Community, Holy in One,
we pray to you as Jesus has taught us,
Our Father . . .

Call to Reconciliation
We've been to the stable, and met the Babe. But tomorrow, when we go
back to work, or school - will others know where we have been? Let us
admit to God our reluctance to reflect transformed lives.

Unison Prayer of Confession
God of Bethlehem:
you bless us richly,
**   forgive our reluctance to share;**
you hold us close to your heart,
**   forgive us for keeping others at arm's length;**
you shine in the shadows of our soul,
**   forgive us for not sharing the Light;**
you lift us from where we have fallen,
**   forgive us for not offering a helping hand;**
you grace us with Joy,
**   forgive us when we worship fear.**

Silence is kept

Assurance of Pardon
If we believe the songs of the angels, and have seen the Child in the
manger, we must go out and tell others this good news.
We will go: glorifying God, praising the Lord, and confessing to
everyone we meet how God has richly blessed us. Amen.

Great Prayer of Thanksgiving
May God be with you.
And also with you.
People of God, lift up your hearts.
We lift them to our God.
Sisters and brothers of Christ, give thanks to our God.
We lift our songs of praise to the One who loves us.

We will indeed sing your praises,
God of Blessings,
creator of heaven and earth.
You brought forth all that is good and beautiful,
   so chaos could not keep hold of us.
You lifted up the dust of creation,
shaping it into your likeness,

34

breathing your life into our lungs.
When we fell into sin,
you did not turn away from us,
   but kept your promises.
You sent prophets to remind us
of our covenant with you,
   but we continued to bow down
      to death's idols.
Finally, you sent your Beloved,
Jesus, the Babe of Bethlehem,
to become one of us,
so we could be made one with you.

So, we join our voices
with the angels in heaven and the beasts in the field,
with those who have gone before us,
and those who will follow,
glorifying you forever:

Holy, holy, holy are you, God of blessings.
All creation glorifies and praises you.
Hosanna in the highest!

Blessed is the One who comes to redeem us.
Hosanna in the highest!

Holy are you, Shining God,
and blessed is Jesus Christ, your Son.
Emptying himself of glory,
   we are filled with grace;
reviled and cursed by coarse humanity,
   he is given the Name above all names;
dying a criminal's death
and cast into death's cold arms,
   he is lifted to your Heart
      to rule over all creation.

As we come to this Table,
we speak of that mystery
we cannot explain:

Christ was obedient to God, even to death;
Christ was exalted by God, raised to new life;
Christ will be proclaimed by all as Lord and Savior.

Come, Spirit of Blessing
upon these gifts of the bread and cup,
and those who come to receive them.
As we bow to receive the Bread of Heaven,
    we would stoop to lift up the fallen;
as we bend to take the Cup,
    we would kneel to comfort your children;
as we worship you,
    we would serve your people.

Then, when all are gathered for your Feast in heaven,
we will sing our glory to you:
God in Community, Holy and One,
now and forever. Amen.

Blessing
The One who blesses you will keep you close:
we will go,
not keeping the blessing for ourselves, but to share it with others.
The One who is gracious to you, shines the Spirit upon you:
we will go,
to reflect the Light of Christ in gracious words and deeds.
The One who turns towards you gives you peace:
we will go, turning to everyone we meet, saying,
"The peace of God be with you."

New Year's Day
Ecclesiastes 3:1-13; Psalm 8
Revelation 21:1-6a; Matthew 25:31-46

Call to Worship
We wake up in the morning
and see the sunrise:
how majestic is your name in all the earth!
We are warmed by the sun;
the rain cleanses all creation:
how majestic is your name in all the earth!
We watch the moon light up the night,
we fall asleep to the lullabies of the stars:
how majestic is your name in all the earth!

Prayer of the Day
You call us
    to be your children;

you gift us
    to serve all people;
you send us to proclaim
    your good news to all:
Glory to you,
Creator of all that is new!

When you are lonely,
    we have a chance to visit you;
when you are hungry,
    we can share our food with you;
when you are naked,
    we can give you
        the clothes off our backs;
when you are sick,
    we can nurse you back to health:
Glory to you,
Savior of the world!

You whisper in our ears,
    so we may praise you;
you fill our souls,
    so we may serve you;
you lead us into the kingdom,
    so we may live with you:
Glory to you,
Spirit of Gentleness!

Glory to you,
God in Community, Holy in One!
Hear us as we pray as Jesus teaches us,
Our Father . . .

Call to Reconciliation
Will this year be a time of new life, new ways for us - or will we continue
to live the same old way? Let us confess to our God our failures, as well
as our hopes, as we begin this year.

Unison Prayer of Confession
**We admit that we always find the time to fill our stomachs, God
of every moment, but not our souls. We spend hours watching
television, but not the wonders of your creation. We arrange
outings with our friends, yet ignore your invitation to sit and talk.
We make resolutions to change every aspect of our lives, except for
that which pertains to you.**

Forgive us, God of Glory, and make us new. In the moments to come this year, remind us that if there is a time for everything, then we do have those moments for grace, for hope, for joy, for a relationship with our Lord and Savior, Jesus Christ.

Silence is kept

Assurance of Pardon
It's over - last year is gone. Our words, our thoughts, our deeds are in the past. Today, we begin anew. Today, and every day, God offers us life and hope.
Here, now, forever - we are forgiven and healed. This year, let us live as such people. Thanks be to God. Amen.

Great Prayer of Thanksgiving
May the God of new beginnings be with you.
And also with you.
People of God, lift up your hearts.
We lift them to the One who makes all things, including us, new.
Children of God, sing praises to the One who gives you new life.
**We praise the One who continues to surprise us
with hope and grace.**

Before there was time,
Hope of Eternity,
you took a moment
    to bring creation out of chaos.
You took time to create mountains,
    and carve deep canyons;
you made the time to fill the oceans
    and to plant food for all creatures;
you found the time to plow rivers
    to water a Garden,
    and to shape us in your image.
But we did not have time for you,
        preferring to spend our days chasing sin,
        and our nights seeking death.
You always made time for us,
speaking of your hopes
    through the prophets,
sharing your dreams
    through the angels.
Then, one day you decided
to do a new thing,
becoming one of us

38

as Jesus became human
to bring hope and grace to us.

So we join with the saints in heaven,
and our sisters and brothers on earth,
who sing of your glory:

Holy, holy, holy Lord, God of every time and place.
All creation sings of your majesty and glory.
Hosanna in the highest!

Blessed is the One who gives us the water of life.
Hosanna in the highest!

Holy are you, Keeper of our days,
and blessed is Jesus Christ,
who is with us in every season of life.
He comes, not to judge us,
    but to forgive us;
he comes, not to cast us out,
    but to gather us into
    the new Jerusalem;
he comes, not to watch us suffer,
    but to die on the cross,
        that we might live with you.

As we give thanks for his life,
and remember his death and resurrection,
we would talk of that mystery which is our faith:

Christ died, so sin would have no more power over us;
Christ rose, destroying death's grip on us;
when the new heaven and new earth come,
    Christ will make all things, including us, new.

In these sacred moments,
send your Spirit
to sanctify the bread and the cup,
and to open the hearts
of those who approach the Table.
As the Bread of life touches our lips,
    may we be strengthened to serve
    those whom the world has forgotten.
As the Cup of salvation quenches our thirst for you,

may we be enabled
to bring relief
to those who wander
the desert wastes of our society.

And when all time ends,
and all people are gathered
around your Table in Heaven,
we will rejoice in your presence,
and sing your praises forever:
One God, Father, Son, and Holy Spirit,
now and forever.
Amen.

Second Sunday after Christmas
Jeremiah 31:7-14; Psalm 147:12-20
Ephesians 1:3-14; John 1:(1-9), 10-18

Call to Worship
However far we have wandered from God:
God comes to find us, and to gather us in generous love.
However broken we have become:
God comes to heal us, and make us whole in hope.
However empty our spirits may be:
God comes to feed us, until we are filled to the brim with grace.

Prayer of the Day
Mirror of Abba:
by light and word,
you come to us,
    so we can hear well enough
    to see your songs all around us.
Through grace and truth,
you teach us,
    so we come to know
    how graciousness is the gift
        we can offer to others.
In promise and hope,
you call us,
    trusting that we will
    accept the joy delivered to us
and count on the fulfillment
    of your dreams for us
    and for all creation.

All this we pray,
God in Community, Holy in One,
as we speak the words
Jesus teaches us to say together,
Our Father . . .

Call to Reconciliation

Our words, our actions, our silence may make it seem that we are on
that path which only hurts others and harms us. But God has destined
us for healing, for hope, for joy. Let us pray to the One who loves us
beyond compare. Please join me as we pray, saying,

Unison Prayer of Confession.

**In the winter of our lives, Tender God, our passion for following
Jesus wilts in the chill of indifference. We could walk in the light,
but tiptoe through the shadows of missed chances. We could look
for your glory in others, but gaze instead in the mirror of
selfishness, seeing our desires staring back at us. We could gather
the broken of the world to our side, but hold them at arm's length
from us.**

**Forgive us, Redeeming Grace. Jesus was bringing life and hope
to all people. With grace and truth, he calls us to follow. Filling us
with peace, he gathers us up and brings us home to you, serving as
our Brother, our Savior, our Friend.**

Silence is kept

Assurance of Pardon

Grace upon grace; mercy upon mercy; hope upon hope: these are the
gifts God pours out on us in this moment, and all the moments of our
lives to come.
**Thanks be to God! We are filled to overflowing with God's tender
love and peace. We are forgiven! Amen.**

Great Prayer of Thanksgiving

May the God of new days be with you.
And also with you.
People of Christmas, lift up your hopes.
We lift them to the one who comes bringing new life to us.
People of hope, offer your thanksgiving to God.
**Joy bubbles from our hearts,
praises dance from our lips to our loving God.**

Into the emptiness of chaos,
Blessing of Imagination,

41

the Word carried all your hopes,
scattering the seeds of goodness
    throughout the universe,
flinging light into the shadows of night,
    planting life in the watery deeps.
You offered us grace upon grace,
    tending to your garden with joy.
But we chose to dance
to the mourning dirges
    played for us by sin and death,
        shutting the doors of our hearts
        in your face.
Prophets came, singing your praises,
telling us of your hopes for us,
    but we would not listen
    to a single word they spoke.
So you sent Jesus to us,
to gather us from the far corners
of despair and loss,
to bring us home to you.

So with those in every place,
and with those through every time,
we join our voices singing to you:

Holy, holy, holy! Lord God of all creation!
Before the foundations of the world were poured,
    you prepared every blessing for us.
Hosanna in the highest!

Blessed is the Word who comes to bear witness to you.
Hosanna in the highest!

Holy are you in every moment, Joyous God,
and blessed is Jesus Christ, Light and Life.
In the beginning,
    he was your Word of creativity,
and at our end,
    he is your Word of hope.
He came among us,
    gifting us with grace and truth,
    whispering of your great love.
Though we rejected him,
he continued to embrace us,
    knowing we were destined for adoption,

42

to be his sisters and brothers.
He carried your light
   into the shadowed recesses
   of our lives;
he was filled with
the emptiness of death,
   that we might receive
   the promise of the resurrection
into life with you forever.

As we begin this new year with hope,
we remember his promise to be with us always,
even as we tell of that mystery we call faith:

At the beginning, Christ was your imaginative Word;
at the right time, Christ was the Word of salvation;
at the end, Christ will be the Word of fulfillment.

As your Spirit rests upon
the gifts of the bread and the cup,
   we pray that you would fill us
   with every spiritual blessing.
As we taste of the life
in the Bread which strengthens us,
   we would be made aware
   of the hunger of our world -
      real, daily hunger for food
      as well as yearning for you -
   and go to bring everyone
      to the feast you offer.
As we drink the sweet
richness of your grace,
   we would reach out
   and take the hands of all
   who are despised and rejected,
      drawing them into your dance of life.
As we are filled at your feast,
   we would go to empty ourselves
   of pride and selfishness,
      as we humbly serve
      that great company of the broken.

And when all things
come to an end in your Word,
as we are gathered in the true Light,

sitting with our sisters and brothers
around the kitchen table
in that life we will have
with you forever,
we will join our voices
singing your praises through all eternity,
God in Community, Holy in One. Amen.

Epiphany of the Lord
Isaiah 60:1-6; Psalm 72:1-7, 10-14
Ephesians 3:1-12; Matthew 2:1-12

Call to Worship
We gather wondering,
'Where will we find the Babe
born in Bethlehem?'
We will find the Babe
 in the laughter of children,
 in the wisdom of grandparents.
We gather asking,
'where will we find
the Child of Christmas?'
We will find the Child
 where the needy are gifted with hope,
 where the oppressed are set free.
We gather wanting to know,
'where will we find the Christ
who has come for us?'
We will find our Hope
 where fear is overwhelmed by grace,
 where hatred is overwhelmed by love,
 where all people are overwhelmed by joy.

Prayer of the Day
We have heard
of your grace,
Shaper of stars:
from those set free
 from injustice;
from our children
 who whisper of your joy;
from greeters
 of dawn's fresh start;
from late risers

who listen to the stories
of the needy.

We have heard
of your Light,
Bright Star of the morning:
which can illumine
    the shadows of our lives;
which can show
    the path to God's heart;
which can point the way
    to where we become
    servants of the gospel.

We have heard
of your promised peace,
Wisdom's Radiance:
that peace
    which can end war,
    as well as heal our hearts;
that peace
    which can conquer our fears,
    and flood us with faith;
that peace
    which can enter our lives
    and overwhelm us with hope.

We have heard of you,
God in Community, Holy in One,
and will proclaim your glory to all,
even as we pray, saying,
Our Father . . .

Call to Reconciliation

Why do we huddle in the shadowed corners of life, rather than running to
the Light of life? Why do we love the wrong we do rather than grasping
the good news offered to us? As we struggle with such questions, let us
speak to God of all we have failed to do, seeking hope and grace as we
pray,

Unison Prayer of Confession

**We search for your light, Star Caster, but too often end up
settling for the dimness of temptation. Our motives for seeking to
find Christ are not always pure, for we expect him to fulfill our**

desires, rather than your hopes for us. We want the gifts of wealth, health, success, fulfillment, rather than those of servanthood, of compassion, of peace.

Forgive us, Shaper of our lives, that we are so foolish to put our needs ahead of your grace. Help us to be like those wise people of so long ago, who found hope, instead of a destination; who found grace, instead of gratitude; who found salvation, instead of a sign. As we journey with your Son, our Lord and Savior, Jesus Christ, fill us with the light of your joy and love.

Silence is kept

Assurance of Pardon
Up, on your feet! Grace has been poured into our hearts, love has flooded our souls, the light of hope shines in us.
This is the light which has come to all, the light we will carry and give to everyone we meet. Thanks be to God. Amen.

Great Prayer of Thanksgiving
People of Advent: the Lord be with you!
And also with you!
People of Christmas, lift up your hearts.
Overwhelmed with grace, we lift our hearts
to the One who was born for us.
People of the Star, offer your songs of joy and thanksgiving to God.
We will sing our praises to the One
who has revealed glory and hope in the Babe of Bethlehem.

In that first moment, you spoke,
Radiant God,
    and the light of creation
    dispelled the thick darkness of chaos.
You whispered,
    and your glory filled the skies.
You sang,
    and the dust of the earth
    was shaped into your image,
as you breathed life into us.
We could have lived
in grace and peace with you
    for as long as the sun endures,
    for as long as the moon hangs in the night sky.
But we were tempted
by the sweet taste of sin,
    and overwhelmed with temptation's

46

wealth of cheap gifts and thrills.
The prophets were sent
to tell of your gifts of joy and peace,
     but we listened to the world's news
     of success, power, achievement.
Finally, in that dark time of despair,
you sent Jesus,
your servant of salvation.

Therefore, we will join our voices
with the wise ones, as well as the foolish,
of every time and place
who forever sing of your grace:

Holy, holy, holy are you, God of bright dawns!
All creation renders tributes of praise to you.
Hosanna in the highest!

Blessed is the One who saves the lives of the needy.
Hosanna in the highest!

Holy are you, God of redemption,
and blessed is Jesus Christ, our Savior.
Overwhelmed with compassion,
he left the glory of heaven,
     to become a prisoner of sin,
          so we could be set free.
Overwhelmed with hope,
he entered death's house,
     to break its forlorn power forever.
Overwhelmed with love,
     he travelled another road,
     walking to Calvary,
          so we might run with joy
          into your waiting arms.

So, as we remember his birth,
as we prepare to journey with him this year,
we speak of that mystery called faith,
which is revealed to us through Christ:

Christ came, the morning star of love;
Christ died, the night star of salvation;
Christ arose, the radiant star of resurrection;
Christ will come again, the constellation of hope.

47

Holy One of stars and sinners,
send down your Spirit of hope
upon those gathered around this Table,
and on the gifts of the bread and the cup,
that they might make us
your faithful and loving children.
Feed us with the bread of hope,
so when we leave,
we will travel another road,
   to defend the weak,
   to speak for the voiceless,
   to assist those cast aside.
Refresh us with the sweet nectar of grace,
so we, overwhelmed with joy,
would go forth
   to enter the houses
      of the strangers in our midst;
   to enter the despair
      of the lonely and forgotten;
   to enter the hearts
      of everyone we meet.

And when eternity's time begins
and we are gathered around your Table,
with friends and family we loved,
with those we ignored and mistreated,
with all our sisters and brothers of grace,
we will lift our songs of glad joy to you,
God in Community, Holy in One. Amen.

Blessing
Let us go to walk with God:
for as long as the sun endures,
for as long as the moon shines in the night sky.
Let us go to walk with Christ:
into the shadows of poverty and need,
into the communities where injustice dwells.
Let us go to walk with the Spirit:
to bring hope to those who have none,
to bring peace to our brokenness.

Baptism of the Lord
First Sunday after the Epiphany/Ordinary Time 1
Isaiah 42:1-9; Psalm 29
Acts 10:34-43; Matthew 3:13-17

Call to Worship
When we are reluctant to dip our toes into faith's river,
Jesus comes, to teach us how to swim.
When we are hesitant to cup our hands
to drink from the fountain of grace,
Jesus comes, to reach in and splash our faces with God's joy.
When we are unwilling to be the pipeline of hope,
Jesus comes, to turn on the faucets God has installed in our hearts.

Prayer of the Day
When we clasp the past
tight to our fading memories,
you come, Glory of Creation:
    to strip us bare
    of all pride and pretense,
        with your future;
    to slip the latch
    on the fears and worries
        which keep us bound
        from following you;
    to stand with us
    when death and sin
        try to bully us.
And we cry, 'Glory!'

When our faith flickers
in the shadows of chaos,
you come, Servant of sinners:
    to be the grace-crier
        through the streets of our hearts;
    to teach eager students
        the songs of peace and hope;
    to open our eyes
        heavy-lidded by indifference.
And we cry, 'Glory!'

When we are dubious
about being disciples,
you come, Baptism's Spirit:
    to journey with peace-walkers
        through the world's violent streets;
    to strengthen us
        when we are bent by doubt;
    to anoint us with rivers
        of grace, hope, and reconciliation.

And we cry, 'Glory!'

God in Community, Holy in One,
we cry 'Glory!' to you,
even as we pray as we have been taught,
Our Father . . .

Call to Reconciliation
The psalmist tells us that the One whose voice can knock trees to the ground listens to our hesitant prayers which speak of our sin, of how we have hurt others, as well as God. Join me, as we pray to the One who will bless us with peace and forgiveness.

Unison Prayer of Confession
You would have all people hear of your grace, Servant God, but we hinder your efforts by hoarding the Word for ourselves. You would have hope flow through our neighborhoods, but we thwart your plans by damming up hope in our hearts. You would have us skip into your kingdom, but we frustrate your future by clinging so tightly to those grudges we have carried for so long.

Have mercy on us, Shaker of our wildernesses, and unlock the shuttered doors of our hearts. Remind us that at our baptism you touch us with the waters of life, promise to be with us always, and call us your beloved, even as you sang your joy to Jesus Christ, our Lord and Savior, at the waters of the Jordan.

Silence is kept

Assurance of Pardon
You know the good news God has proclaimed to you: we are called to let go of the past, and to walk, hand in hand with the Spirit, into the kingdom.
God forgives us, accepts us, and sends us forth to do good, and to testify about the One who baptizes us in the water and the Spirit. Thanks be to God. Amen.

Great Prayer of Thanksgiving
People of the living waters: the Lord be with you!
And also with you!
Beloved of the Lord, lift your hearts to God.
We lift our grace-washed hearts to the One who pours hope into us.
Children of the Spirit, offer your thanksgiving and praises to God.
**We sing 'Glory' to the God who baptizes us
with water and the Spirit.**

50

You immersed chaos
in the waters of creation,
God of new beginnings.
You stretched the sky
to fill it with shimmering stars,
   and taught the planets
   to prance like deer.
The mountains skipped with delight,
   dancing round and round with the rivers.
You took us by the hand
to play in Eden's joy,
   but we broke free
   to go running after
     sin and death.
You asked the prophets
to bear witness to all you did,
are doing, and will do,
   but we were averse
   to listening to their advice.
So, letting go of your glory,
you sent Jesus
to come to us
with your hope and redemption.

So, with those who have wandered
through every wilderness,
and those who have waded
in the waters of life,
we praise you that, in our baptism,
we are made one with those
of every place and time
forever singing of your grace:

Holy, holy, holy, God who blesses people with peace.
Creation skips like a child, coming to praise you.
Hosanna in the highest!

Blessed is the One who comes to fulfill all righteousness.
Hosanna in the highest!

Holy are you, hurler of the heavens,
and blessed is Jesus Christ,
your Beloved, our Servant and Lord.
When the evil one bullied us with fear,

he came to stand with us
    filling us with hope.
When we huddled in the shadows
of despair and doubt,
    he came to be the Light
    showing the path to faith.
When death was convinced
it had won the final battle,
    you gave him the go-ahead
    to leave the grave,
        to lead us back home.

In the baptism of his suffering and death,
in his journey through the waters of resurrection,
we are united with him,
even as we speak of that mystery we call faith,

Christ died, choosing to establish justice;
Christ rose, healing all who are oppressed by death;
Christ will return, taking us by the hand and keeping us for you.

Pour out your Spirit of grace
upon the gifts of the bread and the cup
and on those who gather to eat and drink
with the Risen Lord.
When we have been fed by your life,
and refreshed by your hope,
    may we go forth
    to bear witness to your presence
        in our lives and in our world.
With your Spirit upon us,
send us out:
    to speak of your peace,
        so that all violence might end;
    to bring healing
        to all tyrannized by terror;
    to work for justice
        in all the brokenness of our times;
    to welcome all
        with the inclusive love
        you have shown to us.

And when we gather at the banquet
you have catered with your joy and love,
we will join hands with all

gathered around the Table of grace and peace,
singing 'Glory! Glory! Glory!' to you,
God in Community, Holy in One. Amen.

Second Sunday after the Epiphany/Ordinary Time 2
Isaiah 49:1-7; Psalm 40:1-11
1 Corinthians 1:1-9; John 1:29-42

Call to Worship
In the bleak midwinter, we wait:
for the One who warms us with stories of love and hope.
In the stillness of a snowfall, we wait:
for the One who clears a path so we may follow in faith.
In the shadows of life, we wait:
for the One who lights the way through the world.

Prayer of the Day
Like a teacher
who bends down
to hear a shy student,
    you listen to our hearts;
like a fellow hiker,
    you reach down
    and pull us out
        when we have fallen
        into desolation's pit.
You are faithful,
Steadfast Love.

Like a school custodian,
    you scrub the graffiti
        off our graceless lives;
like a nurse,
    you clean out our ears
        so we can hear
        the hurt and loss around us,
    as well as your gentle reminder,
        "what are you looking for?
        Those are the ones to help."
You are faithful,
Servant of the poor.

Like a best friend,
    you whisper peace
        into our quaking ears;

53

like a debate student,
   you testify about
      God's never-ending love;
like an innocent child,
   you see wonder in every moment.
You are faithful,
Spirit of Salvation.

God in Community, Holy in One,
we proclaim your faithfulness even,
as in faith, we pray as we are taught,
Our Father . . .

Call to Reconciliation

Called to follow, we often trip over our temptations, falling flat on our faith. But God picks us up, sets us on the solid ground of grace, and sends us out as servants. Let us confess our sins to the One who is always faithful.

Unison Prayer of Confession

   Shaped, formed, born to be servants, Faithful One, we spend so much time focused on ourselves. Called to be saints, we deeply despise those with whom we disagree. Challenged to testify about the good news, we keep silent, hoarding stories of joy and hope for ourselves.

   Forgive us, Merciful Lamb. Give us open ears, that we might hear your words of pardon; give us open eyes, that we might see those you would have us serve; give us open hearts, that we might welcome the One who takes away our sins, Jesus Christ, our Lord and Savior.

Silence is kept

Assurance of Pardon

Listen! Before you were born, God called you by name, claiming you as God's child. Pay attention! You are forgiven.
We will not keep silent. We will tell, and we will sing; we will whisper, and we will shout: God is faithful! Amen.

Great Prayer of Thanksgiving

May the grace of God be with you!
And also with you!
Lift up your hearts, people gifted by God.
We offer all that we have to our God.

Let us give thanks to God always, dear ones of God.
We lift our praises to our faithful God,
who calls us into the household of faith.

You called creation into existence,
Gatherer of goodness.
You shaped the hollows
   to hold the waters of life,
you formed the stars
   to glitter in the night sky,
and the suns to warm
   all you created.
Before we were born from dust,
you named us as your own,
   giving us breath that
   we might honor you with our lives.
But when the world asked
about your constant love,
and death wondered if
you were indeed faithful,
   we responded, 'we do not know God,'
      and planted our feet deep
      into the mud of sin and desolation.
Deeply distressed by our rebellion
hoping to bring us back to you,
you sent the prophets
to gather us home.
But we abhorred their advice,
   and silenced them with our laughter.
So you sent Jesus,
the One we were looking for,
even though we did not know it.

So, we join our voices with all who,
in every place and time,
call on Jesus' name, singing:

Holy, holy, holy, God who takes away sins.
All creation tells the glad news of salvation.
Hosanna in the highest!

Blessed is the One whose trust is in you.
Hosanna in the highest!

Holy are you, Gatherer of the lost,
and blessed is Jesus Christ,
Salvation's Servant and our Lord.
He came,
   opening our eyes so we could see
   your light shining in our shadows;
he came,
   testifying that your love and faithfulness
   were the bookends
      holding together our lives;
he came,
   to carry our sins to the cross,
   so they would be left behind
      in sin's grave forever,
as the Risen Lord comes
to lead your people
back into the kingdom.

As we remember his birth, his life,
his words and wonders, his death and love,
we would speak of that mystery we call faith:

**Christ died, hidden in the shadow of God's heart;
Christ rose, delighting to do God's will;
Christ will return, to bring us back to God.**

As you gather us around the Table,
pour out your Spirit
upon the gifts of the bread and the cup,
and upon those who come,
longing to do your will
and to follow you faithfully.
May the bread which has been broken
shape us as servants
   to a world shattered
   by injustice and hopelessness;
as we drink from the cup,
may our hearts be reformed
   so we would hear the cries
   of the lost, the last, the least;
as we are embraced in your grace,
may we be reborn, not as saints
   who can bask in our own glory,
   but as servants who,
   abundant in gifts beyond measure,

would pour them out
for everyone we meet.

And when creation has been reborn
into the new heaven and the new earth,
and we are gathered around
the Marriage Banquet of the Lamb,
we will not keep silent
but will tell and sing, whisper and shout
of your grace and of your peace,
of your faithful and constant love,
God in Community, Holy in One. Amen.

Third Sunday after the Epiphany/Ordinary Time 3
Isaiah 9:1-4; Psalm 27:1, 4-9
1 Corinthians 1:10-18; Matthew 4:12-23

Call to Worship
As he walked by a lake, Jesus called folks to follow him.
And immediately, immediately!,
they left their work and went with him.
As Jesus journeys through our lives, he asks us to follow him.
In this moment, in this moment!,
we have the chance to leave the past behind,
and pursue him into God's future.
As Jesus wanders in our world, he invites others to join him.
We would join him in this ministry, reaching out to our neighbors,
without delay, without delay!

Prayer of the Day
When we get scared
in the middle of life,
    you hide us
    under the blanket of your grace;
when we struggle
with those who don't like us,
    you lift us up
    to see the Prince of Peace
        coming to make us one;
when we are lost,
    you stop playing hide-and-seek
    and call us home.
One thing we ask,
God of our hearts:
be gracious to us!

57

When our sin-parched throats
crack trying to whisper your name,
    you teach us glad songs;
when we are afraid
of what is hidden
in the shadows of life,
    you take our hand
    so we can walk
        in your Light;
when we are alone,
    we discover your face
    in every person we meet.
One thing we ask, Playmate of Peace:
keep calling us to follow!

When we no longer
see eye-to-eye,
    you cleanse our sight
        with living waters;
when we are stooped
by the beams of our burdens,
    you twist and shape them
        into a kids' playground;
when we find ourselves
living in sorrow's city,
    you pack us up and move us
        into hope's neighborhood.
One thing we ask, Foolish Grace:
walk with us!

One thing we ask,
God in Community, Holy in One:
listen to us as we pray, saying,
Our Father . . .

Call to Reconciliation
When we are embarrassed by how we have treated others, God invites
us to seek the face of grace. When we regret foolish words that cannot
be taken back, God reminds us of the hope which comes to us in every
moment. Let us confess our lives to the One who not only hears us, but
answers us with forgiveness.

Unison Prayer of Confession
We are reluctant to admit all the ways we have failed to be your

people. **Created to be one Body, Holy Hope, we are often torn apart by petty squabbles. Called to follow, we push and shove for first place in line. Invited to seek your face, we have trouble looking our sisters and brothers in the eye.**

You have promised to be our Light, Healing Heart, so lead us from the shadows of our sin and silliness. You have promised to be our salvation, so set us free to explore the depths of your heart. You have promised to lead us into your kingdom, so show us how to join hands with one another, as we follow our Lord and Savior, Jesus Christ.

Silence is kept

Assurance of Pardon
Right now, right now!, Christ proclaims the good news to us; Christ teaches us how to live with one another; Christ tears down all the barriers between us.
In God's math, joy is multiplied so that we cannot compute the number - we can only welcome this gift into our hearts, to share it with everyone we meet. Thanks be to God. Amen.

Great Prayer of Thanksgiving
May the Light of God be with you.
And also with you.
In this place and time, encounter the God of wonder.
We offer our hearts to the One we seek in every moment.
Sing glad songs to the God who is your salvation.
We will offer shouts of joy to our God!

Into the gloom of chaos,
a Light burst forth,
God of all time.
This light shone on life
in all its variety;
   it lit the way for the sea
     as it danced along
     the beaches of glory;
   it twinkled in the night,
   reflected in the eyes
     of your beloved children,
     created in your image.
When we could
have been playing leapfrog
in the meadows of Eden,
   we chose to stalk through

the shadows of sin and death.
The prophets came, inviting us
to leave our hidden lives,
so we could dwell in your heart,
　　but we chose to cast our gaze
　　at the temptations of the world.
Finally, your sorrow multiplied
beyond all measure,
you sent Jesus to proclaim the good news.

So, with those who lived in the former times,
and with those who will dwell in the latter moments,
we lift our glad songs of grace to you:

Holy, holy, holy, God who does not forsake us.
All creation shouts with joy to you.
Hosanna in the highest!

Blessed is the One who comes bringing the kingdom near.
Hosanna in the highest!

Holy are you, God of all joy,
and blessed is Jesus Christ, our Lord.
When he could have withdrawn
into your eternal glory,
　　he came to us,
　　　that we might be brought
　　　into your hopeful heart.
When he could have ignored
our foolish fighting,
　　he came to tear down
　　the barriers we have built,
　　　that we might be one with you.
When he could have claimed all power,
　　he emptied himself
　　of your love and life,
　　　that we might be filled
　　　with your peace forever.

As we celebrate his life and death,
as we sing of our joy multiplied
by the wonder of your love,
we speak of that mystery we call faith:

Christ died, crying out to his light and salvation;

Christ rose, breaking all the bonds of death;
Christ will come, making glorious the way to God.

Pour out your Spirit
upon the bread and the cup,
simple gifts with the sole purpose
of restoring us to wholeness,
and making us one with you
and with all our sisters and brothers.
As we gather around your Table,
may we break the boundaries
  of fear, of hurt, of loss
  which separate us,
    so we may serve each other.
As we turn from the Table,
may we see those
  who are lost and alone
  in our neighborhoods and homes,
    so we might carry grace
    to share with them.
As we hear your whispers
of hope and peace
in our hearts,
may we call to everyone we meet,
  'Come and join us;
    we will lead you
    to the hope you are longing for!'

And when all time, former and latter,
has come to an end,
and we have left gloom and desolation behind
to live in your Light forever,
we will join our hands
to dance in your glory,
singing glad songs for all eternity,
God in Community, Holy in One. Amen.

Fourth Sunday after the Epiphany/Ordinary Time 4
Micah 6:1-8; Psalm 15
1st Corinthians 1:18-31; Matthew 5:1-12

Call to Worship
We are blessed when we hunger for justice and thirst for reconciliation.
Our souls are nourished by God's hope and grace.

We are blessed when we grieve over the brokenness of the world,
choosing, as God does, to be
with those who are weak and powerless.
We are blessed when we become God's fools,
willing to do what is right and good, not what is easy.

Prayer of the Day
The hills sing your hopes,
and the valleys echo your dreams,
Holy God, of a world
    where we catch sight of you
       in the innocent hearts of children;
    where we listen to the wisdom
      of souls willing to be weak;
    where we find the home we long for
      in your heart's brokenness.

Teacher of our hearts,
when we are generous to the poor,
    your kingdom of justice is built;
when we love kindness
more than we do power,
    we are heirs of creation's grace;
when we walk hand-in-hand
with the humble-hearted,
    we are in step with you;
when we share a picnic of hope and joy
with the forgotten of the world,
    we follow you up the hill of faithfulness.

Wisdom of Weakness,
when our differences with one another
become stumbling blocks to life together,
    you come
    with your hopeful foolishness
      so your children
      might be at peace,
      and a blessing of life
      to a world in need of healing.

God in Community, Holy in One,
hear us as we pray as Jesus has taught us, saying,
Our Father . . .

Call to Reconciliation

62

Called to be weak,
  we idolize the powerful;
called to be foolish,
  we hunger for the world's wisdom;
called to be poor in spirit,
  we thirst for more and more.
Let us confess to God how following Jesus is often a stumbling block.

Unison Prayer of Confession
  How do we approach you, Exalted God, with our confessions?
We make you weary with our inability to do justice for the poor and
outcast. We gossip about those who are close to us, instead of
being their loving friend. We make promises, and then go back on
our word.
  Forgive us, God of Hope, and bless us with your mercy. By your
peace, we can do justice. By your love, we can act kindly. By your
grace, we can walk with you as humbly, and hopefully, as did our
Lord and Savior, Jesus Christ.

Silence is kept

Assurance of Pardon
It is through foolishness that God makes us wise;
it is through weakness that God strengthens us to serve;
it is through forgiveness that God makes us whole.
We cannot boast in what we have done, but only in the grace
and joy of our God, who showers us with mercy. Amen.

Great Prayer of Thanksgiving
May the God of foolishness be with you!
And also with you!
Blessed of our God, offer your hearts to the One
who has brought us into the kingdom.
We lift our spirits to God, who has chosen us, weak as we are.
Children of God, sing songs of justice, of peace, of kindness to our God.
We offer our praises to the One who fills us with grace and hope.

Blessed is all creation, God on high,
for you brought it out of chaos,
    setting free all that is beautiful and good.
The hills heard you singing in the morning,
calves and lambs danced in the meadows,
    drinking deeply from the rivers of life.
You invited us to live in your love,
building us a home on your holy hill.

63

But we chose the power of sin,
    believing that death was wiser than you.
You sent the prophets, men and women,
to reveal to us what is good,
    but we continued to do injustice,
    to love bitterness and cruelty,
    to parade arrogantly before you.
So, you sent Jesus, the source of life.

With those who are blessed because they trust your future,
and with those who are foolish enough to believe your promises,
we offer our songs of thanksgiving:

Holy, holy, holy, God who walks in our midst.
All creation hungers and thirsts for you.
Hosanna in the highest!

Blessed is the Poor One of your heart,
    who brings the kingdom to us.
Hosanna in the highest!

Holy are you, God of weakness,
for yours is the kingdom given to us.
And blessed is Jesus Christ,
who would not be moved from doing your will.
When he could have danced with the angels,
    he came and sat down among us,
    to teach us how to walk with you.
Blameless in your eyes and in your heart,
    he humbly walked among us,
    so we could find the kingdom's streets.
Sharing the gift of your peace
with those of us who fight with one another,
    he embraces us as sisters and brothers.
With tears flowing down his face at our brokenness,
    he wraps us in your shawl of hope.
Truly pure in heart, he took on our sins,
    so we might discover the freedom you offer to us.
Persecuted for our sake,
    he endured all kinds of evil
    brought against him by sin and death,
        trusting that your weakness
        is stronger than their feared power.

As we celebrate your wisdom in Christ,

as we remember his death and resurrection,
we speak of that mystery we call faith:

Christ died, foolish in the eyes of the world;
Christ rose, the despised One defeating death and sin;
Christ will come, for ours is the kingdom of heaven.

Blessed are the gifts of this Table,
and the Spirit which fills them with your life,
and who is poured into those
who gather in your holy place.
When the bread is broken and we eat of it,
　　we will see the poor in spirit,
　　and open our hearts to receive
　　　　the blessing of the kingdom
　　　　in which they already dwell.
When we drink from the cup
and our thirst for righteousness is filled,
　　we, too, will mourn that your vision
　　of peace, of hope, of mercy for
　　all your children has not been realized,
　　　　and we will join in seeking
　　　　to be taught justice by the marginalized,
　　　　to follow the example of kindness modeled by children,
　　　　to learn the steps of the dance of humility
　　　　　　from the weak of our world.

And when our final blessing comes at the end of time
and we are gathered together on your holy hill
to live with our sisters and brothers through eternity,
we will sing our praises to you,
God in Community, Holy in One,
for we will have inherited all your blessings. Amen.

Fifth Sunday after the Epiphany/Ordinary Time 5
Isaiah 58:1- 9a, (9b-12); Psalm 112:1-9, (10)
1st Corinthians 2:1-12, (13-16); Matthew 5:13-20

Call to Worship
To a society that lives in the shadowed recesses of doubt and fear,
God calls us to be light.
To a world where every appetite is fed until there is no taste to life,
God calls us to be salt.
To a time when loyalties are discarded as easily as the clothes we wear,
God calls us to be faithful.

Prayer of the Day
Creator of the Day,
you rise before dawn
    to make breakfast for the poor,
    to water our parched hearts
        with the joy of grace,
    and to patch the potholes
        poverty has made
        in the streets of the kingdom.

You proclaim
the mysteries of grace,
Voice of Fulfillment,
not with fancy words
    but in weakness,
        which gives strength
        to the weary;
    in compassion,
        which offers the guest room of your heart
        to the homeless;
    in love,
        as you take off your coat,
        and place it around the shoulders
        of a shivering child.

You speak softly,
Revealer of Wonders,
using the alphabet blocks
of grace and hope,
    so all can know
        the hidden heart of God;
    so all may know the words
        to proclaim the Light
        who has come into the world.

God in Community, Holy in One,
hear us as we pray as faithful children,
Our Father . . .

Call to Reconciliation
It is so simple - make a sandwich for the hungry, open our ears to the
crying child, and change unjust laws. These are how we are called to
worship God. Let us confess how we have not answered this call,
as we pray saying,

Unison Prayer of Confession

We admit, Holy One, how in superstition, we will throw salt over our shoulders, but find it hard to flavor a world made bland by the ordinary. We dim our gifts to save our energy, instead of shining as long as we can in society's shadowed corners. We skip a meal once a week to show our faith, but are unable to see those who go through the dumpster to feed their children.

Forgive us, and have mercy, Creation's Goodness. By your grace, heal our brokenness, so we might fix the shattered dreams of our world. With your hope, strengthen our hearts, so we might fill the emptiness of our society. This we ask in the wonderful name of Jesus Christ, our Lord and Savior.

Silence is kept

Assurance of Pardon

God has heard our prayers and comes to us to sweeten our bitterness with hope - to shatter our darkness with the light of mercy.
We will share this good news without being ordered to do so. We will praise God's name because we want to! Thanks be to God! Amen.

Great Prayer of Thanksgiving

May the Lord of the Feast be with you!
And also with you!
You are God's salt here on earth.
We offer our hearts to God, so they may be spiced with mercy, justice, and love.
You are God's light in this time.
We show the world the brokenness in its midst, so that all creation might be healed!

You would not let emptiness remain constant,
God of wisdom and wonder,
but brought forth creation,
    flavoring the seas with your salty tears,
    lightening the shadows of chaos
        so the universe could find the way
        as it unfolded from your imagination.
You shaped us in your image hoping
that, in faith, we would fast with you
on justice, peace, reconciliation, joy.
But when sin laid out its feast,
    we ran, pushing and shoving to the table,

to gorge ourselves on tempting entrees,
to be stuffed by deadening desserts.
Prophets came, reminding us of our stubbornness,
but we only practiced righteousness,
never getting past the first act.
So you sent Jesus to us,
to show us the fast you choose.

So, we join our voices with those
who call out to you in every age,
singing of your hopes for us:

Holy, holy, holy are you, God who holds our hearts.
All creation proclaims that mystery decreed before the ages.
Hosanna in the highest!

Blessed is the coming One, who is taught by the Spirit.
Hosanna in the highest!

You are the holiness of our lives, Loving God,
and Jesus Christ is your Light for all.
The bright morning star of creation,
he would not remain hidden,
but came to light the way for us.
The one who hung the stars in the heavens,
he comes to loosen the knots
tied tightly around the hearts of the oppressed.
The one who received every gift from you,
empties the closets filled with grace and hope,
sharing them with sisters and brothers everywhere.
The one who holds us in his heart,
opens his hands in surrender on the cross,
so that death's clenched fist will release us,
so our healing will spring up to embrace us.

As we remember how his light shone on all,
as we celebrate his spirit which enhances our lives,
we speak of that mystery of faith:

Christ died, to fulfill the law and the prophets;
Christ rose, to give glory to God;
Christ will come, to illumine the way to the kingdom.

Pour out your Spirit
upon the gifts of the bread and the cup,

prepared for those who love you.
As we unclench our fists
to receive your brokenness,
we would open our hearts in love
to those burdened by hopelessness,
we would feed all who hunger.
As we are welcomed at your Table,
and nourished by the cup of life,
we would add a room onto our homes,
to shelter a homeless family,
we would share from our abundance
to rebuild the shattered lives of the poor.

And when the yoke of time has been removed,
and we gather at the feast prepared for us in glory,
our songs of thanksgiving will be like springs of water,
which will flow for all eternity into your heart,
God in Community, Holy in One. Amen.

Sixth Sunday after the Epiphany/Proper 1/Ordinary Time 6
Deuteronomy 30:15-20; Psalm 119:1-8
1 Corinthians 3:1-9; Matthew 5:21-37

Call to Worship
You could have stayed in bed,
you could be eating breakfast out.
We have chosen to be in this place,
feasting on God's words.
You could give a cold shoulder to your neighbors,
you could warm yourself in front of the fire.
We have chosen to see God with more
than just a sliver of our hearts.
You could be chasing after the world's idols,
you could be listening to television's talking heads.
We have chosen to serve the One
who blesses us with life.

Prayer of the Day
Mothering God,
you nurse us with the milk
of blessing and joy,
so we may grow in faith
to feast on grace and hope.
You plow the fields of our hearts,
planting the seeds of love,

so we may be your people.
We hold fast to you,
God of Choices.

You provide the road map for our journey,
    so we will not wander
    down blame's alleys.
When we choose sides
by our quarreling and cliques,
    you reconcile us to each other
    with your words which are true.
We hold fast to you,
Jesus of Reconciliation.

Blessed with the fresh breeze
of your presence and power,
    we will continue to follow you,
    trusting that you will lead us
        into making the right choices
        as the disciples of Jesus.
We hold fast to you,
Transforming Spirit.

God in Community, Holy in One,
we hold fast to you, even as we pray,
as Jesus has taught us, saying,
Our Father . . .

Call to Reconciliation

Following God is not like flipping a coin, and choosing sides. It is intentional; it is difficult; it is risky. That is why we know all the ways we have failed in our discipleship and need to come to God. We choose to confess, so we might embrace the forgiveness God offers to us. Please join me, praying,

Unison Prayer of Confession

Invited to walk in your footsteps, Wanderer of the Universe, we turn away to play hopscotch on the sidewalks of seduction. Given the chance to watch you work wonders of grace and renewal, we fixate on the idols of success and power. When you want to tell us stories of healing and reconciliation, we decline to hear your gentle voice.

Have mercy on us, God of Blessings, and help us to choose to hold fast to your hand; to walk your streets of wholeness and hope;

to follow our Lord and Savior, Jesus Christ, into the life you intend for us.

Silence is kept

Assurance of Pardon
God's forgiveness dwells in our hearts; Christ's love fills us; the Spirit's peace guides our steps.
Our feet are set on the journey. Walking in faith and hope with our God, we will be servants to the world. Thanks be to God, we are forgiven! Amen.

Great Prayer of Thanksgiving
May the God of life be with you!
And also with you!
People of God, come to the Table of blessing.
We seek God's grace whole-heartedly.
Draw near to the word of wonder and hope, children of God.
We praise God with our lips, blessing others with our hearts, serving God's people with our hands.

You set before us those first days, Faithful God,
    the goodness, the beauty,
    the wonder, the mysteries of creation,
    blessing beyond compare,
       all given in hope and love to us.
Created to be with you, invited to walk with you,
our hearts turned away from yours,
    being led astray by sin's desires,
    bowing down at the altar of death.
You sent the prophets to us,
setting before us blessings,
challenging us to choose life.
    But we would not listen to them,
    letting lust continue to clog our hearts.
So you sent your Beloved to us,
letting your words become your Word,
your Servant of salvation for all.

We join our voices this day with all
who have faced the choices before us,
seeking your heart and singing your praise:

Holy, holy, holy, God of the blameless way.
All creation holds fast to your Word.

Hosanna in the highest!

**Blessed is the One who comes to reconcile us to you and others.
Hosanna in the highest!**

Our eyes are fixed on you, Holiness of the ages,
as we follow Jesus Christ, our Savior, our Teacher.
Setting aside his place with you and the Spirit,
he became flesh, fully human like us,
    so we might grow in your faith.
Seeing the broken pieces of our lives
scattered at our feet around us,
he came to put us back together,
    making us one with you.
Knowing we were not ready
to look sin square in the eye,
he chose death on the cross,
    so we might be blessed
    with your life forever.

As we remember how Jesus remained faithful,
as we seek to walk in his blameless ways,
we tell of that mystery of faith:

**Christ has died, seeking God whole-heartedly;
Christ has risen, God's Word being kept for us;
Christ will return, so we might not be put to shame.**

Here in this place, with your people,
you set before us the blessings
of the Cup and of the Bread,
pouring out your Spirit
on your children and your feast.
As we eat the brokenness which makes us whole,
    we will choose to follow your ways,
    into the streets of the world,
        to bring justice and hope to all
        who have been put to shame.
As we drink from the cup of life,
    we will choose to be servants,
        working together to bring reconciliation
        and peace to all shattered by violence.

And when you choose to bring time to a close,
when you choose to gather us around you,

72

we will join our sisters and brothers
from every time, and from every place,
who will forever sing your praises with upright hearts,
God in Community, Holy in One. Amen.

Seventh Sunday after the Epiphany/Proper 2/Ordinary Time 7
Leviticus 19:1-2, 9-18; Psalm 119:33-40
1 Corinthians 3:10-11, 16-23; Matthew 5:38-48

Call to Worship
God would teach us to love, even the imperfect people,
so we can love others as we love ourselves.
God would teach us to deny ourselves,
even walking the extra mile with us,
so we can give ourselves to others
as generously as Christ has been given to us.
God would teach us new ways to journey through life,
so we can follow the footprints of the Word
all the way to the kingdom.

Prayer of the Day
When we see you sharing your hope
    with the poor, the immigrant, the stranger;
when we watch you build a ramp
    for those in wheelchairs;
when we experience your willingness
    to help us in spite of our stubbornness;
when we hear your call to love
    over our yearnings to hate:
we know what holiness looks like,
God of Creation.

When you refuse to speak harshly
    to those who judge you;
when you wipe away the tears
    of those who would hurt you;
when you choose to respond nonviolently
    to those who would crucify you:
we know what peace looks like,
Light of the World.

When we hear you whisper
    of fair play and justice;
when you fill our hands with grace
    to be shared with others;

when you build our lives
    on the foundation of Christ's peace and love:
we know what power looks like,
Spirit alive in us.

We know what you look like,
God in Community, Holy in One,
and so we pray as Jesus has taught us,
even as we yearn to be your image here on earth,
Our Father . . .

Call to Reconciliation

God would teach us all we need in order to live in peace, to love others,
to walk the right paths. Let us confess how foolish we are not to listen to
such wisdom, as we pray together, saying,

Unison Prayer of Confession

A friend hurts us,
    we hurt them back;
someone hits us,
    we strike back;
a family member ridicules us,
    we gossip about him or her.
That is how we have been taught to deal with those around us.

But now, God of mercy,
you call us to a different life:
    the life of forgiving, not avenging;
    the life of peace, not anger;
    the life of love, not hate.
As you forgive us of all we have done,
may we walk in your new ways of living,
as we follow Jesus, our Savior, our Teacher.

Silence is kept

Assurance of Pardon

It begins with God and ends with God - that love which can create,
renew, restore. God loves you and forgives you - now and forever.
As we listen to God's songs of mercy, we are cradled in grace –
now and forever. Amen.

Great Prayer of Thanksgiving

May the God of grace be with you!
And also with you!

You are God's holy people.
We lift our hearts, for the Lord our God is holy.
Children of God, dance for joy.
For God takes us by the hand to lead us into the kingdom.

Master Builder,
you mixed together your Word and Spirit,
    pouring the foundation of creation,
    driving the supports of grace and hope
      deep into the rich soil of wonder,
    clapping in delight as peace carpeted
      the empty spaces, as the trees were framed
      together for the walls, letting the sunlight
        stream through your heart's windows.
These gifts of grace were for us,
but we turned our heads away,
    so we could stare at sin and death.
Prophets came to remind us that we were yours,
    but we mocked them crying, 'we can't hear you!'
    We stuck out our fears, tripping them.
But rather than demanding
an eye for an eye, a tooth for a tooth,
    you sent the delight of your heart, your Child,
    to speak to all your people.

So with those who find it easy to love enemies,
and with those who struggle to love neighbors,
we lift our praises to you:

Holy, holy, holy are you, Crafter of the stars.
All creation longs for your grace and peace.
Hosanna in the highest!

Blessed is the One who comes to judge us with justice.
Hosanna in the highest!

You alone are holy, Artisan of goodness and truth,
and blessed is your Word, Jesus Christ,
who calls us to new life.
When he could have clutched
the jacket of grace tight to himself,
    he took it off, giving it to us,
      handing us the mittens of mercy as well,
      along with hope's overcoat and salvation's scarf.

When he could have wreaked vengeance
on all who rebelled against you,
  he set it aside, taking up the cross,
  following death into its cold emptiness,
    being laid on the barren floor of the tomb,
loving us as if we were best friends,
and not enemies of the kingdom.

As we prepare for the feast of wonder,
as we remember all the Christ offers to us,
we speak of that mystery we call faith:

Refusing to disobey you, Christ died;
laying the foundation of resurrection, Christ arose;
teaching us we belong to you, Christ will come again.

Here, in this place we call holy,
in those moments we call sacred,
  pour out your Spirit upon your Table
  and your people gathered in this place.
You could have given us the scraps of your heart,
but you provide the finest bread which,
  in its brokenness, restores us to life.
Having eaten of its fill,
we can go forth to serve the poor,
  to welcome them as neighbor and friend.
The love which mixed the foundation of the world
overflows the cup which we are given to drink
washing away our pride, our stubbornness,
  so we may remove the impediments
    we have put in the path of those who seek you,
  so we may whisper hope into the ears
    of all deafened by the taunts of the world.

And when the foundations of the world crumble,
when time has faded into a distant memory,
you will gather us as your holy people,
  sitting neighbor next to friend, old enemies
  passing the bread and the cup next to one another,
all voices joining to sing your glory forever and ever,
God in Community, Holy in One. Amen.

Eighth Sunday after the Epiphany/Proper 3/Ordinary Time 8
Isaiah 49:8-16a Psalm 131
1 Corinthians 4:1-5; Matthew 6:24-34

Call to Worship

When our hearts are so heavy, it seems
we cannot carry them through the day,
God will give us compassion through our friends,
so we will not bear the load alone.
When our words are so inadequate
it seems we cannot speak them,
God will give us hope
so we can break forth in songs of joy.
When we have so lost our way
we stumble in the shadows of life,
God will give us light,
so we can find the living waters.

Prayer of the Day

To those who hunger and thirst
in the loneliness of life,
    you nourish us with compassion;
to those who huddle
in the shadows of unhappiness,
    you bring the light of joy.
You love us like a mother, Holy God.

To those held captive
by the stress of daily living,
    you whisper, 'let go; cling to me.'
To those who wonder each morning
what they should wear to school,
    you hand a bouquet of daisies.
You watch over us like a father,
Jesus of our hearts.

For those who stumble through life,
    you fill in the potholes of our worries;
for all those forgotten
as everyone rushes by them,
    you tattoo our faces on your palms,
so you will see us
every time you pray for us.
Like our parents,
you remember us,
Spirit of Joy.

God in Community, Holy in One,

Father, Brother, Mother,
hear us as we pray as we are taught,
Our Father . . .

Call to Reconciliation
Called to be servants and stewards of mysteries, we worry more about
how others will judge our hairstyles or choice of shows. Let us go to
God's store, where we will find grace and mercy, before wasting our
blessings on the trinkets of the world. Join me, as we pray, saying,

Unison Prayer of Confession
**You tell us not to worry, Mothering God, but we cannot seem to
help ourselves. With refrigerators full of food, we still make grocery
lists; with closets so full we cannot shut the doors, we run out and
buy new outfits; with a simple invitation to 'follow me,' we form
committees to help us decide.**

**We lift our hearts to you, Tender God, so you would fill them with
your mercy and hope. May we continue to seek your kingdom in
every moment to come, hoping and trusting in the peace and love
of Jesus Christ, our Lord and Savior.**

Silence is kept

Assurance of Pardon
Like a nursing child fed by its mother, God's mercy calms and quiets us,
so we can receive all that God wants to give us.
**We welcome all that God gives to us, and will share these gifts
with everyone we meet. Amen.**

Great Prayer of Thanksgiving
Hope in God!
Our hope is in the One who feeds us!
Do not be anxious about anything, children of God.
Our hearts are lifted to the One who feeds us at this Table.
Sing for joy, beloved of God, let your voices echo the joy of heaven.
God comforts us with life, with grace, with peace, with hope.

You called, Gentle Heart,
and creation stepped out of
the shadows of chaos
    into the light of goodness.
You would feed us
    from grace's bounty,
you would shelter us
    from the hazards of nature.

78

But we could not stop worrying
   about what to wear,
   or how long our lives would last,
     so we turned to sin and death
     for comforting answers.
Prophets came, assuring us
that you had not forgotten us,
but longed to help us.
   When we continued to trust
   in the world's seductions,
your compassion overflowed
as you sent Jesus
to bring us back to the waters
of life and hope.

So, with those of every time and place,
we lift our hearts to you,
bursting into songs of joy:

Holy, holy, holy are you, God of comfort and hope.
All creation breaks forth into singing.
Hosanna in the highest!

Blessed is the One who comes with compassion for the afflicted.
Hosanna in the highest!

Holy are you, God of Peace,
and blessed is Jesus Christ,
your Compassion, our Savior.
When our days were filled with despair,
   he came bringing the day of hope.
When our days overflowed with grief and pain,
   he came to bring the day of joy and life.
When our names were down on death's calendar,
   he came to bring the day of salvation.

As we remember all the days of his life,
the preaching, the teaching, the healing,
the sacrifice for us, the resurrection for all,
we celebrate that mystery we call faith:

Christ died, our souls engraved on the palms of his hands.
Christ arose, calling to all imprisoned by death, "come forth!'
Christ will come again, to quiet us at God's breast.

Pour out your Spirit
upon these simple gifts
from creation's goodness,
and upon your children
gathered in your name.
Given as a sign of your love,
may the bread we eat
strengthen us to serve those
for whom the world
has no pity.
Given as a seal of your compassion,
may the cup we drink
nourish us so we can
guide our sisters and brothers
to your justice and peace.

And when all time has ended
and there is only that day which lasts forever,
we will gather around your Table,
feeding upon your grace and mercy,
as we lift our hearts singing your praises,
God in Community, Holy in One. Amen.

Ninth Sunday after the Epiphany/Proper 4/Ordinary Time 9
Deuteronomy 11:18-21, 26-28; Psalm 31:1-5, 19-24
Romans 1:16-17; 3:22b-28, (29-31); Matthew 7:21-29

Call to Worship
Here is the promise:
when you ask for help, God will respond.
We will put these words in our hearts.
Here is the promise:
God's salvation is for all, a gift of grace.
We will share these words with our children.
Here is the promise:
whether we are foolish or wise, God loves us all.
We will carry these words with us through life.

Prayer of the Day
When we get trapped
in the shifting sands of prejudice,
you build fairness as a model for us;
when we stumble over the marginalized
sinking in their oppression,
you build justice in our hearts;

80

when we would choose the easy way
of cursing others and ourselves,
you whisper blessings into our souls.
Holy are you, God of Creation.

When we have no words to offer
to all those who suffer,
you write compassion on our hearts
so we may serve them.
When we wonder what we can say
to our children as they ponder
a future they cannot see,
you write hope onto our hearts,
so we may teach them.
Holy are you, Friend of the forgotten.

When we think that only fools
would believe in this thing called the gospel,
you wisely give us mentors
to show us the way.
When we think we have earned
enough bonus points to get into heaven,
you wisely remind us
that it is what God has done for us
that makes all the difference.
Holy are you, Spirit of Joy.

Holy, holy, holy are you,
God in Community, Holy in One,
and we lift the prayer Jesus has taught us, saying,
Our Father . . .

Call to Reconciliation
Each moment, and every moment; each day and every day, we face
choices. Will we help, or hurt another; will we speak in anger, or love;
will we see God in the other, or ignore them altogether? Let us confess
to God the poor choices we have made in our lives, as we pray, saying,

Unison Prayer of Confession
    **Why do we worry so much about earning points with you, Heart
of Holiness, when it is your grace which sets us free? Why is it we
can glide so gracefully through temptation, yet trip when we try to
follow Jesus? Why do the false promises of the world tantalize our
souls, while we cannot remember your words of blessing?**

81

Forgive us, Foundation of Faith, when we make the wrong choices. Write your words of grace and hope on the doors of our hearts, so we can open them to the love and mercy, Jesus Christ, our Lord and Savior, brings to us.

Silence is kept

Assurance of Pardon

It is not because of anything we do, or by some great human endeavor on our part, that God forgives us. It is finally, and simply, because of God's gracious love for us.

Now, we stand on solid ground; now, we find our sins forgiven; now, we find our shattered lives put back together. Thanks be to God. Amen.

Great Prayer of Thanksgiving

May the God of blessings be with you.

And also with you.

People of God, offer your hearts to the One who loves you.

May God write words of courage and hope on them.

Sing glad songs to the One you love.

We rejoice, as we commit our lives to God.

In that first moment,
you spoke, Ingenuous God,
and your creation was revealed:
> fall's kaleidoscope of colors;
> winter's frost-tipped bushes and icy streams;
> spring's bouquets of every fragrance;
> summer's fireflies flickering in the night.
All was created for those shaped in your image,
whom you would shelter in Eden's wonders,
> but we turned away from all this beauty,
> crying out, "we never knew you!"
> as we built our lives on temptation's shifting sands.
Seeking to untangle us from sin's snares,
the prophets came, calling us to choose
between your blessings and evil's curses,
> but we continued to fall short of your hope.
So you sent Jesus into the world,
to reveal your righteousness to us.

With those who kept your words in their hearts,
and those who have tattooed them on their souls,
we lift our voices in praise to you:

Holy, holy, holy are you, God our Rock and Redemption.
All creation is filled with your overflowing goodness.
Hosanna in the highest!

Blessed is the One who came to do your will.
Hosanna in the highest!

You are holy, God of every moment,
and Jesus Christ, our Savior, is blessed forever.
Seeing us sinking in sin's sands,
    he came with the blueprints
    of how we can build our lives on you.
Refusing to boast of his glory and wonder,
    he whispered the songs of salvation
    and shouted the good news of redemption.
Gathering up the curses of death,
    he carried them into the grave,
    leaving them behind to turn to dust,
    as he strode out into your new life.

As we see your righteousness revealed in Jesus,
as we are justified by the grace he offers,
we proclaim that faith which is a mystery:

Christ died, being faithful to your will;
Christ is risen, revealing the power of your salvation;
Christ lives in us, so we are not ashamed of the gospel.

Here at this Table of love,
as your children gather to be fed,
pour out your Spirit upon the simple gifts
of the bread and the cup you prepare for us.
As we come to the Table,
may the Bread of Life, broken for us,
    strengthen us, so we may
    commit our lives to serving others.
As we drink from the Cup of Grace,
    may we listen to the cries
    of the broken and the lost,
    and become blessings to them.

And when our journey through this life has ended,
when we gather in the shelter of your eternity,
we will join our voices with our sisters and brothers

at the Feast of Heaven which is offered to us,
forever singing our praise and joy to you,
God in Community, Holy in One. Amen.

Transfiguration/Last Sunday after the Epiphany
Exodus 24:12-18; Psalm 99
2 Peter 1:16-21; Matthew 17:1-9

Call to Worship
On glory's mountaintops
of wonder and delight, we wait:
for God's amazing grace
to transform our shadowed lives.
In the valleys of everyday life,
where noise overwhelms us, we wait:
willing to waste time
simply being in God's presence.
In the devouring fires of fear,
in the mist of misguided living, we wait,
for the One who comes in majesty,
to lead us down the paths of humility.

Prayer of the Day
When you could stay
hidden behind your glory,
    you send Jesus,
    to show us your heart.
When you could
remain silent for all time,
    you whisper your hopes
    to us in every moment.
When you could remain
on the pinnacle of our praises,
    you enter the depths
    of our shadowed lives.
Splendor's glory:
You are holy!

When we bump along
over the potholes of impatience,
    you smooth out our lives
    with your wisdom.
When we live in
the hollows of hopelessness,
    you would transfigure us

with your joy.
When we wander the lonely
valleys of grief and death,
    you are beside us,
    holding our hearts.
Humility's Lover -
You are holy!

You transform every day events
    into miracles of awe;
you text message joy
    onto the emptiness of our souls;
you enter the fog
of our feeble, fear-filled faith,
    to reveal to us
    the Morning Star of hope.
Glory's Mystery -
You are holy!

God in Community, Holy in One,
you are the glory of our mountaintops
and the comfort of our valleys,
even as we pray, saying,
Our Father . . .

Call to Reconciliation
Sometimes it seems that we wait for God to astound us with mighty
wonders, while God knows that what we need is grace. God waits
to forgive us, so let us hold nothing back, but trust in the One who listens
to our prayers and answers us with mercy,

Unison Prayer of Confession
    **God of mountaintops, the din of the world can harden our hearts
to your Word. We watch news, reality TV, silly sitcoms, yet have
trouble bearing witness to your presence in our lives. Our faith is
placed in those who fail us, our trust is given to those who misplace
it.**
    **Forgive us, Revealer of Mystery. You offer mercy to us, that we
might hear your call to discipleship. You whisper our names, that
we might know how loved we are. Caught by the surprise of your
never ending love for us, how can we not follow our Lord and
Savior, Jesus Christ, onto the mountaintops of worship and into the
valleys of sacrifice and service!**

Silence is kept

85

Assurance of Pardon
On mountaintops and in the valleys, in our homes and in our hearts, God knows us better than we know ourselves, and God forgives us when we cannot forgive ourselves.
By God's mercy, we are forgiven.
By God's mercy, we are made whole.
By God's mercy, we are equipped to serve others.
Thanks be to God. Amen.

Great Prayer of Thanksgiving
The Lord of the dawning day be with you.
And also with you.
People of God, open your hearts to the One who feeds you with grace.
Our hearts tremble with delight for the feast which awaits us.
People of God, give thanks to the One who meets us on the mountaintops of glory and in the valleys of service.
We praise God's great and holy name.

Shaper of mountains and Carver of rivers:
it is our greatest joy to offer you
our praise and thanksgiving in these moments.
    All things in every place were created by you
    to rejoice in your radiant splendor.
Created by you to live in your garden of hope and joy,
    we believed in the shrewd schemes of the world,
    and wandered into the valleys of death and sin.
But you did not forsake us, but became one of us
that we might be transformed into new life.
You gave us the Breath of life and the Word of grace
so all the living could find voice to sing your glory.

Therefore, we join with those of every time and place
singing the ancient hymn of majesty and glory:

Holy, holy, holy are you, Lover of justice.
You are exalted over all creation.
Hosanna in the highest!

Blessed is the One who comes to touch us,
    whispering, 'do not be afraid.'
Hosanna in the highest!

Mighty God, shelter of all who love you,
you are seated upon the praises of your people.

On the mountain of holiness
    you proclaimed Jesus Christ as your Beloved,
    the hope of all your children.
He descended the mountain of glory
to climb up a garbage heap called Calvary.
When he could have stayed with Moses and Elijah,
    he chose to be crucified between two thieves.
When he could have taken shelter
within your love and hope,
    he endured the cross of pain and suffering.

And so, we proclaim our faith
as we come to your Table:

Christ died, defeating the power of sin;
Christ rose, God's love overshadowing death;
Christ will come again, for all who have waited for him.

Descend upon us, Holy Spirit,
and on these gifts of the Bread and the Cup.
As we share them with one another,
may we be restored to wholeness.
Strengthened by the broken bread,
    may we greet each dawn with the resolve
    to be such lovers of justice,
        that none will remain oppressed.
Nourished by the overflowing cup of grace,
    may we work through the long hours of night
    to feed the hungry, to shelter the homeless
    until, together, we welcome the Morning Star
        into our hearts.

And when all our waiting is done,
when the stars of creation join in song,
we will get up from the Table of the Lamb,
    joining our hands with our sisters and brothers
    from every time and from every place,
        forever dancing in joy with you,
God in Community, Holy in One. Amen.

Ash Wednesday

(Note that while we use Taize songs for our worship, other songs can
be substituted)

Silent Prayer in Preparation for Worship
As you begin this service, take a few moments to bring yourself before
God - your present state of mind and preoccupations, as well as your
desire to meet God during this time.

Call to Worship
God's people have been called to gather.
From breast-feeding infants to aged grandparents,
all are welcome.
God's people have been called to repent.
From those who wear their faults on their sleeves,
to those whose secret hearts are broken,
all are welcome.
God's people have been called to be reconciled to our God.
From those who have turned away,
to those whose pain whispers in the night,
all are welcome.

Taize song "Wait for the Lord"

Prayer of the Day and our Lord's Prayer
God of holiness:
your day comes near,
and we tremble,
not out of fear,
but from awe and gratitude.
    For on your day,
    we are fully known,
    completely restored,
    reconciled to you forever.

Jesus Christ,
Grace Bearer:
as we come to your fast,
    may we be filled with your hope;
as we receive your gifts,
    may our hearts be opened to others;
as we begin our journey with you,
    may we put no roadblocks
    in the path to Jerusalem.

Holy Spirit,
Creator of clean hearts:
as water rushes
into an empty hole,

may your sacramental silence
fill the emptiness of our souls.

God in Community, Holy in One,
our Treasure, our Hope, our Joy,
hear us as we pray as Jesus taught us, saying,
Our Father . . .

Taize song "In the Lord, I'll Be Ever Thankful"

Joel 2:1-2, 12-17

Taize song "Our Darkness"

Psalm 51 (read in unison)

Taize song "In God Alone My Soul"

2 Corinthians 5:20b - 6:10

Taize song "Our Eyes"

Matthew 6:1-6, 16-21

Silence is observed (10 minutes)

Invitation to Lenten Disciplines
Beloved in Christ,
at the time of the Christian Passover,
we celebrate our deliverance from sin and death
through the death and resurrection
of our Lord Jesus Christ.
Lent is the season of preparation
for this great celebration,
the means by which we renew our life
in the Paschal mystery.
We begin our Lenten journey
by acknowledging our need for repentance,
for in penitence,
we name those things
which damage us and others
for what they really are,
and we open ourselves
to the One whose love knows no boundaries
and whose mercy is demonstrated to us

89

in the life of Jesus Christ.

By taking an honest look at our lives,
and repenting of our humanness;
by praying quietly
but with full hearts;
by letting go of those things that harm us
and by taking on works of love for others;
by reading and feasting on God's Word,
we observe a holy Lent,
and prepare ourselves for the passion of Holy Week
and the joy of Easter.

Let us prepare ourselves
to come to our God.

Taize song "O Lord, Hear My Prayer"

Call to Reconciliation
God begs us to turn from those words, those acts, those obstacles
which keep us from being God's people. As we begin our Lenten journey,
I invite you to join with me, with words and in silence, as we bring
our brokenness to God who desires to make us whole.

Unison Prayer of Confession
**Too long have we traveled our own ways, Approaching God, too
long have we sought to satisfy our hidden desires. We have trusted
the falsehoods of the world, and relied on that power which would
consume our souls. We have sought healing from impostors, and
rejected the One who was broken for our wholeness.**

**Have mercy on us, God whose love overflows our deepest
hopes. Let our hearts be a sanctuary for your Spirit; let our lives
abound in service to others; let our spirits reflect the One we call
our Lord and Savior, Jesus Christ.**

Silence is kept

Assurance of Pardon
God lets go of the punishment we deserve and gives us mercy in its
place. Willingly, God puts a new spirit into us, the spirit of hope and joy.
**We will sing to the One who has delivered us from our sins. We
will praise God with cleansed hearts. Thanks be to God. Amen.**

Imposition of the Ashes
Our ancestors in the faith

used ashes as a sign of our repentance,
a symbol of the uncertainty and fragility
    of human life.
Like them,
    we have tasted the ashes of hopelessness;
    we have walked through the ashes
        of our loss and pain;
    we have stood knee-deep
        in the ashes of our brokenness.

God of our lives,
out of the dust of creation
you have formed us and given us life.
May these ashes not only be a sign
of our repentance and death,
but reminders that by your gift of grace
in Jesus Christ, our Redeemer,
we are granted life forever with you.
Amen.

(A period of silence will follow. Those who wish to do so, may come
forward to have the sign of the cross placed on their foreheads or
hands. The ashes are from palm branches used at Palm Sunday
services in the past, mixed with oil).

Responsive Invitation to the Table (from Isaiah 58)
We try, God knows, we try.
We show up at church, hoping God will notice.
We study Scripture, pretending God is reading aloud to us;
we put on those masks to show everyone
    how proper we are,
    how law-abiding,
    how religious;
and we wonder - does God even care?
Not when we clench our fists in anger,
    rather than opening them in love;
not when we work people too hard,
    and pay them too little;
not when we speak bitter and harmful words
    to those we are given to love.
So tonight, as we begin our Lenten fast,
God offers us a feast. Why?
So that the broken bread will strengthen us
    to break the chains of injustice,
    to take the burden of poverty off our neighbors,

to stop trying to control those around us,
to fix a meal for the hungry.
God offers us a feast
so that the cup of grace will free us
to take coats out of our closets
and wrap them around shivering shoulders;
to offer shelter to the homeless
without judging them;
to spend more time with our families
and less on the internet.
So, come to this Table and eat.
Then, you will see the light God offers to your darkness;
then, you will find the path God calls you to walk;
then, you will discover God waiting to help you,
even before you say a word.
We will come to this Table and feast.

Great Prayer of Thanksgiving
People of God, the Lord be with you.
And also with you.
People of dust, lift up your hearts to God.
We lift them up to the One who created us.
People of ashes, give thanks to the Lord our God.
Praise and thanks are offered to the One who restores us to life.

Now is the right time to praise you;
now is the moment to sing your praises,
Holy God of Creation.
You formed us to live in joy
and peace with you,
but we tore your heart
when we chose our desires
over your dreams for us.
We prefer to swim in the cesspool of the world
than to be cleansed in your living waters.
We hunger more for the adulation of others
than for the quiet intimacy of your grace.
Yet you did not turn away from us
but remained true to your covenant,
calling us to return in the words
trumpeted by the prophets;
inviting us to gather in your kingdom,
entreating us to accept your overflowing love.

Therefore, we glorify you,

joining our voices with those
who had wandered far from you,
but who were brought home;
and with those who seek you now
in this time and place:

Taize song "Bless the Lord"

Holy are you, Steadfast Love,
and blessed is Jesus Christ, Bread of Life.
Considered a pretender to David's throne,
    he is your heart's true Son.
Taking on the poverty of the human spirit,
    he shared the abundance of your heart;
weeping over our broken relationships,
    he reconciles us with your saving joy;
having nothing he could call his own,
    he gives us more than we ever need;
dying like a common criminal,
    he gives us life,
        releasing us from the grip of sin and death.

Preparing to journey with him once again,
we remember the mystery
of his faithful obedience to your heart:

Taize song "Jesus Christ, Bread of Life"

Holy Spirit,
Heart of Compassion:
as the ashes of our humanity
are placed upon your baptismal seal,
so the brokenness of our lives
is placed on the Table of grace,
so the bread might make us whole,
and the cup might fill us with hope.
Then, in your wisdom,
    may we turn to serve others;
in your joy,
    may we bear the burdens of others;
in your grace,
    may our love overflow to others.

Through Christ, with Christ, in Christ,
in the community of the Holy Spirit,

all glory and honor are yours,
God of holiness, now and forever. Amen.

The Breaking of the Bread
The Sharing of the Cup
(while receiving communion, you are invited to sing the Taize song,
"Eat This Bread")

Prayers of Petition

Taize song "Jesus, Remember Me"

Please depart the sanctuary in silence

First Sunday in Lent
Genesis 2:15-17; 3:1-7; Psalm 32
Romans 5:12-19; Matthew 4:1-11

Litany for Lent
O Christ,
led by the Spirit
to wander temptation's wilderness,
you show us how
to turn our backs
on the wrong ways of the world,
so we can follow you faithfully:
Walk with us, Lord Jesus.
O Christ,
Wellspring of wonder,
you let go of your glory,
so you might hold
our shattered hearts.
Cradle us, Lord Jesus.
O Christ,
grace-full and truth-full,
you empty yourself
to fill us with the bread
which makes us whole,
with the living waters
which burst the banks
of our faded dreams.
Fill us, Lord Jesus.
O Christ,
shatterer of sin's death grip,
into our despair, you bring hope;

into our fear, you come with peace;
in our loneliness, you become our brother.
Save us, Lord Jesus.
Jesus Christ, Lamb of God:
have mercy on us.
Lamb of God, who takes away
the sins of the world:
pour our your grace upon us.
Jesus Christ, gift of salvation:
grant us your peace.

Silence is kept

You hold nothing, nothing!
back from us, Gardener of Grace.
Your very self came to us,
your very heart was broken for us,
your life was poured out for us,
in Jesus, our Brother, our Savior.
We seek to do your will,
to share your truth,
to sing of your faithfulness,
to proclaim the good news,
as we follow Jesus
into the wonder of your kingdom,
praying as he taught us, saying,
Our Father . . .

Call to Reconciliation
Like a parent, God seeks to set boundaries for the children of God. And,
like children, we are stubborn enough to want to do things our own way.
So we become easy prey for the evil one. But Jesus, our Brother, shows
us how to find the will, the strength, to resist and to know the mercy of
God. Together, let us confess our sins, so God might fill us with hope
and joy.

Unison Prayer of Confession
    **God of Eden's morning, we know that Lent is a hard time for us.
In a culture which showcases success, you call us to sacrifice
ourselves for others. In a world which promotes power, you invite
us to deny ourselves. In a society which encourages us to 'feel
good,' you point us to the struggles of our sisters, the burdens our
brothers bear.**
    **By your mercy, forgive us, Hope of our lives. Remind us that as
we journey with Jesus, we learn the steps of discipleship. As we**

95

listen to his call to obedience, may we learn how to say 'no' to all that tempts us. As we see his suffering, may we live out the good news which has come to us through our Lord and Savior, Jesus Christ.

Silence is kept

Assurance of Pardon
By ourselves, we would be controlled easily by sin and temptation. But God has given us the free gift of grace, and so we are set free to live as disciples.
This is the gift which brings us hope;
this is the gift which brings us joy;
this is the gift which brings us life.
Thanks be to God, we are forgiven! Amen.

Great Prayer of Thanksgiving
The Lamb of God be with you!
And also with you!
All who search for God, lift your hearts.
We offer them to the One who comes searching
for us in the wilderness of life.
People of God, sing praises to the Lord.
We worship our God, and will serve God alone.

You tilled the barrenness
of chaos, Gardener of Genesis,
freely giving life to all
that is good and beautiful.
    Shade trees with ripe fruit,
    flowing streams, and creeping things,
    skies bright with your joy,
    clouds scudding across your hopes -
        all were formed for our safe keeping.
But what was a delight in your eyes,
was a disappointment in ours,
    and so we looked to the world,
    finding the bread which
        cannot fill our emptiness,
    drinking from temptation's cup,
        which only increases our thirst.
You sent the prophets
to lead us out of our wilderness,
    but we clung to the rocks

96

which gave us no foundation.
Then you sent Jesus,
to carry the free gift of grace
into our hearts.

Therefore, with all those
who have journeyed with you
in every time and place,
we lift our glad cries of deliverance:

Sung: **Creator of the stars of night,**
Your people's everlasting light,
O Christ, Redeemer of us all,
We pray you hear us when we call.

Holy are you, God of goodness and glory,
and blessed is Jesus Christ, your Holy Child.
Fluent in the language of grace,
he speaks to us of
    your steadfast love for us;
passing every test and temptation offered to him,
he teaches us
    obedience and faithfulness;
willing to be the one to carry the sins of others,
he went to the cross,
    faithfully serving only you,
    even into suffering and death.

Risen in glory from the grave,
he welcomes us to this Table,
even as we sing of that mystery called faith:

Sung: **At your great name, O Jesus, now**
All knees must bend, all hearts must bow:
All things on earth with one accord,
Like those in heaven, shall call you Lord.

Pour out your Spirit
upon the bread and the cup,
and upon your children
gathered around this Table.
As we turn towards Jerusalem,
may we reject the temptation
to focus only on ourselves,

97

but engage in
radical acts of obedience:
    feeding the hungry around us,
    nurturing the children left behind,
    comforting the lonely and ignored,
    picking up the brokenness
    and restoring our world
        with your peace and reconciliation.

Then, when our journey has ended,
and we are surrounding your Table in glory,
we will welcome our family and friends,
as we share peace with our enemies,
singing through all eternity
of the One who has brought us home:

Sung: **To God the Father, God the Son,
And God the Spirit, Three in One,
Praise, honor, might, and glory be
From age to age eternally. Amen.**

(sung responses are from a Latin hymn dating back to the 9th century "Creator of the Stars of Night")

Second Sunday in Lent
Genesis 12:1-4a; Psalm 121
Romans 4:1-5, 13-17; John 3:1-17

Call to Worship
In this season of discipleship,
God calls us to leave our comfortable lives,
**to journey, like Abraham and Sarah,
into that unknown, yet strangely certain,
country called faith.**
On sleepless nights, in fear's shadows,
we toss and turn with doubt's questions,
**hoping, like Nicodemus, to find Jesus
and to listen willingly to his responses.**
Reluctant to deny ourselves, convinced
that everything, every thing, depends on us,
**we struggle to affirm, as Paul did,
that everything, every thing, is in God's hands,
and we can let go of all to which we cling.**

98

In this season of discipleship,
we long to follow Jesus,
wherever he may go, wherever he may lead,
just like Abraham, Sarah, Nicodemus, Paul,
and so, so many others.

Prayer of the Day
Every moment is a gift,
from you, Keeper of our lives.
When we would foolishly
slip away from your side,
    you take our hands,
      and lead us into that adventure
        we call obedience.

Every day which races by,
every moment which drags
through the night, you are with us,
Watcher of our souls.
When our thoughts get
tangled with temptations,
    you unravel the knots
      so we can listen to you.
When we toss and turn
with our doubts and fears,
    you lullaby us to sleep
      with God's promises.

Every breath we take,
every grace born in us,
is our immersion in you,
Spirit which never rests.
    In the words we speak,
      you sing of hope;
    in the prayers we whisper,
      you bring healing;
    in the service to which you call us,
      we find our peace and purpose.

God in Community, Holy in One,
hear us, in this and every moment,
as we pray as Jesus teaches us, saying,
Our Father . . .

Call to Reconciliation

Late at night, in the shadows and the silence, we know ourselves for who we truly are: people who have stumbled over sin, those who wander the wasted walkways of the world. Knowing this truth, let us come to God, not to boast of who we think we are, but to confess our failures and our foolishness.

Unison Prayer of Confession

We want to brag about how good we are, and all the good we do, but you do not want to hear it, Generous Grace. You know how easily we slip off the paths of discipleship, as we come near the distractions of the world. We seem to be more comfortable in the shadows of doubt, than basking in the warm sun of trust. We try to control the Spirit, so she blows when we choose, and works according to our directions.

Forgive us, and fill us with new faith, Keeper of all hearts. If we will but listen to you, we will know your ways. If we know your ways, we can go to others to proclaim the gospel. If we proclaim the good news with our lives, we will bear witness to the One who came to save not only us, but all the world - Jesus Christ, our Lord and Savior.

Silence is kept

Assurance of Pardon

Lift up your eyes! God loves the world - God loves YOU! - so much that Jesus was given to grace us with life.
Our salvation comes from God, who will lift us up when our faith has fallen, to place us on the paths to the kingdom. Thanks be to God. Amen.

Great Prayer of Thanksgiving

The God of faith journeys be with you.
And also with you.
People of God, offer your hearts to the One who keeps them.
We open ourselves to the Watcher of our nights and days.
Sing praises to the One who transforms despair into hope.
We join in the glad chorus of joy to the One who keeps our lives in every moment.

Holy Eternal One:
in that moment when time began,
you took life by the hand,
    bringing it out of chaos's night,
    to be a blessing to all creation.
You lifted up mountains we could climb,

100

puddles in which we could play,
trails on which we could walk with you.
But we became star-struck
by the performances of sin and death,
believing their lies to be words of truth,
trusting their boasts of success and power.
You called the prophets
to show us how
to find our way back to you,
but our feet kept skipping after
those who would destroy us.
So, out of your great love,
for us - and for all creation -
you sent Jesus,
who came by your Light to save us.

Therefore, we would lift up our voices
with Abraham and Sarah, with Paul and Phoebe,
with all the saints (and sinners) of every time and place,
forever singing to the One who watches over us:

Holy, holy, holy are you, God who calls into existence
the things that do not exist.
All creation lifts its eyes to you.
Hosanna in the highest!

Blessed is the One who comes to redeem
all the families of the earth.
Hosanna in the highest!

Holy are you, Watcher of our nights,
and blessed is Jesus Christ,
Answerer of all our questions.
He came,
to teach us wonders
we could never imagine;
he came,
to show us that grace
is not the bonus we earn,
but the hope given
to the out-of-luck;
he came,
to silence the boasting
of sin and death,

by being lifted on the cross,
lowered into the grave,
and raised to new life -
for us and for all the world.

As we sing of your help which comes in every moment,
as we remember that life which graces us forever,
we would testify about that mystery we call faith:

Christ died, in order that we might be saved;
Christ rose, to keep our lives;
Christ will come, to keep our going out and coming in forever.

Though we cannot direct her,
we pray the Spirit chooses
to grace the bread and the cup,
and those who gather for this feast.
Made whole by the Bread of life,
may we go to the brokenness
where you would send us.
Nourished by Christ's Spirit,
may we go to the needs
of our neighbors around us.
Saved by your love
which we dare not control,
may we go to the strangers
who are all around us, so
that hand-in-hand
we may enter the kingdom.

Then, when our moments
are folded into your eternity,
when our boasting is silenced
and our eyes are lifted to your glory,
we will sing forever to the One
who has kept us safe in Love's heart:
God in Community, Holy in One. Amen.

Third Sunday in Lent
Exodus 17:1-7; Psalm 95
Romans 5:1-11; John 4:5-42

Call to Worship
We come, our souls thirsting for God,
our spirits longing for love.

**We come to the One who supplies every need;
we come to the One who gives us living water.**
We come, with prayers in our hearts,
and with words too painful to speak.
**We come to the One who listens to our hearts,
who carries our suffering through eternity.**
We come, with our brokenness and loss,
with our hope to be made whole.
**We come to the One who knows all our secrets,
who brings peace to all of us - and to each of us.**

Prayer of the Day

When we were determined
to remain at war with you,
    you sent the Prince of Peace.
When our relationship with you
was lying in pieces on the floor,
    you offered the broken Bread
    to restore us to wholeness.
When petty pride
stiffens our necks so much
we cannot bow down
in your holy presence,
    you massage our souls
    with grace's tender touch.
We worship you in joy,
God, our God.

When our ears become stuffed
with our selves,
    you open them with songs
    of grateful praise.
When our mouths overflow
with rich, sweet whine,
    you wash them out
    with living waters of hope.
When all we can say
is 'Give me! Give me!'
    you challenge us
    to submit to servanthood.
We worship you in sprit,
Jesus, Water Giver.

When our souls are empty,
    you fill them with living water.

When we are reluctant
to follow Jesus,
    you steer us in the right direction.
When we are tempted to boast,
    your whispers of grace silence us.
We worship you in truth,
Comforter of our hearts.

God in Community, Holy in One,
our joy, our truth, our spirit,
we worship you, as we pray, saying,
Our Father . . .

Call to Reconciliation

Walking the dog, reading a bedtime story, recycling newspapers - in
every moment, in every place, God is there. Let us confess how often
we do not see God in our lives, especially in how we live them.

Unison Prayer of Confession

**God of eternity, you know how often we travel down the rocky
roads of doubt and fear. We pester others with our worries; we hurl
bitter words at those we love. We have chances to offer ourselves
in service, but give only our contempt to those in need. We could
share the living waters with the world, but want to store it in jars for
safe-keeping.**

**Fountain of Grace, you turn towards us, to meet us wherever we
are. You break open our rock-hard sin, so we might be made whole.
In Jesus Christ, our Lord and Savior, our thirst for hope and joy is
quenched.**

Silence is kept

Assurance of Pardon

God does not disappoint us. Our sins are forgiven, our lives are made
whole, we are sent forth to serve.
**In Jesus Christ, living water breaks through the roof of our hearts,
in such abundance that we don't have enough buckets to hold it all.
Thanks be to God. Amen.**

Great Prayer of Thanksgiving

May the God of love be with you!
And also with you!
May the God of dolphins and little children fill you.
Our hearts swim in the depths of God's joy.

Sing praises to the One who saturates our arid souls with peace.
Our voices are lifted in glad songs of thanksgiving.

With the Spirit,
you struck stony chaos,
and creation gushed forth,
    to fill the hollows of heavens,
    to seed the mountains
        you cradled in your wisdom.
You longed to sit by Eden's well,
telling us stories of the world
you were shaping for us.
    But we tested you
    with our quarreling ways.
Hearing the boasts of sin and death,
    we bowed down and
    worshiped at their altars.
Prophets came to lead us
through despair's desert
back home to you,
    but our ears were clogged
    with temptation's seductive songs.
Finally, you sent Jesus
to meet us in our brokenness,
to save us by your grace.

Therefore, we join our voices
with saints and sinners,
with testers and pesterers,
who forever sing your praises:

Holy, holy, holy, God of rocks and rebels!
From the depths of the seas to the far reaches of the stars,
    all creation praises you.
Hosanna in the highest!

Blessed is the One who comes to be among us.
Hosanna in the highest!

Holy are you, Grace-giving God,
and blessed is Jesus Christ,
the Fountain of our hope.
When we were too weak to resist,
    Christ came to take on sin and death.
When we are unfaithful,

Christ shows us your constant love.
When our fears and failures stain our souls,
    Christ cleanses us.
When our hopes for life had faded,
    Christ died that we might live forever.

As we remember his gentle touch,
as we recall his words of hope and grace,
we speak of that mystery called faith:

Christ died, that we might have hope;
Christ rose, God's hope not disappointing us;
Christ will return, that we might have peace forever with God.

Pour out your Spirit
upon your children
gathered in this place,
and on the gifts
of the Bread and the Cup.
May they be the grace
which nourishes and sustains us.
As we come to reconciliation's table,
    may our broken relationships
    be made whole again.
As we see you in these gifts,
    may we go and proclaim the good news.
As we open our hearts
to your never-ending love,
    may we offer our selves
    to everyone we meet.

And when all time is ended.
when hunger and thirst is no more
as we are fed at the Lamb's feast,
    we will join our hands and hearts,
    bowing down to worship you forever:
God in Community, Holy in One. Amen.

Fourth Sunday in Lent
1 Samuel 16:1-13; Psalm 23
Ephesians 5:8-14; John 9:1-41

Call to Worship
Here, in this place, with these people,
we find the One who leads us into God's Kingdom.

Here, in God's Kingdom, with our sisters and brothers in Christ,
we find a Feast prepared for us.
Here, in God's sanctuary, at this Table,
we eat of the good news which heals us,
we drink of the mercy which is God's gift.

Prayer of the Day
Shepherding God:
you create life
    from the mud of the earth;
you draw forth light
    from the shadowed corners of chaos;
your goodness and mercy
    are our closest friends.
Great is your name.

Jesus our Shepherd:
you open eyes
    shuttered by sin
    and prejudice;
you heal lives
    shattered by bitterness;
you create pools of still grace
    in our stress-filled hearts.
Great is your love

Holy Spirit,
our companion in every shadowed valley:
you plant seeds of goodness and mercy
deep within our souls,
    so we would bear fruit for others;
you awaken us from
our troubled sleep,
    so we might be a light to the world.
Great is your peace.

God in Community, Holy in One,
hear us as we pray as Jesus taught us, saying,
Our Father . . .

Call to Reconciliation
How quickly we notice the mistakes of others, but never see our own
faults! Before we judge others, we need to pray that our blindness might
be healed by God's gracious love. Please join me as we pray together,
saying,

107

Unison Prayer of Confession

God our Great Shepherd: it is easy for us to lose sight of your kingdom, and your way for us. We hope that love conquers hate, that light shines in our shadows, that life is stronger than death--yet our lips are filled with bitter words, our lives are weak and shallow, the shadowed corners of the world beckon to us.

Have mercy on us and lead us to the still waters of your grace and the healing garden of your heart, Tender Shepherd. Restore our sight to see you living with us, restore our hope that we might trust you, restore our speech that we might praise you for your great gift to us in Jesus Christ, our Lord and Savior.

Silence is kept

Assurance of Pardon

With a gentle touch, with the anointing of the Holy Spirit, with the joy of love, God reaches out to forgive us and make us whole.
Touch us, eternal Spirit;
heal us, Light of Love;
fill our lives with new meaning, God of joy,
as we receive your forgiveness and grace. Amen.

Great Prayer of Thanksgiving

May the Lord of green pastures be with you.
And also with you.
People of God, open your hearts to the One
who leads us to pools of serenity.
We are transformed by the One who restores our souls.
Goodness and mercy are our companions on our journey.
We offer songs of praise to the One who leads us home.

It is our greatest joy to offer you praise,
God of all hope and power:
you whispered your goodness,
    and the stars leapt for joy;
you spoke your tenderness,
    and all creatures sang your name;
you sang your love,
    and we were created in your image.
But placed in the Garden of heavenly delights,
    we hungered for the unfruitful ways of the world.
Bathed in the radiance of Eden's light,
    we walked into the shadows of our sin.
But your mercy is like the river

which flows through the new Jerusalem,
and never fails to bring us hope.

So, with the choirs of angels
and with every generation of believers,
we proclaim your glory:

Holy, holy, holy are you, Shepherd of us all.
Still waters and green pastures, far-flung stars
    and daffodils sing your praises.
Hosanna in the highest!

Blessed is the Lord's Anointed who comes to us.
Hosanna in the highest!

Holy are you, Glorious God,
and blessed is your Son, Jesus Christ, our Lord.
Through him, you spoke the words
    which transformed our unbelief;
you mixed the waters of baptism
with the dust of the world
    and smeared grace on our eyes
    that we might see your glory;
you walked the paths of the world,
stopping at a cross,
    that death might lose its power over our hearts,
    and sin its grip on our souls,
        so we could follow Jesus into your kingdom.

As we gather to remember his love for us,
may we proclaim the mystery of our faith:

Christ died, going into that valley we fear;
Christ is risen, that we might live as children of the light;
Christ will come again, so we might dwell in God's house forever.

Healing God, send forth your Spirit
upon these gifts of the bread and the cup,
so that as we taste their goodness and mercy,
    we would be transformed into your holy people.
Open our eyes to the suffering of all your people;
    open our ears to the cries of the lost and lonely;
open our hearts to the brokenness of the outsiders;
    open our hands in service to all your children.

Then, bring us to that Table of Grace
where we will sit with all your children in eternity,
feasting on your goodness, living in your light,
one people, one heart, in joy and at peace with you,
God in Community, Holy in One, now and forever. Amen.

Fifth Sunday in Lent
Ezekiel 37:1-14; Psalm 130
Romans 8:6-11; John 11:1-45

Call to Worship
The psalmist tells us if we will but wait,
God will whisper hope to us.
Do you believe this?
We believe God's Word is not a pipe dream,
but the river of love which flows forever!
Paul reminds us that it is foolishness to think
only of ourselves and our wants.
Do you believe this?
We believe that when we pay attention to God,
we will find joy, peace, love!
Jesus calls us to walk in the light,
so we will not continue to stumble over our sin.
Do you believe this?
We believe he is the One
who leads us out of Hopeless Valley
into the kingdom of grace and life!

Prayer of the Day
With you,
there is that life
    broken enough to make us whole;
with you,
there is that gentleness
    strong enough to save us from sin;
with you,
there is that grace
    powerful enough to defeat death.
Bone of our bone:
    our hearts hear your voice
    and do handsprings of hope.

In you,
our death-stained souls
    are cleansed by your tears;

110

in you,
we are brought out of
    the graves of our bitterness;
in you,
our broken relationships
    are knitted together
    into the Beloved's community.
Flesh of our flesh:
    our hearts hear your voice
    and do handsprings of grace.

Through you,
our dried-up lives
    are refreshed;
through you,
the valley of No Hope
    becomes the Garden of Grace;
through you,
our exhausted souls
    are filled with joy's breath.
Spirit of our spirits:
    our hearts hear your voice
    and do handsprings of laughter.

God in Community, Holy in One,
may your heart do handsprings
as we pray as Jesus has taught us, saying
Our Father . . .

Call to Reconciliation
If God was intent on keeping score, we would end up losing every time. But God loves us so much, that we are invited to join in that game of grace which never comes to an end. With such hope for our lives, let us confess our sins to God.

Unison Prayer of Confession
Like the disciples, Holy One, we drag our feet when it comes to following you. You would have us face conflict, and we look the other way. You would lead us into those hopeless valleys where so many of your children live, and we would build homes on the mountaintops. You would bring all of us into your peace and reconciliation, but we stay entombed in our troubles and fears.

Forgive us, Creator of new lives. As Lazarus was brought forth from the grave, unbind every worry which keeps us from living as

111

your children. As the Spirit led Jesus from the tomb into the joy of the Resurrection, fill us with the power to walk in the light of this hope. As Jesus offers us the life and resurrection we need, help us to believe the good news which comes from our Lord and Savior.

Silence is kept

Assurance of Pardon
Jesus loved Lazarus so much, he brought him back from the grave. God loved Jesus so much that he was raised to new life. See how much God loves us - loves you! - by forgiving and saving us.
We thank you for hearing our prayers, Lord God, and for setting us free from everything which would bind us to sin and death. Amen.

Great Prayer of Thanksgiving
May the God of old graves and new life be with you!
And also with you!
People of God, lift up your hearts.
We offer them to the One whose Spirit is placed within us.
Wait for God, children of the resurrection,
wait with hope in your souls.
We sing to the One who rolled away the stone,
and who will open the graves.

Into the barren valley of chaos,
you breathed, River of Love:
    joy raced through the heavens
    flinging stars into the night;
grace danced upon the earth,
    springing up in every place
    in which it was planted.
Gathering up creation's dust,
you formed us as your image,
    bone of your bone,
    flesh of your flesh,
    heart of your heart.
You gave us the garden of your heart
in which to dwell with you forever,
    but we became entranced
    with the world's seductive valleys,
    and wrapped ourselves in death's gravecloths,
        finding them a perfect fit.
Though your heart was broken,
you sent prophets to call us forth

112

from all those places littered
with our faithless hearts and souls.
But we would not breathe
the new grace you offered,
turning over to sleep in our dried-up dreams.
So, with tears running down your face,
you sent Jesus to become
our hope, our life, our salvation.

Therefore, we join our voices
with those whose dried bones were given new life,
and all who cry out to you for hope,
singing of the glory of your name:

**Holy, holy, holy are you, Breath of new life.
All creation waits, hoping in your Word.
Hosanna in the highest!**

**Blessed is the resurrection and the life who comes to us.
Hosanna in the highest!**

Grace is who you are, God of Every Heart,
and blessed is Jesus Christ,
our Brother, our Redeemer, our Hope.
Weeping over the brokenness
of your dreams for us,
he came to make us whole.
Weeping over the pain we cause,
he came to heal us.
Weeping over Jerusalem,
he came to bring forth
the new kingdom of peace.
Weeping over Lazarus,
he wipes away the tears
of all who grieve.
Weeping over the power
of sin and death,
he left them behind at the grave,
as your Spirit raised him
to the life of your new hope.

As we remember his life, his death, his love,
as we long for the promise of our resurrection,
we sing of that mystery called faith:

Christ died, and God wept;
Christ arose, and the angels rejoiced;
Christ will come, untangling us from sin and death.

Send your Spirit upon those gathered
around your Table of joy,
and upon the gifts of grace and peace.
As we are fed by the Bread of Life,
    may we be serve all
    who live around us.
As we drink from the Cup of hope,
    may we share it
    with all who long for your presence.
As your Spirit moves into
the guestroom of our hearts,
    may we welcome those
    who have no family or home.
As you listen to our prayers,
    may we open our hearts
    to the cries of the broken of our world.

And when we are awakened from sleep,
to live forever with you,
as we join hands and hearts
around your Feast in heaven,
may we sing your praises forever and ever,
God in Community, Holy in One. Amen.

Passion Sunday/Palm Sunday
Isaiah 50:4-9a; Psalm 118:1-2, 19-29
Philippians 2:5-11; Matthew 21:1-11

Call to Worship
Here in this place, with these people,
we begin that week we call Holy.
We crane our necks to see the parade,
we will bow our heads as the funeral
procession winds through the streets.
We have been with Jesus on this journey;
we long for courage to go to the end.
In one hand, we clutch the palm branches;
in the other, we cradle our broken hearts.
As children dance excitedly around him,
Jesus humbly enters our lives.

**Hosanna! We welcome the kingdom
bearer into our midst. Hosanna!**

Prayer of the Day
Our hearts are wounded
by the nails we carry in them,
    yet you would heal us
    with your love.
We are worn to the quick
by the struggles of our lives,
    yet you carry us in your heart.
Our souls are emptied
by the loneliness of our lives,
    yet you would fill us
    with sisters and brothers.
Blessed are you,
who comes to live with us!

You could have remained
in Nazareth, caring for your family,
    but you journeyed through our lives
    to bring us home.
You could have stayed
at home in glory,
    but you vacated God's heart,
    to serve us with grace.
You could have come
clutching unbearable power,
    but you filled your pockets
    with humility's wealth
    to share it with us.
Blessed are you,
who comes to save us!

When we would puff up with pride,
    deflate us with your gentleness.
When we would go home,
after the parade has ended,
    walk us to the foot of the cross.
When we would put
our "Hosannas" away
for another year,
    teach us to sing
    our gratitude for new life.

Blessed are you,
who comes to help us!

God in Community, Holy in One
we bless you, as we lift our prayer, saying,
Our Father . . .

Call to Reconciliation
We sing, we wave our branches, we shout 'Hosanna!' Then, we turn
away, to go back to our old ways, our old lives, our old sins. But God
is in the business of granting forgiveness and filling us with new life.
Let us confess to the One who comes to fill us with grace,

Unison Prayer of Confession
**With eager hearts and open hands, Holy One, we welcome
Jesus, until he refuses the power we offer him, choosing to become
our servant. We pick up the faith we had laid on the ground before
him, and put it back on the shelf where it belongs. Our pride keeps
us from being able to follow him all the way to Calvary.**

**Hosanna, Steadfast God, save us! Help us to let our fears, our
doubts, our faithlessness slip from our lives to fall at your feet, so
we may stand with our Lord and Savior, Jesus Christ, who comes
in your name, in your glory, in your grace to save us.**

Silence is kept

Assurance of Pardon
Tell the daughters of despair, proclaim it to the sons of sadness: Christ
has come to save us!
**Hosanna! We will give our thanks to God, who comes to bring us
grace, hope, life. Hosanna in the highest. Amen!**

Great Prayer of Thanksgiving
The Lord of parades be with you.
And also with you.
People of God, open your hearts to the One who comes with hope.
**We would receive the joy and grace
the prophet from Nazareth brings us.**
Give thanks to God, for God's love endures forever!
God is our God, the One who comes to make us whole.

Joy is indeed the highest praise
we can offer to you,
Steadfast Love.

116

On that first morning,
you woke creation
   from its slumbering sleep,
   to give light to chaos' shadows.
Morning by morning,
you shaped your dreams
   into everything that is true,
   turning hopes into your justice.
You asked simply that we rejoice
in your gifts and glory,
   but we chose to sing the choruses
   of sin and rebellion,
      following death as it paraded
      through the world.
Prophets struggled to awaken
our dulled ears
with whispers of peace,
   but we laughed at their ideas
   that we should return to you.
When you could have set your face like flint,
when you could have hardened your resolve,
you sent your Child, your Joy,

Therefore, we join our voices in thanksgiving,
with those who shouted "Hosanna"
and with those who ran away from you,
with those in every moment, and in this moment,
singing with all creation to your glory:

**Holy, holy, holy are you, Opener of our ears.
All creation proclaims, "God's steadfast love endures forever."
Hosanna in the highest!**

**Blessed is the One who opens the gates of righteousness.
Hosanna in the highest!**

You are holy, God our Creator,
and blessed is Jesus Christ,
who comes in your grace.
When he could have filled your heart,
   he poured himself out for us;
when he could have remained by your side,
   he came to be a servant, raising us to glory;
when he could have watched from heaven,
   he came down to show us your heart;

when he could have taken the easy way,
he chose to be faithful to you,
even to the point of shameful death.
As he gathered up our brokenness
to make us whole,
you raised him to new life,
and he stands with us in eternity,
glorifying you forever.

As we remember the joy and excitement of the parade,
as we remember the gentle words he taught,
as we remember the spirit with which he died,
we proclaim the One who is the Bread of Life:

Christ died, emptying his life for us;
Christ rose, defeating our old adversaries sin and death;
Christ will come, to fulfill what has been promised.

Here, at this Table,
we would receive the gifts
of the bread and the cup,
and your Spirit which anoints us with peace.
Nourish us with the Bread of hope,
that we might go into
the brokenness of our world;
fill us with the cup of grace,
so the weary would discover us
standing by their side;
fill us with the overflowing joy
of the good news,
so we might sing forever
of your heart's desire
for justice and peace for all people.

Then, on that final morning,
when we gather for the Feast of the Lamb,
when we are seated with those
who shouted their hosannas,
as well as those who yelled for death,
we will join our voices in eternity's anthem,
giving our thanks to you forever and ever,
God in Community, Holy in One. Amen.

Holy Thursday

Exodus 12:1-4, (5-10), 11-14; Psalm 116:1-2, 12-19
1 Corinthians 11:23-26; John 13:1-17, 31b-35

Call to Worship
In remembrance, we gather:
to be with the One who teaches us the meaning of faithfulness.
In remembrance, we worship:
lifting our voices to the One who calls us to love one another.
In remembrance, we feast:
breaking the Bread which makes us whole,
drinking the Cup which fills us with grace.

Evening Prayer
It was the beginning of hope
on that night long ago,
Liberating God,
　　as you prepared to lead
　　your people to freedom.
As they readied themselves,
you fed them
with your unblemished grace,
　　so all sin, pain, and bitterness
　　could be set down and left behind
　　　　when it was time
　　　　to follow you.

It was the beginning of salvation
on that night long ago,
Servant Lord,
　　as you prepared your disciples
　　for all the things which were to happen.
You humbled yourself
by washing their feet,
　　so they could follow you
　　in service and love
　　　　into a world which would reject you
　　　　and hang you on a cross.

We tell these stories once again
on this night of remembrance,
Servant's Spirit.
Here is the Bread
　　which gives us life;

119

here is the Cup
    which slakes our thirst for justice;
here is the towel
    with which we wipe the tears
        of the broken-hearted;
here is the basin
    which cleanses the stains
        of the world.

Prepare us for our journey of discipleship,
God in Community, Holy in One,
as we pray as our Servant, Jesus Christ, teaches us, saying,
Our Father . . .

Call to Reconciliation
How is it people will recognize us as followers of Jesus? Simply by how we treat one another. Let us confess how we have not loved as Christ loves us.

Unison Prayer of Confession
Creator and Loving God, you kneel to wash our feet, yet we are reluctant for you to see all the places we have gone in our attempts to escape you. You would bathe us in the warm, living waters of your love, even though we splash and play in the puddles of temptation. We have received all the gifts you have to offer, yet we are tempted to think they are only for us, rather than sharing them.

Forgive us, Holy One, and have mercy on us. What can we give you for all your wonderful graciousness towards us? As you have broken your heart for us, may we open ours in service to others. As you have given your life for us, may we offer ours to bring healing to the world. As you have called us together around your Table, may we go forth to feed a world hungry, not only for food, but for that Spirit which brings peace and reconciliation. This we pray as servants of Jesus Christ, who came to serve us in life, in death, in resurrection hope.

Silence is kept

Assurance of Pardon
On this holiest of nights, we have received the good news: God has come in Christ Jesus, to fill us with hope and peace, to bathe us in grace and mercy.
In remembrance, we go forth:
  to bring hope where despair resides;
  to be servants to those who are broken;

**to love as selflessly as we are loved by Jesus Christ,
our Lord and Savior. Amen.**

Great Prayer of Thanksgiving
May the God of last suppers be with you.
And also with you.
Open your hearts to God this night.
We open them to the One whose heart is broken this night.
In the midst of uncertainty and fears, we will praise God.
**Our thanks are offered to the One who walks and waits with us
through long nights.**

When the hour had come, Creator of the heavens and earth,
you lifted up the cup of creation,
pouring it into the emptiness of chaos.
    Rivers played tag through the valleys,
    stars spangled the blue-black night,
    joy danced in the fields of grace.
Given that fountain flowing with living water,
    we drank from betrayal's bitter cup;
offered the feast of faith,
    we sat down at sin's groaning table.
You asked the prophets to remind us of promises made,
    but we continued to embrace the pangs of hopelessness.
Then, because we are your own, you sent Jesus
to glorify you by saving us from ourselves.

Therefore, with those whose feet are covered with sin,
and those who hearts are gripped by fear,
we join the choirs of every time and place, forever singing your praises:

**Holy, holy, holy Lord, God of towels and basins.
We join heaven and earth in praising your name.
Hosanna in the highest!**

**Blessed is the One who became a servant for us.
Hosanna in the highest!**

Holy are you, God of Redemption,
and blessed is Jesus Christ, our Servant, our Savior.
When the hour had come,
    he got up from grace's side,
    took off his glory,
        tied humanity around his heart
        to cleanse us of our sins.

121

In the midst of his friends,
in the congregation of his enemies,
    he kept the promises made to you,
        to love us to the very end.
Our friend,
    he welcomed all;
our teacher,
    he modeled the life of obedience and faith;
our Redeemer,
    he endured the snares of death,
        that we might have life with you.

Every time we eat the bread, our brokenness is made whole;
every time we drink from the cup, we receive unceasing grace;
every time we come to the Table,
we remember that mystery called faith:

In remembrance, we mourn Christ's death;
in remembrance, we look to the Day of Resurrection;
in remembrance, we await his return to us.

Now that the hour is come,
send your Spirit upon the gifts
of the bread and the cup.
As you cradle the bread in your gentleness,
break it, give it to us, feed us with your compassion
    that we might be made whole
    and, in our healing,
        become servants to a shattered world.
As you take the cup,
mingle its juices with your tears of hope,
    so we might carry this gift
        to all who have lost everything.

And when there are no more hours to come,
when there is only eternal peace and life with you,
we will gather in that upper room called your heart,
serving our families and friends with grace,
receiving forgiveness from our enemies,
singing your joy, forever and ever,
God in Community, Holy in One. Amen.

Good Friday
Isaiah 52:13 – 53:12; Psalm 22
Hebrews 10:16-25; John 18:1 – 19:42

Call to Worship
Here, in the midst of these people, we come to worship you.
We come with the groans of our life,
and the whispers of hope in our hearts.
Here, in the midst of these people, we come to remember you.
We come, trusting you have not forgotten us;
that here, promises will be fulfilled.
Here, in the midst of these people, we come to have our hearts touched.
We come, knowing you hear our souls;
we come, to praise you for your steadfast love.

Prayer of the Day
On this day, God of all tears,
you call us in the midst
of our busy lives
    to look at the suffering and death
    of the One who came to carry
        the pain of the world into your heart.
Give us eyes to see your love
        this day.

On this day
you would gather everyone
to your side,
Grace of Calvary,
    but we leave you
        to carry the cross alone.
You came simply as love incarnate,
    but hate and bitterness
        were the gifts we offered to you.
You poured out your love
    so our emptiness might be filled.
Give us ears to hear your pain
        this day.

On this day,
you would pray for us,
for we cannot find the words
on our own,
Shattered Spirit.
    Hear the cries of those in need.
    Listen to the lament of the lonely.
    Cradle the whispered hopes of children.
    Set free the dreams of prisoners and captives.

Give us hearts to pray with you
this day.

God in Community, Holy in One,
we lift our prayers to you in the name of the One
who suffered and died for us
this day
and who teaches us to pray, saying,
Our Father . . .

Call to Reconciliation
Confident of the hope received by the death of Christ, we bring our
hearts - broken, stained with sin, filled with failings - to the One who
sprinkles them with grace, cleansing them with the waters of life.

Unison Prayer of Confession
**Like little children who can wander off in a crowded store, we
have lost our way, God of this grim day. We betray you when we
do not befriend the poor; we deny you when we are afraid to speak
up for the voiceless; we turn our backs on you when we do not do
good for others; we crucify you when we harm our family and
friends.**

**At the foot of the cross, we stand with all who have forgotten you
and forsaken the way which you offer to us. Forgive us, Lamb of
God, and fill us with the mercy, the hope, the grace you poured out
for us, as you gave your life for the sins of the world.**

Extended silence is kept

Assurance of Pardon
Christ has lifted our suffering onto his shoulders, carrying all our hurts
and rejections into God's heart. There, God casts them away into the sea
of forgetfulness, so we may be restored to hope and live as new people.
**Fed with grace, carried in God's arms, we know that we are
forgiven. Thanks be to God. Amen.**

Easter Day
Jeremiah 31:1-6; Psalm 118:1-2, 14-24
Colossians 3:1-4; Matthew 28:1-10

Call to Worship
This is the day:
**when healing touches the suffering;
when loneliness discovers a family;**

124

when peace caresses the stressed.

This is the day the Lord:
breaks free of death's clutches,
rolls away the stone,
folds the grave clothes into a neat pile.
This is the day the Lord has made:
the day of sin's defeat,
the day of resurrection,
the first day of the new creation.
This is the day!
Christ is risen! Hallelujah!

Prayer of the Day
Early in the morning
before chaos was awake,
you tiptoed quietly past,
Surprising God:
and whispered the Word
which caused grace and love
to blossom into creation.

Early in the morning
while the disciples slept,
Jesus, Son of the Living God:
you prepared a feast
to fill their emptiness;
you rolled away their hardened hearts
to open them to your grace;
you whispered their names
to awaken them to new life.

Early in the morning
while we are still drowsy,
you sing your songs to us,
Holy Spirit:
hymns of hope,
cantatas of compassion,
psalms of peace,
litanies of love.

God in Community, Holy in One,
early this morning we bring our prayer to you
as Jesus has taught us, saying,
Our Father . . .

Call to Reconciliation

It was early in the morning, when God created all the good and beauty in the universe. It was early in the morning that a baby cried in a manger. It was early in the morning on that first day, when a voice told us that death has been defeated and Jesus is alive in our midst. Let us confess the fear, and the great joy, we bring with us, early in the mornings . . .

Unison Prayer of Confession

This morning, Wonderful God, in the company of your church - saints and sinners - we gather to celebrate your life, your ministry, your death and resurrection, your great love for us. Yet, we know we often leave the celebration here in the sanctuary, as we go back to our homes, our jobs, our fears, our doubts, our lives.

Bring us new life, God of the living, where we are tired and stressed; transform our hardened hearts into fountains of love; forgive us the hurts and harms we have caused; fill us with the joy of your Holy Spirit in the hollows of our souls.

Silence is kept

Assurance of Pardon

God, our Creator, gives us new life;
Christ, our Reconciliation, invites us to a Table;
Holy Spirit, our Peace, teaches us the Way, the Truth, the Life;
this is the Good News: the tomb is empty,
death is conquered, sin has lost its power.
 We are a new people, shaped by the Risen Lord into new life forever! Thanks be to God. Amen.

Great Prayer of Thanksgiving

The God of early mornings be with you.
And also with you.
People of the first day, lift up your hearts!
We lift them to the One who makes every day Easter!
People of Easter joy, give thanks to the One who is your salvation.
We offer our hallelujahs to the God of steadfast love.

We lift our praise to you,
Gardener of Creation.
On the first day,
    your Light split the shadows of chaos,
    and all goodness flowed forth.
Gently and tenderly,
    you gathered up the dust of the earth
    and shaped us into your image.

126

But the day came when we chose
to run away from you,
     preferring our petty schemes
     to your dreams for us.
You sang to us through the prophets,
hoping we would join you
in the heavenly chorus.
     But we kept silent,
     believing our wisdom
     was far superior to your love.
And when we dug our heels in
through blind stubbornness,
refusing to follow you,
you became one of us.

Therefore we join our glad songs of Easter
with those in every time and in every place,
who sing to you their praise:

Rejoice, heavenly powers!
Sing, choirs of angels!
Jesus Christ, our Lord, is risen!

You alone are holy, Steadfast God,
and blessed is your Son,
Jesus Christ, our Lord and Savior.
God's true Light,
     he wandered the shadows of hell
     to bring us out;
God's own Beloved,
     he endured our sin,
     to heal us forever;
God's own Glory,
     he went into the grave,
     that we might enter
     the gates of righteousness.

As we remember you raising him
from the dead and giving us life,
we proclaim our faith:

Sin is conquered;
death is defeated;
Christ is risen!
Alleluia!

Here at this Table
we are nourished by your steadfast love,
God of new mornings.
As you pour out your Spirit
upon the bread and the cup,
    fill us with the grace of Jesus.
As we have been raised to new life,
    may we reach out to those who have fallen;
as we have been fed,
    may we fill the hunger of the world;
as we have seen the empty tomb,
        may we bear witness to the presence
        of the Risen Lord in our lives.

Then, when we are united with all the saints,
may we gather around your Table,
one people, lifting our voices in praise to you,
Father, Son, and Holy Spirit,
one God, forever and ever. Amen.

Second Sunday of Easter
Acts 2:14a, 22-32; Psalm 16
1 Peter 1:3-9; John 20:19-31

Call to Worship
Alleluia! Christ is risen!
Christ is risen indeed! Alleluia!
We have not seen the risen Christ,
**but we see him in the lives
of those transformed by grace.**
We have not seen Jesus face-to-face,
**but we have seen him in the faces
of everyone whose love encourages us.**
We have not touched the wounds from the cross,
**but we have been called to bring healing
to the scarred of the world.**

Prayer of the Day
On the evening
of the first day of creation,
Holy God,
    you held out your hands,
        filled with all the grace
        we would ever need;

you began to surround us
    with all that is good and pleasant.

On the evening
of the first day of Easter,
Defeater of Death,
    you walked through
        the closed doors
        of our doubts and fears;
    you held us tight
        until the warmth of your grace
        softened our hardened hearts;
    you handed us the gift of peace
        to calm our frightened faith.

On the evening
of the first day of following you,
Breath of Peace,
    you open our eyes
        to the bright color of hope;
    you teach us
        the glad songs of grace;
    you share the most
    valuable gift of all:
        faith.

God in Community, Holy in One,
we lift our prayers to you
as Jesus has taught us, saying,
Our Father . . .

Call to Reconciliation
While it is true that we did not put Jesus to death, we are quite aware of
all the ways in which we have not followed the paths of life that have
been offered to us by God. Let us confess our sins, as we pray, saying,

Unison Prayer of Confession
    **We lock the doors of compassion, God of Easter, so that we may
share it only with those we believe to be deserving. We harden our
hearts to the cries around us, because we cannot be completely
sure of who is in need. We close our eyes to the suffering around
us, believing it will all go away if we don't look.**
    **Forgive us, Hope of the Ages. You fill us with all the grace we
need, not because we are so special, but because we are servants,
called to hold out our hands to all in need, even as Jesus Christ,**

our Lord and Savior, holds out his hands to us, to lead us into your kingdom.

Silence is kept

Assurance of Pardon
From the shadows of life, God brings us into the Light of Christ. From the prison of sin and death, God sets us free to live in hope.
The God and Father of our Lord Jesus Christ has raised him from the dead, and given us new life. Thanks be to God. Amen.

Great Prayer of Thanksgiving
The Lord of Easter be with you.
And also with you.
People of the God of Joy, lift up your hearts.
We offer them to the Lord who gives us peace.
The Joyous Feast of the Lamb has been prepared for you.
We rejoice, clapping our hands and singing praises to our God.

Into the darkness of chaos,
you stepped, Creation's Joy.
You opened your hands,
    and rivers flowed through
    the deserts of delight;
you spoke a simple Word
    and a universe complex
    with beauty and diversity was formed.
You birthed us
from the dust of earth,
    with the Breath of peace
    filling our lungs.
Yet, we were attracted
by the deeds of sin and death,
    and drank from their sweet cup.
You sent holy ones called prophets
to make known to us
your ways of life and grace,
    but we multiplied your sorrow
    by turning our backs on them.
By your great mercy,
you would not give up on us,
but sent Jesus Christ
for the salvation of our souls.

And so, we join our voices

with those of every time and place,
who forever sing your praises:

Holy, holy, holy are you, God our chosen portion.
All creation rejoices in your peace.
Hosanna in the highest!

Blessed is the One who has been raised from the dead.
Hosanna in the highest!

Holy are you, Path of life,
and blessed is Jesus Christ,
Right Hand of the righteous.
With signs and wonders,
    he pointed to your hopes for us;
with simple words of invitation,
    he welcomed us into your family;
keeping you ever before him,
    he looked sin direct in the face,
        and broke its power over us;
with that hope grounded in you,
    he entered into that locked room of death,
        believing what he had not seen,
        that you would bring him to new life,
our inheritance awaiting us
in your kingdom.

As we remember his life, his death, his resurrection,
as we seek to believe what we have not seen,
we tell of that mystery called faith:

Christ died, birthing us into a living hope;
Christ arose, breathing peace into our lives;
Christ will come, that we might receive the outcome of our faith.

Stir this cup with your grace,
and warm this bread with
the Breath of Peace,
Joy of our hearts.
You hold these gifts in your hands,
and offer them to us
as the living hope of our lives.
As you fill us with
the gladness of your presence,
    may we go forth to be with those

131

who are forsaken by the world.
As you pour out your Spirit
into our hearts,
    may we be sent to bring healing
    to those whose brokenness
    is ignored by our society.

And when, by your great mercy,
all time has ended
and we rest secure in your grace,
    we will gather around the Table
    joining hands with your children
    of every time and place,
who will rejoice with glad hearts,
singing your praises forever,
God in Community, Holy in One. Amen.

Third Sunday of Easter
Acts 2:14a, 36-41; Psalm 116:1-4, 12-19
1 Peter 1:17-23; Luke 24:13-35

Call to Worship
Where shattered hearts are made whole,
where wounded souls are healed,
where life is stronger than death:
there, the stone has been rolled away.
Where the lonely become our friends,
where a stranger is welcomed home,
where hope is stronger than despair,
there, we find Jesus walking.
Where closed wallets are opened,
where the anxious find serenity,
where love is stronger than hate:
there, Jesus is opening our eyes.
The stone has been rolled away!
Jesus is our companion on the journey!
Our eyes are opened to the needs of others!
Alleluia! Christ is risen!
Alleluia! Christ is with us!

Prayer of the Day
Splattering the black-blue night
    with the twinkling stars
and spinning fluffy clouds
    out of the fabric of your hope,

132

you raised creation out of chaos,
Gracious God,
　　giving life and calling it good.

Walking with disciples
down grief's lonely road,
　　you sang of how
　　God had raised you from the dead,
so that listening,
　　they might believe;
believing,
　　they might understand;
understanding,
　　they might obey;
going forth to invite all
　　to follow you,
Bread of Life,
　　to feast on your love forever.

Reaching out your love to us,
　　so we would touch others;
filling us with your gifts,
　　so we could be a blessing to the world;
piercing our darkness with hope,
　　so we might bring healing
　　to the broken;
you raise us to new life,
Spirit of God.

God in Community, Holy in One,
hear us as we pray, saying,
Our Father . . .

Call to Reconciliation
Here! Christ is here! In our hearts, in our lives, and in our midst. As on
that road to Emmaus, Jesus is with us--teaching, loving, leading, feeding.
Let us confess how we have overlooked the presence of the living Christ,
and ignored the words he whispers to our hearts, as we pray, saying,

Unison Prayer of Confession
　　**We become comfortable, Joyous God, with our lives, with our
faith, with our friends and family. We are so secure, your gospel
jars us with your hopes for us. We know we should tell your story,
but doesn't everyone who matters know it already? We could invite
others to your table, but then we might have to share. We could**

welcome the strangers, but worry they might feel uneasy among so many unfamiliar faces.

Forgive us, God of Easter. Walk with us, so we can become companions to the lost. Welcome us, so we can include the hopeless and the homeless. Love us, so we can share that love with everyone we meet on our journey, as we follow Jesus Christ, our Lord and Savior, into life with you.

Silence is kept

Assurance of Pardon
God loves us so much, God will listen to our cries, our prayers, our hopes, and our dreams. God's promises are for all, those who are right beside us, as well as those who live on the other side of the world. **What can we give to God for such grace? We will lift our hearts to God, giving thanks for the mercy that has been given to us. Thanks be to God! Amen.**

Great Prayer of Thanksgiving
May the Risen Christ be with you!
And also with you!
Disciples of the Lord of Easter, lift your hearts.
We offer them to the One who warms them with love.
Children of God, offer praises to the One who is in your midst.
We will lift our songs of thanksgiving to the One
who is known to us in the breaking of the bread.

When silence was caught
in the traps of chaos,
you spoke a Word,
Heart of Hope,
    and the rivers sang
        sonnets of joy,
    the stars rang with laughter,
        and the valleys echoed
        the choruses of all creation.
Made in the image of your love,
    you considered us more valuable
    that the finest jewels and metals.
You cupped your ear
to listen to our praises,
    but heard only our complaints,
    as we foolishly interpreted
    the stories sin and death told us
        as being the truth we should follow.

You longed to open our eyes,
   but we were blinded by disobedience.
Your heart broken,
you sent Jesus to come to us,
to lead us back to you.

Therefore, we join our hearts and voices
with those right next to us, and those far way,
of every time, and from every place,
who sing forever your praises and glory:

Holy, holy, holy are you, God who listens to us.
All creation pays its vows to you.
Hosanna in the highest!

Blessed is the One who is your servant.
Hosanna in the highest!

Holy are you, ever listening God,
and blessed is Jesus Christ, our Lord and Savior.
Having learned compassion
while sitting on Spirit's lap,
   he came to be our Servant.
Walking by your side in creation's gardens,
   he came to travel pain and loss with us.
Listening to your promises
to all your children,
   he came to tell us
   of their fulfillment in hope.
Your Beloved Child,
   he showed on the cross
   that grace and love
   are able to defeat sin and death for all time.

Remembering his compassion and service,
made whole by his brokenness,
we proclaim that mystery we call faith:

Christ died, that we might be born anew;
Christ is risen, that our eyes might be opened;
Christ will come, so we, our children, and all who
   are far way may be gathered together in you.

As we lift the Cup of salvation,
as we grasp the Bread of life,

pour out your Spirit
upon these simple gifts
and all who seek your presence.
As our eyes are opened
by the breaking of the bread,
    may we see those around us
    whose lives have been shattered
        by an uncaring world.
As our hearts are thawed
by the sweet taste of grace,
    may we serve
    all who hunger for healing.

And when all time has come to an end,
when we are gathered around
the feast you prepare for all your children,
    we will lift our hearts and voices,
    singing your praises forever and ever,
God in Community, Holy in One. Amen.

Fourth Sunday of Easter
Acts 2:42-47; Psalm 23
1 Peter 2:19-25; John 10:1-10

Call to Worship
Day by day, God leads us:
to the deep, deep pools of peace,
to the green, lush lawns of grace.
Day by day, Jesus calls us:
to pour out ourselves in service,
to anoint the stranger with hope.
Day by day, the Holy Spirit shows us:
the community we could be,
the family we are called to become.

Prayer of the Day
Day by day, Gate of grace,
your love is poured
into the emptiness of our souls.
You share your joy
so we might be a blessing
to those all around us.
You are generous to a fault,
that we might have
glad and gracious hearts.

Day by day,
Doorway to God's Heart,
you would lead us
down the streets of
discipleship and service,
uncomfortable as they
may seem to us,
knowing that at the
end of our journey,
we will find ourselves
at home with goodness and mercy.

Day by day,
Spirit of openness,
you watch over us,
so we will not wander
into the busy traffic
at the corner
of sin and death,
but will find our life
in the front yards
of the kingdom.

God in Community, Holy in One,
we open the gates of our hearts to you,
even as we pray, saying,
Our Father . . .

Call to Reconciliation
It is not just material things, but the 'stuff' that makes us who we are - our
hearts, our hopes, our dreams - that we have trouble sharing with others.
But the more we hoard, the less we trust God to use us, and all our gifts,
in the work of the kingdom. Let us entrust our brokenness to our God,
that we might be made whole, as we pray saying,

Unison Prayer of Confession
   **Why is it so hard to trust in your grace, Generous Heart? You
promise to pour out blessings upon us, but we are reluctant to let
go of what we have. We put a lock on our hearts and feelings, while
you share your precious Child with us. You call us home to dinner,
but we would rather keep playing in the shadows of life.**
   **Forgive us, Goodness and Mercy. Anoint us with the oil of
grace, until our hearts overflow with praise. Fill us with the living**

waters of hope, so we can share with others. Feed us at your Table of joy, so we might follow Jesus Christ, our Lord and Savior, with glad and gracious hearts.

Silence is kept

Assurance of Pardon
When we would stand on sin's shoulders, trying to peer through the windows, God throws open wide the front door, so we can come in and live forever in joy.
We are led through death to life; we are fed at grace's table; we are forgiven. Thanks be to God. Amen.

Great Prayer of Thanksgiving
May the Gate of Easter be with you!
And also with you!
People of God, live with glad and generous hearts.
We open our hearts to the One who prepares the Table for us.
Day by day, rejoice in the Restorer of your souls.
We will praise God, while seeking good for all people.

You stilled chaos,
Compassionate God,
so creation could burst
forth in joyous song.
You planted lush carpets
of grace where we could rest;
you filled pools with
the waters of peace;
you showed us
the hiking paths
through Eden's gardens.
But we chose
to devote ourselves
to that skimpy existence
offered by the world,
playing in the revolving door
of sin and death.
Prophets listened
to your heart breaking,
and called us back
to fellowship with you,
but we ignored their hopes.
When you could no longer
stomach our disobedience,

138

you sent Jesus
to re-open the door
to the kingdom.

Therefore, we would join our voices
with those of every time and place,
who lift their songs of praise to you:

Holy, holy, holy, God of bread and prayers.
All creation overflows with your goodness and mercy.
Hosanna in the highest!

Blessed is the One by whose wounds we are healed.
Hosanna in the highest!

Holy are you, Soul Shepherd,
and blessed is Jesus Christ,
Heart Opener, Grace Giver.
Ridiculed and rejected by us,
he offers back friendship and hope;
trusting in you alone,
he devoted himself
to setting us free from sin;
braving the pain of death,
he healed the wounds
we caused ourselves,
to lead us hand-in-hand
to play in Joy's Garden.

So, as we remember his coming to find us,
as we celebrate his opening his heart to us,
we would tell of that mystery called faith:

Christ died while suffering unjustly;
Christ arose, becoming the Gate to eternal life;
Christ will return, calling us by name and leading us home.

Come, Holy Spirit,
to fill these gifts
of the bread and the cup
with your goodness and mercy
which never end.
As we are fed by hope,
open our gated hearts
that we might welcome

139

the weak and weary of our world.
As the cup of life
restores our arid souls,
may we follow Jesus,
that we might lead others
to the One who sings
the glad choruses of grace.

And when we gather
around that Table in eternity
which has been prepared for us,
and for those we have ignored,
we will break bread together,
our wounds healed, our hearts made whole,
forever singing your praises,
God in Community, Holy in One. Amen.

Fifth Sunday of Easter
Acts 7:55-60; Psalm 31:1-5, 15-16
1 Peter 2:2-10; John 14:1-14

Call to Worship
The One who shaped the universe,
crafts us into a community of faith:
a people to shelter the homeless,
a family to feed the hungry.
The One who made kittens and elephants,
shapes us in the divine image:
so we can grow with grace
as we welcome the hopeless and helpless.
The One who blesses us with flowers and waterfalls,
gifts us with the way, the truth, the life:
so we can go to tell the story,
to bring healing to a broken world.

Prayer of the Day
In you, Glory of Grace,
we will find that heart
    which shelters us
    when grief overwhelms us.
In you,
we will find the Parent
    who crouches down on one knee,
    to listen to us more carefully.

In you,
we discover that Face
   which glows with joy
   every time you catch
    sight of us.

Through you, Servant's Heart,
we can hear that truth
   which will cut us loose
   from the world's net of lies.
Through you,
   we will find our way
   back to the paths of peace.
Through you,
   we will have the lives
   God envisions for us.

With you, Spirit of welcome,
we find the nourishment
   we need to follow Jesus.
With you,
we are cemented,
   by your grace and love,
   with others into God's
    community of hope.
With you,
we embrace all the nobodies
   rejected by our world.

In you, through you, with you,
God in Community, Holy in One,
we lift our prayer as Jesus taught us,
Our Father . . .

Call to Reconciliation
The Stone tossed aside by the architects of sin and death, is the One
who becomes the foundation for redemption, the cornerstone for grace
and hope. We can confess freely and openly to God, who will not shame
us, but forgive us and welcome us home.

Unison Prayer of Confession
   **In humility, we must confess how we have not matured as your
children, Gentle Parent. The hurting and helpless of our world cry
out, and we cover our ears with hands which could be serving
them. The forsaken and ridiculed of our neighborhoods and**

141

schools are looking for a community of acceptance, and we cover our eyes with hands which could welcome them. The lonely and grieving are listening for hope, and we cover our mouths with hands which could embrace them, and sing gentle songs of grace to them.

Forgive us, Refuge of the broken. Our times are in your hands, so help us to believe we can be healed in this moment. Our hearts are in your heart, so transform ours that we can serve your children. Our lives are redeemed by the death and resurrection of Jesus Christ, our Lord and Savior, so call us to give them away in his name.

Silence is kept

Assurance of Pardon
The good news is that in Christ, our sins are forgiven, our lives are made whole, we become God's own people. Do you not believe? **We believe. And in believing, we will live as those chosen, not only to tell a Story, but to live it out each and every day. Thanks be to God. Amen.**

Great Prayer of Thanksgiving
May the Way, the Truth, the Life be with you.
And also with you.
Precious and chosen by God, offer yourselves in joy.
We open our hearts so we may grow into salvation.
God's own people, proclaim the mighty acts of God.
We sing the praises of the One who calls us into the light.

Chaos covered its ears,
Crafty God,
as you began constructing creation.
Joyous noise filled the air,
    as rivers cascaded
    through verdant valleys.
From the heavens
    came love's raucous laughter,
    echoing down mountain passes.
You would gladly guide us
along Eden's paths of peace,
    but we shook off your hand,
    rejecting your dreams for us.
Women and men were called
to tell the story
of your love and grace,

but we covered our ears
as we continued to drink
the soured milk of sin.
But continuing to believe in us,
you sent Jesus,
to show us the way back to you.

So, with saints and sinners,
with seniors and newborn infants,
with all called to be your people,
we sing our loud songs of praise:

Holy, holy, holy are you, God our shelter.
All creation has received your mercy.
Hosanna in the highest!

Blessed is the One whose times were in your hands.
Hosanna in the highest!

In you, Foundation-building God,
we can find a safe haven;
and a guide for our lives
in Jesus Christ, our Lord and Savior.
With you at the beginning of time,
he became a newborn babe,
    longing to share the milk
    of grace and peace with us.
He became the cornerstone
of mercy and hope,
    that rock standing forever,
    while sin and death crumble
    at the foot of the cross.
Believing in your promises,
he opens us to the beauty and life
    you shape out of our grief and sin.

So, as we come to this Table of hope,
as we remember the truth of that life given for us,
we sing of that mystery called faith:

Christ died, showing us the Way through death;
Christ rose, the Truth of God's promises;
Christ will come, bringing Life for all of us.

And now we pray you
would fill these gifts
of the bread and the cup
with your welcoming Spirit.
As you open your heart
to feed us with your grace,
we would place our hearts in yours,
      as we would go out to heal
      the brokenness of our world.
As you pour the Cup of joy
into our arid souls,
      we would see the rejected around us,
      and rush together to embrace them.

And when we have followed the Way home,
when we gather around the Table
you have prepared for us,
we will sing our songs of thanksgiving, ever praising you,
God in Community, Holy in One. Amen.

Sixth Sunday of Easter
Acts 17:22-31; Psalm 66:8-20
1 Peter 3:13-22; John 14:15-21

Call to Worship
Here, in this place, in these moments,
we can speak of what God has done:
the One who is closer than our imagination tells us.
Here, in these moments, with this people,
we will sing of what God is doing:
the One who lives in us, and calls us the Beloved of the Lord.
In every place, at every moment, with every person,
we dare imagine what God will do:
the One who will move us to serve others,
to be with them as surely as God is with us.

Prayer of the Day
Your imagination
cannot be confined
      to any buildings, boxes,
      or barricades we try to shape.
Your hope
cannot be captured
      in any stone, wood, or
      artifact we might create.

You live, you move,
you are our joy,
and we adore you,
　　　God, our Creator.

Your love
cannot be intimidated
　　by any reluctance
　　in our hearts.
Your grace
cannot be incarcerated
　　in any prison our fears build.
You live, you move,
you are our salvation,
and we thank you,
　　　Jesus, our Friend.

Your peace
cannot be overcome
　　by any anxiety
　　in our souls.
Your truth
cannot be drowned out
　　by sin's seductive songs.
You live, you move,
you are our hope,
and we worship you,
　　　Spirit, our Lover.

You live, you move, you are our
God in Community, Holy in One,
and we pray together saying,
Our Father . . .

Call to Reconciliation
If our consciences were clear, we would have no need to confess. But
we stand transparent before God, who knows our thoughts, our hearts,
our misdeeds. Let us speak to the One who has promised not to put us
to shame, but to forgive us of our sins.

Unison Prayer of Confession
　　**As painful as it may be, God of our lives, we will try to speak our
hearts. Called to live gently with our families and friends, we cause
great hurt by our words and actions. Created in your image, we live**

145

as if it were the evil one who shapes our hearts. Given the simple command to love, we complicate it with our expectations, our fears, our doubts.

You cannot overlook our sin, Loving God, and so you sent Jesus to redeem us. Through the waters of baptism, the fire of our failings is extinguished. Through the grace of your heart, we are made whole. Through the gift of Jesus Christ, our Lord and Savior, we do indeed live, and move, and have our being with you.

Silence is kept.

Assurance of Pardon
Do not be afraid of God. In love, God forgives us; in grace, God redeems us; in hope, God sends us forth to share this good news.
Through Christ's resurrection, we become new people. Amen.

Great Prayer of Thanksgiving
May the God who loves us be with you.
And also with you.
People of God, offer your hearts to the One
who is known in love and wonder.
We lift them to our God who cradles us in grace.
Sing praises to the One who has shaped you in joy.
**We lift our songs of thanksgiving to the God
whose hope is greater than we dare imagine.**

When chaos was all
that was known,
you became Lord
of heaven and earth,
as you poured your imagination
into creation's rich variety:
    mountains and trees
    casting long shadows
    in the light of suns and stars.
You longed for us
to inhabit this goodness and beauty,
    as your offspring formed
    by your love and hope.
But we chose to live
with sin and death,
    their altars of temptation
    the objects of our worship.
In times of human rebellion,
you sent the prophets

to call us back
from those sin-splattered places,
     but we could not obey.
Though you could not
overlook our disobedience,
you would not leave us parentless,
and so sent Jesus
to come to us in grace.

So, with the angelic choirs,
with those of this time and every moment,
we lift our songs of praise:

Holy, holy, holy are you, God of heaven and earth.
All creation echoes with the sound of your praise.
Hosanna in the highest!

Blessed is the One who will not leave us orphaned.
Hosanna in the highest!

Holy are you, God of imagination,
and blessed is Jesus Christ, our Savior.
When he could have
remained in glory,
     he came to visit
     those imprisoned by sin.
When he could have
stayed in heaven,
     he wandered through
     our fears and doubts,
          to proclaim your love for us.
When he could have
been cradled in your right hand,
     he took our side
     against sin and death,
          defeating their power
          and authority over us.

As we remember the words he spoke,
as we recall his death and resurrection,
we will sing of that mystery we call faith:

Christ died, suffering for doing what was right;
Christ arose, God's steadfast love surrounding him;
Christ will come, the hope that is within us.

Pour out your Spirit
upon these gifts
of the Bread and the Cup,
and upon your children
who gather for your feast.
Welcomed by the Spirit,
     may we become friends
     with those the world rejects.
Fed by your love,
     may we become joy
     for those hurt and saddened.
Nourished by your grace,
     may we become advocates
     for those society has silenced.

And when we are led to
that abundant Table in heaven;
when we gather to feast
with everyone we love,
and everyone we have rejected,
     your heart will echo
     with our praises,
     as we sing to you,
God in Community, Holy in One. Amen.

Ascension of the Lord
Acts 1:1-11; Psalm 47
Ephesians 1:15-23; Luke 24:44-53

Call to Worship
We gather in this place,
some empty, some filled, some whole, some broken:
yearning for the Holy Spirit to fill us.
We come, with these ordinary people, who have shown us the way:
trusting that God will continue to illumine our hearts.
We surround the Table of grace, so we might be fed by the Bread of life:
that graced, we may serve others;
that healed, we may bring hope to the world.

Prayer of the Day
Exalted God,
you are the constant lover
     who never forsakes us;
you are the mother

who cradles her children,
you are the teacher
    patiently repeating your words for us.
We worship you.

Jesus Christ:
in you
    we are convinced
        God loves us;
through you,
    we are formed
        into your people;
with you,
    we serve those
        the world has forgotten.
We follow you.

Holy Spirit:
you are the power
    that gives us peace;
you are the wisdom
    that reveals the broken
        in our midst;
you are the spokesperson
    of the voiceless
        to whom we are deaf.
We welcome you.

God in Community, Holy in One,
we lift our prayers to you
as Jesus taught us, saying,
Our Father . . .

Call to Reconciliation
Called to proclaim repentance, we are reluctant to look at our own
failings. Invited to witness to God's loving forgiveness of sins, we would
rather not speak aloud of our own. Let us trust in the One who offers us
hope and healing, as we pray together, saying,

Unison Prayer of Confession
    **You call us to proclaim a gospel we find difficult to practice, God
Most High. We watch our clocks to make sure we spend more time
with ourselves than with you. We are hesitant to witness to your
power from on high, as we are uncertain of your presence in our
lives.**

149

Forgive us, God of Light. Fill us with the healing presence of your Spirit, that we may proclaim your good news, as we participate in the life and suffering of our world, as did your Son, our Lord and Savior, Jesus Christ.

Silence is kept

Assurance of Pardon

Choosing to set aside judgment, God gives us justice; choosing to let go of punishment, God fills us with peace; choosing to release anger, God's steadfast love rests upon us.
Forgiven, redeemed, restored - we will tell everyone, through the lives we lead, what God has done for us. Thanks be to God. Amen.

Great Prayer of Thanksgiving

The Ascended Lord be with you.
And also with you.
Lift up your hearts to the One who gives us a spirit of wisdom.
We offer our hearts to Jesus who opens God's words to us.
Clap your hands, God's people! Sing songs of praise to our God!
We sing praises to the One who blesses and blesses us!

We do indeed lift loud songs of joy to you,
Awesome God!
Everything in heaven, and on earth,
provides all the proof we need
   of your goodness and mercy.
But closing our hearts to such evidence,
we looked to our own wisdom,
   devising foolish ways to save ourselves.
Patiently you waited, hoping
   we would return to you,
but when you could no longer wait,
you came to us
   in your Word made flesh and blood.

Therefore, with all your people
of every time and every place,
we sing our glad songs to you:

Holy, holy, holy Lord God, Sovereign over all the earth.
The riches of your glorious creation forever praise you.
Hosanna in the highest!

150

Blessed is the One who will return for us.
Hosanna in the highest!

All glory is due to you, God on High,
and blessings on your Son,
our Lord and Savior, Jesus Christ.
Stripping himself of glory
    he came that we might be clothed
        in the power of the Holy Spirit.
Wearing the thorny crown of death,
    he is the Head of all the Church,
        his Body made whole for the world.

As we remember his life, his service,
his death, his resurrection, his ascension,
we speak of that mystery called faith:

Christ died to reveal salvation to us;
Christ arose to reveal resurrection life to us;
Christ ascended and will return to reveal glory to us.

We will not stop giving thanks to you,
Generous and Wonderful God,
as we pray that you
would pour out your Holy Spirit
upon your children gathered at the Table,
and upon the gifts of the bread and the cup.
We are filled with Christ's presence,
so we may go to empty ourselves:
    telling your story of grace and hope,
    carrying your mercy to those
        who cannot forgive themselves,
    pouring cups of cold water,
    embracing the untouchables of our time.

Then, when we gather at your feast in glory,
seated with our sisters and brothers from all time,
we will clap our hands, shouting our joy to you,
God in Community, Holy in One,
now and forevermore. Amen.

Seventh Sunday of Easter
Acts 1:6-14; Psalm 68:1-10, 32-35
1 Peter 4:12-14; 5:6-11; John 17:1-11

Call to Worship
The hour has come to worship our God:
to gather together as people of faith,
to glorify the God of all grace.
The time has come to devote ourselves to prayer:
to bring the burdens we carry,
to lift our hopes to the God who hears us.
The hour has come to rejoice and make God's name known:
to lift a song of thanksgiving,
to praise God for all our blessings.

Prayer of the Day
Your love is so limitless
that the needy receive goodness,
    and the prisoner finds
    a well-paying job;
the homeless find your heart
open to them,
    and all can place their worries
    in your hands.
Parent of Orphans,
we will make your name known
through all the world.

We gaze at the sky
looking for you,
    when you can be found
    in the laughing play of children;
we wonder where you have gone,
    while you are all around us
    in our sisters and brothers.
Cloud Rider,
we will sing your name
to all the world.

When our hearts
are hardened by fears,
    you melt them
    with your hope;
when our lips
can only utter boasts,
    you teach us songs
    of humility.
Caregiver of Widows,
we will exult your name

in all the world.

We will make your name known,
God in Community, Holy in One,
even as we pray as we have been taught, saying,
Our Father . . .

Call to Reconciliation
When we look to God in prayer, are we looking for condemnation and
punishment? Or do we look for the One who promises to forgive us
and make us new? Let us pray to God for mercy, as we offer our
confessions, saying,

Unison Prayer of Confession
**We cannot put it off any longer, Gracious God, it is time to
confess our unfaithfulness. Our appetites for all things threaten to
devour us like hungry animals. We are reluctant to humble
ourselves to serve others, believing we are special. We are afraid
to share in the sufferings of children and the elderly.**

**Forgive us, Voice of Mercy and Hope. Bless us with grace and
life, so we might rejoice in your love, tell of your faithfulness, and
join Jesus Christ, our Lord and Savior, in making you known to all
people.**

Silence is kept

Assurance of Pardon
Unfailing love, the Spirit of healing, the life of faith in Christ - all are
Easter gifts God offers to us.
**We rejoice and are glad. We are blessed: with mercy, with hope,
with joy. Thanks be to God. Amen.**

Great Prayer of Thanksgiving
May the Lord of Easter be with you!
And also with you!
People of God, exult before the Lord.
Our hearts overflow with God's never-ending showers of grace.
Children of God, sing to the One who blesses you.
We will offer glad songs of thanksgiving in every moment.

On that first morning of creation,
Rider of the Cosmos,
you rose up and scattered chaos
    and it melted into the silence
    and beauty of the universe.

153

You hiked the valleys,
　　and rivers raced to keep up;
you showered goodness on the earth,
　　and planted a garden of grace
　　for your beloved children.
You would provide
all we could ever need,
　　but we looked longingly
　　after the delights of sin and death,
　　　letting them devour us
　　　with their hungers.
You sent the prophets
to remind us of your name,
　　but we were too busy
　　gazing at our exalted opinions
　　of ourselves to listen.
Then, you humbled
yourself to save us,
sending Jesus into our midst.

So, with those who share in Christ's suffering,
and all who make your name known
in every word they speak, in every act they undertake,
we sing loud songs of praise to you:

Holy, holy, holy are you, God of wonder and joy.
All creation is jubilant with joy before you.
Hosanna in the highest!

Blessed is the One who gives eternal life to all.
Hosanna in the highest!

Holy are you, Pilgrim guide of prisoners,
and blessed is Jesus Christ,
brother to all orphaned by sin and death.
When we were destined to be lost,
　　he came to find us;
when we thought
nothing could ever surprise us,
　　he shouldered our sins
　　carrying them to the cross,
　　　where he was lifted up to his death.
Rising from the grave,
　　your spirit of resurrection
　　rested upon him,

so we might know you forever.

As we come to this Table remembering his life,
as we humble ourselves in the face
of his death and resurrection,
we will tell the world of that mystery called faith:

**Christ died, resisting the evil prowling all around him;
Christ rose, the spirit of glory resting upon him;
Christ will come, to restore all creation.**

Here at this Table,
where the Bread and the Cup wait,
bless these gifts with your Spirit,
so salvation might fill our emptiness,
and grace might overflow our hearts.
As we eat the simple loaf,
    may we humble ourselves
    to exalt the broken and forsaken
        the world has cast aside.
As we drink from the common cup,
    may we become alert
    to those opportunities
    we are given
        to provide for the needy,
        to learn from the prisoners,
        to be adopted by the orphans
            of this time and place.

And when we are seated around
the Great Feast of Heaven,
with those who suffered to know glory,
and those who humbled themselves
in order to lead us to faithfulness,
we will join our hearts and voices
in never-ceasing praise to you,
God in Community, Holy in One. Amen.

The Day of Pentecost
Acts 2:1-21; Psalm 104:24-34, 35b
1 Corinthians 12:3b-13; John 20:19-23

Call to Worship
On this first day, the Lord's Day,
we gather in this place, with this people:

though we have different gifts,
we are blessed by the same God.
On that great day of Pentecost,
the disciples gathered together:
though uncertain, they trusted God's future,
though many, they were one in Christ.
On the last day of all time, God's daughters
and sons will be together, in one place:
until then, we will talk of God's dreams,
with every breath we take, with every moment we live.

Prayer of the Day
Astonishing Creator,
at Pentecost,
you could have been
calm, cool, analytical -
but you decided to no
longer play it safe,
    but once again
    (and for all time),
    unleashed the Spirit
        into our babeling
        and humble-jumble lives.

Like an artist using
a variety of mediums,
Living Water,
    you proclaim good news to us:
to those who hunger for hope,
    you feed them
    from the banquet of justice;
to those parched by loneliness,
    you hold that precious cup
    overflowing with your tears
        to their cracked lips.

Unbridled Spirit,
you calm us when
we are racing around
    like four-year-olds
    playing tag;
you come rushing
through our soul's backyard,
    knocking our dirty lives
    off the closed-lines,

to shawl us in
salvation's spring garb.

May our words please you,
God in Community, Holy in One,
as we pray as Jesus taught us,
Our Father . . .

Call to Reconciliation
Called to be one body, we live as fragmented members. Our selfish
desires, our lust for more, our belief we have no need of others, leads
not to unity, but to division. Let us confess our brokenness to the God
who saves us.

Unison Prayer of Confession
**In the arguments which divide us, Hope's Heart, we cannot hear
your voice calling us to be one. In the rush to judge others who
speak, dress, or look different from us, we cannot stop to
experience your grace. In our devotion to ourselves and our
needs, we cannot open our hearts to receive your gifts.**

**Silence our babeling lives, Sculptor of Salvation, so we might
hear the clear, sweet voice of the Spirit, announcing that we are
forgiven, calling us to proclaim the good news to all the world,
baptizing us into the Body of Jesus Christ, our Lord and Savior.**

Silence is kept

Assurance of Pardon
On this day, as on every day, God stands, arms wide open to embrace
us; heart wide open to forgive us. Friends, this is the good news.
**God's glory is forever; God's grace will never end. We will rejoice in
God's healing hope, as long as we have breath. Amen.**

Great Prayer of Thanksgiving
May the Spirit of Pentecost be with you.
And also with you.
People of Pentecost, lift up your hearts.
**Come, Holy Spirit, and fill our hearts with
the flames of your justice for others.**
Spirit's Children, join your voices in praise.
**Come, Holy Spirit, to teach us new songs
of compassion and service.**

Architect of the universe:
when chaos had grown old and wrinkled,

157

you sent Spirit to give it a new face -
imagining, shaping, painting -
    until the starlight shimmered
    on the watery deeps,
        until the earth trembled
        from the trees dancing in delight.
You created critters which tip-toe
across our floors at night,
and great whales that play
hide-and-seek with submarines.
You formed humanity in your image,
and filled us with your Spirit,
so we could sing praises
to you every moment.
    But sin and death
    took our breath away
        with their fireworks made
    of futility and fear,
        and we chased after them
        clapping our hands in delight.
Prophets came, entreating
your daughters and sons to come home,
    but we thought they were drunk
    on ecstasy's sweet wine.
So, you sent Jesus,
hoping to get our attention
with glory made flesh.

So, with all who have gone before us,
and all who will come after,
we sing our songs of praise:

Holy, holy, holy are you, God who sweeps away all barriers.
All creation trembles as it rejoices in you.
Hosanna in the highest!

Blessed is the One who breathes the Holy Spirit on us.
Hosanna in the highest!

Holy are you, our only Hope,
and blessed is Jesus Christ, your Son.
When our souls thirsted
for your presence,
    he came,
        to offer us a drink of grace.

158

When our hearts cracked
from the strain of unbelief,
   he came,
     to mend us with faith.
When we had lost our way,
   he came,
     to follow agony
     to its bitter end,
so we could begin
our journey home to you.

As we remember his life, his death, his rising,
as we celebrate the fulfillment
of the Spirit he promised,
we sing of that mystery we call faith:

Christ died, giving his last breath for us;
Christ rose, the fresh breath of resurrection filling him with life;
Christ will come, breathing new life into us forever.

Pour out Pentecost's Spirit
upon these gifts of the bread and cup,
and on your daughters and sons
who hunger for your goodness.
As we eat of the Bread,
may grace dance in our hearts,
   so we will want
    to rush out with healing
    for a broken world.
As we drink for hope's Cup,
may it cascade through us,
   filling us with your
   undying compassion,
     till we become lives
     of flowing love
     to a parched people.

And when that great day comes
when you gather your children
in one place, around one great Table,
we will receive the Spirit,
being fed by your Servant, Jesus,
and sing to you
with one voice, one heart,
God in Community, Holy in One. Amen.

Genesis 1:1 - 2:4a; Psalm 8
2 Corinthians 13:11-13; Matthew 28:16-20

Call to Worship
Called to be faithful stewards of creation,
we come to worship:
to sing to the One who has created all
that is good, beautiful, and true,
and who has shared everything with us.
Called to be disciples of Jesus Christ,
we come to learn:
to follow the One who meets us
in every moment of our lives,
in every place where we find ourselves.
Called to proclaim the good news of Easter,
we come to find the words:
to be taught by the Spirit who moves
in and through us, as we serve the world.

Prayer of the Day
Hearing your whisper,
creation tingles with anticipation,
knowing that goodness
and wonder are your heart's desires.
Listening to your instructions,
the universe shimmers with delight,
and all creatures fall down
to worship you.
Imaginative God,
you are as close
as the early morning breeze.

God spoke,
and you ran forth
to sprinkle the heavens
with the shimmering stars;
you poured the waters of grace
into the hollows of the earth,
so all life might emerge.
Bone of our bone,
flesh of our flesh,

you are as close
as the love which
fills our hearts.

God dreamed,
and you flowed over chaos,
shaping, spinning, weaving
peace, wonder, and joy
into the fabric of all life.
Your passion for hope
became flames which
dance in our hearts.
Spirit of fanciful faith,
you are as close
as a butterfly's wings
brushing our cheeks.

You are closer to us
than we ever dared hope,
God in Community, Holy in One,
and so we lift our prayer to you, saying
Our Father . . .

Call to Reconciliation
When God looks at us, the One who created us sees hope, joy, grace,
life. But all too often, others see us as we are - broken, hurtful, sinful.
Let us confess our deeds and words to the One who loves us, and longs
to recreate us in the image of true life.

Unison Prayer of Confession
**Why do you pay us any attention, Artist of Creation? Created in
your image, we show faces filled with desire, and offer hearts filled
with anger to those around us. Called to be disciples of Christ, we
all too often are seen chasing after the false promises of the easy
life. Offered the role of being stewards of creation, we think that
everything that you have created is to be used up so we can enjoy
life, with no thought about future generations.**

**Yet you have declared everything you created to be good, even
us, God of unexpected grace. So we know that, in Christ Jesus our
Lord and Savior, you will reshape our greed into generosity, our
bitterness into blessings, and our brokenness into lives poured out
in service to our sisters and brothers.**

Silence is kept

Assurance of Pardon
Lives that are chaotic become cradles of peace; hearts malformed by meanness are reshaped into goodness; souls filled with despair are cleansed with grace.
This is the good news: the God who created us is the God who redeems us; the God who redeems us, is the God who sends us forth to serve. Thanks be to God! Amen.

Great Prayer of Thanksgiving
May God in Community be with you!
And with you as well!
Shaped in the divine image, let us open ourselves to the Creator.
With grace-filled hearts, we come to the Redeemer's Table.
Called to be God's household, let us offer our praises.
**We rejoice that, from many places,
the Holy Spirit has brought us here to our home.**

At the beginning,
God of Imagination,
you finger-painted
sunrises and sunsets
on the blank canvas of chaos.
You sang creation's cantata,
while suns, moons, and stars
kept watch over your delights.
You laughed, while
lions, tigers, and bears
danced joyfully in the meadows,
and everything that
wiggles, creeps, crawls
clapped their hands in time.
When you would have
clothed us in glory,
we found sin and death
to be a more comfortable fit.
Prophets came teaching obedience
and calling us to faithful lives,
but we continued to insist
on having control of our souls.
So, you sent Jesus,
to make our brokenness
whole once again.

So, with grace, love and unity
our faithful companions and teachers,

162

and with all the saints of every time and place,
we lift our songs of thanksgiving:

How majestic is your name in all the earth, Holy One.
All creation greets you with glad songs of praise.
Hosanna in the highest!

Blessed is the One who comes to make us disciples.
Hosanna in the highest!

Holy are you, God over us,
and blessed is Jesus Christ, God with us.
He took off glory's garb,
to put on humanity;
he set aside heaven's honor,
to be crowned with disgrace;
he spoke of love and hope,
silencing our enemy, pride;
he went into the grave,
to free us from death's grasp.

As we remember his life, death, and resurrection,
as we celebrate his recreating power in us,
we would speak of that mystery called faith:

Christ died, crowned with death's thorns;
Christ rose, crowned with resurrection's wonder;
Christ will come, to crown us with glory and honor.

Send your Spirit to move over
the gifts of the bread and the cup,
and to bring light and goodness
to those who gather around your Table.
As we break the Bread of life,
may we become living hope
to a world mired in despair.
As we drink from the Cup of grace,
may we cradle your kindness and peace
in our hearts and souls,
so we might be poured out
to those who thirst for your
peace and gentleness in their lives.

And when your dreams which began at creation
are realized when all time comes to an end,

when we gather around your Table,
with saints and sinners, disciples and deniers,
we will find ourselves closer to you
that we ever thought we might be,
singing our praises forever and ever,
God in Community, Holy in One. Amen.

Charge and Benediction
God, who created you in the divine image, sends you forth:
we go, to reflect the presence of our
Creator to everyone we meet.
Jesus, who has redeemed you,
has established God's Kingdom in our midst:
we go, to bring healing
to the broken of the world.
The Holy Spirit, who calls you to be
God's people, goes with you to many places:
We go, to tear down the walls that divide us,
and to build lives of hope for all of God's children.
And now,
may the peace of the rolling waves,
the peace of the silent mountains,
the peace of the singing stars,
and the deep, deep peace of the
Prince of Peace,
be with you now and forever.
Amen.

Pentecost 2/Trinity 1/Proper 4/OT 9
Genesis 6:9-22; 7:24; 8:14-19; Psalm 46
Romans 1:16-17; 3:22b-28 (29-31); Matthew 7:21-29

Call to Worship
Be still!
The One who cradled the remnant of creation
in the cleansing waters calls us here.
Be still! And know this:
at the present time, God cradles us in safety
even as fear floods all around us.
Be still! And know who God is.
The One who is with us in every moment:
past, present, and future.

Prayer of the Day
In every city center

where lives teeter on the edge;
in every suburban home
where lives can be trapped
in the quicksand of complacency:
you are there, Helping God.

In every corridor of power
where nations hurl insults
or whisper hope;
in every prejudice
rooted in fear;
in every grace-filled conversation
between strangers:
you are there, Strength of the World.

In every heart that welcomes
the broken and beaten-down of the world;
in every reconciling embrace
of those we once boasted
were our enemies:
you are there, Spirit of Refuge.

God in Community, Holy in One,
early in the morning, your glad rivers
of hope and joy flow through us,
as we lift our prayers, saying,
Our Father . . .

Call to Reconciliation

When we gather to praise our God, we remember that we are people
who tend to choose our will over God's. Accepting God's power to create
us as new people in Christ, let us confess our sins before God and one
another, as we pray,

Responsive Prayer of Confession

In the lonely neighbor next door, you come to us,
but we do not recognize you;
in the cries of the children sleeping in the street, you call,
but we do not hear you;
in the laughing hug of an old friend, you bless us,
but we cannot feel you.
Forgive us, and make us new.
In the immigrant who sits beside us on the bus, you accept us,
but we will not shake your hand;
in the family member who tells us to 'forget it,' you forgive us,

but we dare not let go of what they have done to us.
Forgive us, and make us new.
In a broken world, we see your mission,
but we insist on doing everything our way;
in the outcast, the poor, the needy, we find you,
but we do not care what is happening to you;
in your death and resurrection, we find life,
but we are unable to believe you.
Forgive us, and make us new.

Silence is kept

Assurance of Pardon
There is no shame in the good news - only hope, only life, only joy, only peace.
Even now, God is forgiving us; even now, God is making us new.
Thanks be to God. Amen.

Great Prayer of Thanksgiving
May God our strength be with you!
And also with you!
Lift your hearts to the One who is in our midst!
Our hearts overflow and make glad our God!
Sing glad songs to our God!
For the God of all people invites us to this Feast!

You put an end
to the corruption of chaos,
Ark of our hearts,
filling its emptiness
with creation's beauty.
You whispered your dreams,
and the mountains echoed with praise;
you shaped us in your image
and the heavens saw your work.
You placed us right
in the center of your goodness,
giving us the solid foundation
of your heart as our home.
But we decided to stand
on the shifting sands of sin,
not fearing death's flood.
You sent the prophets
to remind us that
you were not ashamed

166

of your hopes for us.
But we would not keep
our covenant with you,
and so you sent Jesus,
to offer us the justice
of your righteous love.

So, with those who have found
their refuge in you in every time and place,
we lift our songs of thanksgiving:

We will be still and know that you are God.
Every animal, every creeping thing, everything that lives and moves
in all creation praises you.
Hosanna in the highest!

Blessed is the One who comes with your authority.
Hosanna in the highest!

Holy are you, Creator of all life,
and blessed is Jesus Christ, our Peace.
He could have stayed
in the haven of glory,
but came to walk our streets,
bringing the dawn of redemption.
He could have prided himself
on his signs and wonders,
but faithfully did your will.
Making no distinction
between your children,
he went to the cross,
willing to sacrifice his life,
to put an end to
death's control over ours.

As we remember his life, his death, his resurrection,
as we long to not be ashamed of his gospel,
we speak of that mystery we call faith:

Christ died for all who fall short of God's glory;
Christ rose so all might be justified by God's grace;
Christ will come for all of God's children.

167

Here, on this Table
are your gifts -
the bread and the cup.
But even more,
are the gifts of grace,
of hope, of peace.
So pour out your Spirit
upon all these gifts,
and those who gather
in this place and this time.
As we eat of the Bread of life,
may we reach out to those
starving for justice and peace.
As we drink from the Cup of joy,
may we live out our faith
by serving those damaged
by the violence of our world.

And when we enter heaven,
our feet on the firm foundation
of your love and grace,
we will gather around your Table once more,
singing our praises to you forever,
God in Community, Holy in One. Amen.

Pentecost 3/Trinity 2/Proper 5/OT 10
Genesis 12:1-9; Psalm 33:1-12
Romans 4:13-25; Matthew 9:9-13, 18-26

Call to Worship
The sinners, the saints;
the broken, the whole:
**We all come seeking the One
who offers grace and hope.**
The doubters, the devout;
the wonderers, the wanderers:
**We all seek to follow the One
who works for justice and hope
for all of God's people.**
The hesitant, the heroic;
the grandparents, the little children:
**We all listen for the songs of joy
all creation sings to the One
who gives life and peace.**

Prayer of the Day
When we begin
our journey of faith,
you are there,
Constant Love,
    pointing the way
    to the promises you offer.

When we stumble
over our own silliness,
and skin our knees
on the hardened pavement
of our pride,
you are there,
Companion of the world's riff-raff,
    to take us by the hand,
    to lift us to our feet,
    to bandage our bleeding egos.

And you continue to call us,
Breath of life:
to follow,
    even when our faith falters;
to drink
    the living waters bottled
    with your grace;
to serve
    those whom the world
    easily discounts;
to see
    you waiting at the end
    of our pilgrimage.

God in Community, Holy in One,
we will seek to follow you always,
even as we pray as Jesus teaches us,
Our Father . . .

Call to Reconciliation
In this place, in this moment, we wonder, "is it true?" God's hopes, God's
promises, God's grace - are they really for you, for me, for us? God
invites us to bring our questions, as well as our fears and failures, so we
might discover the truth for ourselves, as we pray, saying,

Unison Prayer of Confession

When we look for our place cards at the table of honor, do we see you standing at the back of the room with the servers? When we walk around the homeless on the way to the ballgame, do we see you sitting in the doorway with the hungry children? When we tell others to pull themselves up, have we forgotten how many people reached out their hands to us along the way?

Forgive us, God who offers mercy to us, and desires that we share grace with others. If we would truly follow, we must be willing to take off our Sunday best and put on the aprons of service, offering everyone we meet the bread of life and cup of hope which have come to us through Jesus Christ our Lord and Savior.

Silence is kept

Assurance of Pardon

Here is the good news: it is *not* up to us. God has not wavered in keeping the covenant of grace, of hope, of mercy, of life.
By God's grace, we are forgiven;
by God's healing, we are made whole;
by God's constant love, we are restored to life.
Thanks be to God. Amen.

Great Prayer of Thanksgiving

May the God who gives life to the dead be with you.
And also with you.
Open your hearts to God's steadfast love.
Hoping against hope, our hearts are glad in God.
Let joyous melodies be offered to our God.
Loving righteousness and justice, we rejoice in God.

You saw the well-laid plans
chaos had devised, Faithful Worker,
and laughed out loud,
the heavens bursting forth
with each great guffaw,
the stars spilling into places
with each breath of joy.
Filling the earth with
that love which never ends,
you created us so we might
live in your garden of grace.
But we reached out to grasp
the garment of sin,
letting it drag us through

the mud of despair and death.
Even then, you sent those
who spoke in your name
to remind us of the promises
made so long ago.
When we continued to cling
to trying to save ourselves,
you sent Jesus to us,
knowing his faith in you
would never weaken.

So, knowing praise is the only response
which we can make to such love,
we join our voices in this place and moment
with those in every time and place
who forever sing your joy:

Holy, holy, holy are you, God who desires mercy.
All creation sings new songs of thanksgiving.
Hosanna in the highest!

Blessed is the One who eats with people like us.
Hosanna in the highest!

Holy are you, God of Grace,
and blessed is Jesus Christ, Desirer of mercy.
He walked among us,
calling us to follow
that we might know
the way to your heart.
Sitting with the outsiders,
he fed them with that love
which welcomed and embraced them
as sisters and brothers.
Following your hopes,
he went into the grave
where death was waiting,
so he might take us
by the hand and lead us
into life forever with you.

As we remember your ancient promises
fulfilled in the One who will never die,
we would sing of that faith which is ours;

171

**Trusting God's faithfulness, Christ died on the cross;
giving God the glory, Christ rose from the grave;
calling us to follow, Christ leads us into God's kingdom.**

Pour out your Spirit
upon these simple,
yet so very precious, gifts
of the bread and of the cup.
By your grace,
when we would sanitize
our hands with piety,
the bread transforms us
so we would reach out
to the untouchables of our time.
By your compassion,
when we would sit at home,
at ease, in comfort, with plenty,
the cup alters our attitude
so we will get up
and follow Jesus into
the brokenness of our world.

And when we are gathered
around the great Table in heaven,
seated beside Abraham and Sarah,
Paul and the psalmists, Jesus and Joanna,
we will lift our voices together,
praising you forever,
God in Community, Holy in One. Amen.

Pentecost 4/Trinity 3/Proper 6/Ordinary Time 11
Genesis 18:1-15 (21:1-7); Psalm 116:1-2, 12-19
Romans 5:1-8; Matthew 9:35 – 10:8 (9-23)

Call to Worship
On an ordinary Sunday,
we come to worship God:
**we come, trusting God will speak to us;
we come, hoping God will surprise us.**
On this day, like every other day,
we seek to follow Jesus:
**we follow, believing Jesus will be with us;
we follow, hoping Jesus will work through us.**
On this day, we lift our souls to God's Spirit:

we open our hearts, that the Spirit may fill us;
we open our hands, that we might be a gift to others.

Prayer of the Day
The mother watching
her son packing for camp,
the father teaching
his daughter how to drive;
the spouse worrying
over their spouse's addiction to work,
the child closing
her ears to her parents' arguing:
    each is precious in your sight,
    Compassion of Creation.

The grandmother hoping
for a telephone call,
the neighbor frantic
about selling his house;
the teenager struggling
with choices she cannot share,
the retiree wandering
the empty hours of daytime:
    each is welcomed into your heart,
    Haven for the hopeless.

The kids on the corner selling
lemonade to help a classmate,
the teacher already preparing
for next year's classes;
the parent wondering
how to pay for groceries,
the unemployed hoping
for good news this week:
    each is cradled in your peace,
    Spirit of Serenity.

God in Community, Holy in One,
each of us, all of us,
lift our prayers to you, as Jesus taught us,
Our Father . . .

Call to Reconciliation
If you are looking for proof of God's love, here it is: at the very moment

we realize we cannot help ourselves, that is the time we discover God
has saved us in Christ Jesus. Join me as we pray to our God, saying,

Unison Prayer of Confession
**How easily we pat ourselves on the back, Listening Love, for the
lives we lead. We welcome the praise of others, but have little
compassion for those who have failed us. We assume that a
comfortable life is our birthright, yet believe poor choices produce
suffering for those around us. We boast of the good we do, but
forget to thank you for all that you have given to us.**

**Forgive us, Companion of Compassion, for breaking your heart,
and disappointing your hopes for us. As we seek to follow your
Child, may we be found with those whose lives are barren, with
those who know little laughter in their day, with those who have
received no love from others - for in their presence, we will find
Jesus Christ, our Lord and Savior.**

Silence is kept

Assurance of Pardon
Listen to the good news - the kingdom of God is very near. As close
as a child's laughter, as embracing as a father's love, as enfolding
as a mother's caress.
We are God's people:
called, that we may follow;
gifted, that we may serve;
forgiven, that we might bring hope.
Thanks be to God. Amen.

Great Prayer of Thanksgiving
May the gracious God be with you!
And also with you!
In the presence of God's people, lift up your hearts.
We call on God's name with joy in our hearts.
Offer God songs of thanksgiving this day.
We love God, who hears our voices of praise.

When there was no time,
when there was only chaos,
you knew it was the right moment,
Ingenious Love,
to bring forth creation
in all of its glory.
    Butterflies dancing from
        flower to flower,

174

birds harmonizing in praise,
gentle breezes caressing grass,
kittens chasing bugs they will never catch.
Given this bounty of goodness,
we returned your graciousness
with blatant betrayal,
tossing aside your hopes for us,
proclaiming sin and death
as the authorities for our lives.
Heart-broken,
you sought to provide a way
for us back to your grace
through the words of the prophets,
but we laughed to ourselves
as we continued skipping down
that never-ending road of rebellion.
But you proved your love for us
by sending Jesus to die for us,
an act we would not do
even for those we loved.

So, with those of every time and place,
with those in this place, and in this moment,
we will sing our praises to you
knowing you incline your ear to listen:

Holy, holy, holy are you, God of mercy.
Your servants join all creation in praising you.
Hosanna in the highest!

Blessed is the One who tells us of the kingdom's nearness.
Hosanna in the highest!

Holy are you, Compassion's Heart,
and blessed is Jesus Christ, our Savior.
You sent him to travel
our cities, our lives, our hearts
to teach us of your hopes for us.
He did not laugh
at our foolish ways,
but, with great compassion,
he reached out to help us.
Asking no payment,
he gave himself to death,
dying for all of us sinners,

that we might discover
the kingdom of heaven
which is nearer to us
than we would ever imagine.

As we remember his life and death,
as we seek to respond to his calling for us,
we would proclaim that mystery called faith:

**Taking nothing but his faith, Christ went to the cross;
precious in God's sight, Christ was raised from the grave;
keeping faith, Christ will deliver us from death.**

Here, in these moments
as we prepare to feast on your love,
pour out your Spirit
upon the bounty of your grace,
this bread and this cup,
and upon those for whom they are given.
You would feed us
on the Bread of life,
　　so we might go out
　　to bring hope to all
　　whom the world has disappointed.
You offer us the cup of grace,
so, as your love is poured
deep within our parched souls,
　　we can become that offering
　　of peace and reconciliation
　　for which all creation longs.

And when time has come to an end,
and we are all one with you,
we will call on your name,
God in Community, Holy in One,
offering our thanks forever and ever. Amen.

Pentecost 5/Trinity 4/Proper 7/Ordinary Time 12
Genesis 21:8-21; Psalm 86:1-10
Romans 6:1b-11; Matthew 10:24-39

Call to Worship
There is no hope like you, O God!
Hope for those who cry out from the deserts of their lives.
There is no grace like you, O God!

Grace for those rejected, ignored, and cast aside by the world.
There is no love like you, O God!
**Love for those who have known days of trouble
and nights of loneliness.**
There is no one like you, O God!
No one! No one! No one!

Prayer of the Day
When we are filled
with loss and despair,
    you gladden our hearts
    with your hope.
When everyone around us
turns a deaf ear,
    you lean over and put
    your hand to your ear,
        to hear our cries.
There is no love like you,
Compassionate God.

When we long
to continue in sin,
    you call us
    to live with you
    in the kingdom of God.
When we have fallen,
our souls parched by death,
    you lift us up,
    holding us tight to your heart,
        carrying us to drink at
        the deep well of living water.
There is no grace like you,
Brother of the hopeless.

When the world would stuff
our pockets with fears,
    you turn them inside out,
    and fill them with the
        smooth stones of hope.
When we see nothing
on the horizon of life,
    you hold up the sign
    which reads 'follow Jesus!'
When we are weakened
by our foolish choices,

you strengthen us with
joy overflowing from your heart.
There is no peace like you,
Spirit of wisdom.

God in Community, Holy in One,
there is no one like you in our lives.
This we know, as we pray together,
Our Father . . .

Call to Reconciliation
When we would keep our faults and failings in the shadows, you call us
to bring them into the light of your grace and forgiveness. With such a
promise, with such a hope, how can we not confess to the One who
loves us so much? Join me as we pray together, saying,

Unison Prayer of Confession
**It is never easy to confess our sins to you, Listener to our words.
When we have a chance to speak up for the outsider, we too often
join in sending them away into the wilderness of hopelessness.
When we could shout good news to a needy world, our voices drop
to a whisper. When we could abound in grace, we continue to
wallow in wrongdoing.**

**Forgive us, Hearer of our hearts, and have mercy on us. You lean
over to listen to our words, and then to cast them into your sea of
forgetfulness. You show us your signs of hope, that we might point
others to you. You help us when we are weakest and, in Jesus
Christ, our Lord and Savior, you save us when we cannot save
ourselves.**

Silence is kept

Assurance of Pardon
Do not be afraid. God cherishes us, God treasures you, beyond all else
in creation. You are graced, you are forgiven, you are healed.
**We will not keep this good news to ourselves. We will shout our
hope from the rooftops of our hearts. Thanks be to God, we are
forgiven! Amen.**

Great Prayer of Thanksgiving
May the God of Abraham and Sarah be with you.
And also with you.
There is no one like the God of Hagar and Ishmael.
And so we lift our hearts to God.

God will gladden the souls of all people.
We sing to the One who is always gracious.

There is none like you,
Everlasting Grace,
    shaper of goodness and beauty
    out of the shadows of chaos.
You gladdened the soul
of all creation
    with stunning sunsets,
    clear-streamed valleys,
    mountains towering into the sky.
These gifts, as well as your
hopes and dreams, were for us,
    but we sent them away into
    the wilderness of forgetfulness,
      choosing to live in
      the long days of rebellion.
The God of forgiveness,
your words calling us back
overflowed from the mouths
of the prophets,
    but we continued to sin.
Seeking to unite us
with you once more,
you sent Jesus,
to baptize us with your life,
even as he was baptized
into death for us.

Therefore, we join with those in this place,
as well as our sisters and brothers
throughout all creation
in singing your praises:

Holy, holy, holy, God of every time and people.
All creation kneels, glorifying your name.
Hosanna in the highest!

Blessed is the One who lost his life for our sake.
Hosanna in the highest!

Holy are you, Steadfast Love,
and blessed is Jesus Christ, our Savior.
He could have remained

179

the Child of your heart,
    but came to be with
    his sisters and brothers.
Seeking to glorify your name,
    he was called a blasphemer,
    accused of usurping your power.
Longing to lead us out
of despair's deep desert,
    he willingly went to the grave,
        that we might be raised
        to life with you forever,
        walking the streets of the kingdom.

As we remember his baptism at the Jordan,
as we recall his baptism into death,
as we celebrate his resurrection to life,
we sing of that mystery called faith:

Christ gave his life, for the sake of all;
Christ rose, for death lost its power over him;
Christ will come, for we have been baptized into his death.

As we come to your
Table of peace and hope,
pour out your Spirit upon
the gifts of the bread and the cup,
and upon your children
gathered in your name.
As we are nurtured
by the Bread of Life,
    may we have no fear,
    but boldly go to serve
    those cast out by our world.
As we are nourished
with the wine of wonder,
    may we not keep
    your love and grace a secret,
    but shout the good news
        of your salvation for all.

And when we have been
baptized into death like Christ,
and raised into life with you,
we will join our voices
with our sisters and brothers

singing your glory forever,
God in Community, Holy in One. Amen.

Pentecost 6/Trinity 5/Proper 8/Ordinary Time 13
Genesis 22:1-14; Psalm 13
Romans 6:12-23; Matthew 10:40-42

Call to Worship
With joy and celebration, God welcomes us to this place.
How good it is to gather in God's house!
With joy and celebration, we welcome one another.
We greet each other by name; we are equal in God's Kingdom.
We open our hearts, to welcome God's love;
we open our arms, to welcome God's people.
Here, every single one of God's children is welcome.

Prayer of the Day
You have invited us to this place,
Accepting God,
for this is where you want us.
Here, we learn to trust you,
    and to faithfully follow where you lead us.
Here, we learn to listen to you,
    and hear the words of life,
    of hope, of healing.
Here, we learn to bring everything to you -
    even our pain, especially our brokenness -
    that we might be made whole.

Pilgrim Jesus:
you are with us in this place,
    and in every place
    where we live, work, play, pray.
And, if we dare to trust
this good news,
we discover that grace
which sets us free:
    to treat one another
        as sisters and brothers;
    to use that grace
        to break down every barrier;
    to live that grace
        in every moment of our lives.

We would receive you
into our hearts, Abiding Spirit,
knowing that you have brought us together,
for by the gift of your presence,
   we are no longer strangers
   but friends and neighbors
      in your Kingdom.

God in Community, Holy in One,
hear us as we pray as Jesus taught us, saying,
Our Father . . .

Call to Reconciliation

Created to live with one another and our God, we know the truth about our shattered lives and relationships. Yet, out of this brokenness, God shapes new people, giving every one of us a new start. Let us confess those things which separate us from one another, that we might be made one in Christ.

Unison Prayer of Confession

In your house, there is room for all; at your Table, we find a place set for us. But we admit, Inviting God, that we find it difficult to be as accepting as you and we find it easy to shoulder others away from your feast. You fling wide the doors to your kingdom, Welcoming God, but we are quick to try to shut them to those who are different from us. Your heart is open so that all might experience your grace, and we reluctantly remember our ungracious words and deeds.

Forgive us, God of every person: heal our broken lives; mend our fragmented souls. Open our hearts to your vision of the Kingdom where all are welcome, all are affirmed, all are beloved - even as we receive these gifts from Jesus Christ, our Lord and Savior.

Silence is kept

Assurance of Pardon

Can it be any clearer? God has created us to be a family - sisters, brothers, neighbors, friends. No longer strangers, we are all welcome in the kingdom of love, grace, and hope.
In Christ, we are one. There are no barriers, no differences, no divisions. We are a new people, forgiven and made whole. Thanks be to God. Amen.

Great Prayer of Thanksgiving

The Lord who provides be with you!
And also with you!
Lift your hearts to the One who frees us from sin.
We rejoice in God, who delivers us from death's power.
Offer songs of joy and wonder to the One
who welcomes you to this Table.
**We will sing to God, whose bounty fills our lives,
our hearts, our souls.**

With great joy and thanksgiving,
we lift our songs of praise to you,
God of all life.
You did not withhold
your treasures from us,
    but poured them out
    in overflowing abundance for us:
        sparkling streams, rolling clear and clean;
        carpets of grass,
            through which the wind tiptoes;
        crystal blue skies freckled
            with bright, billowing clouds.
All was created and called good by you,
and offered as gifts for us.
But when we could have danced
through Eden, free and joyous,
    we chose to let sin bind us,
    placing us on death's altars.
When we refused to answer you
when you called in the night,
when we turned deaf ears
to the prophets you sent to us,
    you did not withhold your only son,
    the Child you loved most of all,
        but sent Jesus to come to us,
providing a way home to your heart.

So, we lift our voices, filled with joy,
joining them with the glad songs
of every place and generation,
all creation praising your name:

**Holy, holy, holy are you, God who does not forget us.
All creation trusts in your steadfast love.
Hosanna in the highest!**

Blessed is the One who gives a cup of living water to the thirsty. Hosanna in the highest!

Holy are you, God of constant love,
and blessed is Jesus Christ, our Savior,
and the love of your heart.
When we thought you had forgotten us,
    he came to remind us
    of your eternal promises;
when we would lay in
the cradling arms of pain,
    he came to make us whole;
when we prepared to sleep
in death's comforting bed,
    he came to shine the light
    of your love upon us,
and to welcome us home
into your kingdom of eternal life.

As we remember his hospitality to all,
as we would not forget his dying for us,
as we would celebrate his resurrection,
we would tell of that mystery we call faith:

**Christ died, welcoming death on our behalf;
Christ rose, welcoming the gift of resurrection on our behalf;
Christ will return, on our behalf, so we might not lose our reward.**

You send your Spirit
to rest upon the gifts
of the bread and the cup,
and to welcome all your children
to the feast of the Lamb of Life.
As we eat of that Bread
which makes us whole,
    we would make room
    for all of your children,
        welcoming all who have been
        rejected by the world.
As we drink deeply from
that Cup which gives us life,
    we would leave this place
    to go and be with all
        who are bound by fear and failure,
        by hunger and hopelessness,

by hate and persecution,
not withholding our
most precious possession,
but sharing our lives with them.

And when all time has ended,
when we are gathered as your family
at the table which you have prepared for us,
we will feast on the grace you provide,
praising you forever and ever,
God in Community, Holy in One. Amen.

Pentecost 7/Trinity 6/Proper 9/Ordinary Time 14
Genesis 24:34-38, 42-49, 58-67; Psalm 45:10-17
Romans 7:15-25a; Matthew 11:16-19, 25-30

Call to Worship
We stand here today, in the presence of the Holy:
who will show us the way to hope and grace.
We come today to the spring of hope:
where Jesus will draw for us all the living water we can drink.
We speak from our hearts, lifting our praise and prayers:
leaning over to listen, the Spirit hears us, filling us with peace.

Prayer of the Day
You bless us
beyond all reason,
    that we might give
    all we have
    (and all we are)
        in service to you.
You speak hope
to our hearts,
    that we might hear
    the cries of your
        little ones in our midst.
Your love is celebrated
in all generations,
Joyous Creator.

You befriend
    all the outsiders
    of every time and place;
you lead us by
the right way,

if we would but follow;
you rescue us
from our foolish wisdom,
    carrying us like babies
    into the kingdom.
Your grace is revealed
to every generation,
Servant of the weary.

You are the goodness
    from which we draw life;
you are the comforter
    who warms us
    when death's chill comes;
you are the common sense
    which helps us to live
    God's gracious ways.
Your peace is celebrated
through all generations,
Spirit of rest.

With every generation, in our generation,
we would sing your praises forever and ever,
God in Community, Holy in One,
even as we pray as Jesus teaches us,
Our Father . . .

Call to Reconciliation
When we could delight in God's ways, we seem to wander down the
paths of failings and foolishness. When we could dance in joy, we shuffle
our feet through despair's dry dust. Let us confess our wayward lives to
the One who longs to forgive us, as we pray, saying,

Unison Prayer of Confession
**We are sinners, Creator of gentleness, and cannot make good
choices. We know what is the right thing to do, yet end up acting in
wrong ways. We know the gentle words a friend needs, yet raise our
voices in anger and hurt. We hear you inviting us to crawl up into
your gracious lap, but run outside to play with our old friend, evil.**

**Forgive us, Blesser and Blessing of our hearts, and rescue us
from our foolish lives. Speak to our aching spirits with your healing
hope. Yoke us with Jesus Christ, our Lord and Savior, so we might
lead gentle and gracious lives in the days to come.**

Silence is kept

Assurance of Pardon
God deals faithfully and truly with us. Choosing to forget our mistakes, and to forgive our sins, God blesses us with love and hope.
Blessed, forgiven, healed - we are God's new people, going out to bring others to the waters of life. Thanks be to God. Amen.

Great Prayer of Thanksgiving
May the Lord of rest be with you.
And also with you.
All who are weary, yoke yourselves to the Lord of life.
We join our hearts with God's Heart of compassion.
People of God, lift your glad songs to the One who loves us.
Praise is on our lips, thanksgiving overflows from our hearts.

At the first moment of time,
you drew from the deep wells
of gentleness and goodness,
Compassionate Creator.
You wandered the fields,
    planting the seeds which blossomed
    into rainbows of beauty;
you walked in evening's coolness,
    scattering the stars and moons
    into the deep blue-black skies.
All that you made
was given to us that
we might eat, drink, and dance
with you forever and ever.
    But we did not understand
    all the blessing you offered,
    choosing to sit in sin's marketplace,
        as death played its
        mournful tunes for us.
You offered us rest
from our wandering ways,
whispering to our souls
through the prophets' heartaches.
    When we could not, or would not,
    turn back to you,
you sent Jesus to
rescue us from ourselves.

So, with every generation before us,
with all who will come after us,

we lift our voices in praise to you:

Holy, holy, holy, God of the weary soul.
Creation celebrates your name in all generations.
Hosanna in the highest!

Blessed is the One who offers our souls rest.
Hosanna in the highest!

Holy are you, God of every moment,
and blessed is Jesus Christ,
friend of the forsaken, Savior of all.
Graced with your glory,
    he humbled himself to come to us,
    to lead us back to you.
Yoked with your heart,
    he came to bear our burdens,
    so we might find rest
        in your hope and healing.
Fed by your love,
    he came to eat and drink
    with all the outsiders,
        so we might dance forever
        in your kingdom of love.
Embraced by your gracious will,
he handed himself over to death,
    carrying the heavy burden of our sins,
    so the joy of resurrection
        might be revealed to us.

As we remember his life, his death, his rising,
as we come to this meal prepared for us,
we celebrate that mystery of faith
given to every generation:

Christ died, gentle and humble to the end;
Christ rose, delighting in the new life given to him;
Christ will return, offering us the yoke of resurrection.

To what shall we compare your grace,
God of all hope and joy?
You pour it out upon us,
and upon the simple gifts of the Meal,
through your Spirit of gentleness.

You feed us with the Bread of hope,
not that we might be satisfied,
   but so we would go forth
   to embrace the outcasts of our world,
      eating and drinking with them,
      offering your love to them.
You tilt the Cup of mercy to our lips,
not that we might become smug,
   but so we would be dissatisfied
      until all the broken are healed,
      until all the homeless are sheltered,
      until all the hungry are fed,
      until all the lost are found,
      until all the least are celebrated.

Then, when the last moment of time has come,
and creation is restored to goodness and beauty,
we will sit at the Table with the Lamb,
with all the sinners and saints,
with all the winners and losers,
with all our sisters and brothers,
celebrating your peace and joy forever and ever,
God in Community, Holy in One. Amen.

Pentecost 8/Trinity 7/Proper 10/Ordinary Time 15
Genesis 25:19-34; Psalm 119:105-112
Romans 8:1-11; Matthew 13:1-9, 18-23

Call to Worship
Your grace is a lamp for our hearts, O God.
Light our way through the shadows of this world.
When we struggle with questions and doubts,
tell us your stories of hope and grace.
When we are about to wander off into the wilderness,
show us the paths to your peace and joy.

Prayer of the Day
When we wonder
why life is the way
it seems to be,
   you teach us how
   to live for others.
When we would sell
our birth gift of grace

for a bowl of sin's stew,
    you nourish us with
    a serving of hope.
Prayer Granter,
listen to our hearts and words.

When we are convinced
we are only barren soil,
    you plant seeds of grace
    deep within us.
When our souls are as
parched as arid deserts,
    you refresh us
    with the waters
    of goodness and mercy.
Story Teller,
fill our hearts with your words.

You come into our hearts,
to remove the bricks and mortar
from that great wall of hostility
we have built over the years,
    setting us free to play
    in the kingdom of peace.
You help us to let go
of our focus on ourselves,
    so we may reach out
    to share with others.
Emancipator,
send us forth to live your words.

God in Community, Holy in One,
with our hearts and with our words,
we lift our prayers to you, saying,
Our Father . . .

Call to Reconciliation

We talk about lives of faith, but are usually found walking down the streets of seduction and temptation. God sends the Spirit to live in us, so we might have life with God. Let us confess our mis-steps as we pray together,

Unison Prayer of Confession

We walk through the world, Life Giver, so focused on ourselves, that we do not notice sin laying traps for us. We choose favorites,

hurting folks looking for love. In our rush to grasp what we want, we let go of your promises given for us. In resisting your claims on us, we turn our backs on your dreams for us.

Forgive us, Promise Keeper, and have mercy. Like Isaac and Rebekah, we are heirs of your trust; like Jacob, we receive your grace even when we have done nothing to deserve it; like Esau, we share in your promises. May Jesus Christ, your Son, our Lord, sow seeds of faithfulness and hope in our hearts.

Silence is kept

Assurance of Pardon
God leans over so that great heart of forgiveness and hope might touch our own, healing us and restoring us to new life.
Not condemnation, but God's compassion;
not judgment, but God's justice;
not a punishment, but God's grace.
We are forgiven and loved. Thanks be to God. Amen.

Great Prayer of Thanksgiving
The God of seasons be with you!
And also with you!
Offer your hearts to God, heirs of the promise.
We lift them to the One who sows seeds of grace in us.
May hope and wonder be on your lips this day.
We sing songs of grace and love to the One
who waters us with peace.

Into the rocky heart of chaos,
    you sowed the seeds of beauty,
Heart's Imagination.
Into the thorny soil of nothingness,
    you cast hope and grace.
Creation sprang forth,
your goodness bubbling up
    in streams flowing down
    to crystal clear oceans;
your compassion planting all
we would ever need to live.
You sowed,
so we might feast
on your peace and grace,
    but once we had tasted
    the fruits of the flesh,
        we hungered for more and more.

191

Prophets came to teach us
how to live your will,
    but their words fell on thorny hearts.
So then, you sent Jesus,
to call us home to you,
doing for us what we could not do.

Therefore, with those who hunger for your word,
in every generation, in every time, in every place,
we lift our songs of thanksgiving to you:

Holy, holy, holy are you, Light and Lamp to all.
All creation is filled with your Spirit.
Hosanna in the highest!

Blessed is the Sower of salvation who comes to us.
Hosanna in the highest!

Holy are you, Giver of all life,
and blessed is Jesus Christ, our Hope and Joy.
When he could have come
with words of condemnation,
    he sat down and told stories
    of forgiveness and hope.
When he could have claimed
the birthright due your own true Child,
    he poured out his inheritance
    of grace upon all sinners.
When we could not -
when we would not -
submit to your will,
    he gave himself up
    to sin and death
defeating their power
as he walked out of the tomb,
    gripping our hearts
    to lead us back to you.

As we remember his life, death, and resurrection,
as we listen once more to his words for us,
we would reflect on that mystery we call faith:

Christ died, severely afflicted for our sake;
Christ rose, given life according to your promise;
Christ will return, holding our lives in his hands forever.

192

As you send your grace
upon the gifts of your Feast,
may this Spirit of life
rest upon your children gathered here.
As the Bread of Life
feeds us with hope,
    may we go out
    to walk with all who stumble
        along the paths of life.
As the Cup of Salvation
nourishes the rock gardens
of our barren souls,
    may we become the foundation
    of justice and peace for our communities.
As your Word of grace
prunes our thorny hearts,
    may we welcome all those
    who have sold their hopes
    for a meal of broken promises.

Then, when all time comes to an end,
when we are called to your Table
for that great feast with our sisters and brothers,
we will grip one another's hands,
and join our voices in praising you,
God in Community, Holy in One. Amen.

Pentecost 9/Trinity 8/Proper 11/Ordinary Time 16
Genesis 28:10-19a; Psalm 139:1-12, 23-24
Romans 8:12-25; Matthew 13:24-30, 36-43

Call to Worship
Early in the morning, we gather
at the edge of heaven,
finding the gates flung wide open
by the One who welcomes all.
Early in the morning, we come
to this holy place of worship,
to be touched by the One
who offers us grace and love.
Early in the morning, we worship God,
who adopts us into the family,
to be filled by the One who would
pour us out in service to the world.

Prayer of the Day
God-who-keeps-promises:
every word you have spoken
of hope found in the depths of life,
of healing surprising our pain,
of grace jumping rope with children,
will all come true -
> even when our stubbornness
> deafens us to your whispers.

Jesus-who-sows-seeds:
every hope you have for us
of kindness never ending,
of persistent patience,
of sacrificial service,
can be found -
> even when others cannot
> see them in us.

Spirit-who-leads-us-into-life:
every dream you have
of peace becoming our best friend,
of joy bubbling from our hearts,
of strangers welcomed as kin,
will happen -
> even when we insist on
> living out our fantasies.

Behind us, under us, beside us, over us,
you are ever and always with us,
God in Community, Holy in One,
and so we lift our prayer to you saying,
Our Father . . .

Call to Reconciliation
Hiding in the cobwebbed corners of our lives, we hope God cannot find
us and see how we truly act and speak. But God's light of righteousness
shines on us, so that we might find comfort, hope, forgiveness. Let us
confess our sins together, saying,

Unison Prayer of Confession
I've tried to hide from your searching gaze, Love's Delight:
I've climbed mountains,
> **and burrowed deep into earth's caverns;**

194

I've fled to the farthest edges of my soul,
 and longed to sail in my fears to the dark side of the moon.
And wherever I go -
you are waiting for me!
 Even in the dimmest corners of my heart,
 your light is able to find me.

Lost,
 I am found;
afraid to speak of my sinfulness -
 you hear my stumbling words
 before I shape them in my mind;
unable to help myself -
 you redeem me through the gracious love
 of Jesus Christ, my Lord, my Savior.

Silence is kept

Assurance of Pardon
In sorrow so deep we cannot find our way out, God cradles us in comfort;
in moments so dark, we stumble over ourselves, God lights the way;
in joy which cascades into our souls, God fills us with healing.
**Even when we cannot see it, God's hope is all around us,
surrounding us with peace and healing. Thanks be to God, we are
forgiven. Amen.**

Great Prayer of Thanksgiving
May the God who knows you best be with you!
And also with you!
Worship the One who is with us at this Table,
as well as in our hunger for hope.
How blessed we are to open our hearts to God.
Sing songs of wonder to the One who whispers in your soul.
We praise the One who surrounds us in every moment.

Into the shadows of chaos,
you shine your light of righteousness,
Creation Blesser.
You looked, and saw the sun
 shimmering over green meadows;
you watched, as the moon
 gleamed in the night sky.
When your Spirit came to lead us
through the gardens of your grace,
 we ran and hid ourselves

195

under the shelter of death,
        believing you would never find us.
You sent the prophets
to sow seeds of hope
in our shallow and barren souls,
    but we collected them
    and threw them out with the trash.
So, groaning with the pain
of your shattered heart,
you sent Jesus to gather us up
and to bring us home to you.

So, with those who have gone into the deserts,
and found you waiting for them;
with those who have journeyed to the center
of faithful living, led by your Spirit;
we lift our voices, to sing your praises:

Holy, holy, holy, God who knows us completely.
All creation hopes for what is not seen.
Hosanna in the highest!

Blessed is the One who comes, laying his hand on us.
Hosanna in the highest!

Holy are you, God of all joy,
and blessed is Jesus Christ, our Savior.
When our lives had touched
the bottom of despair,
    he came to lift us up
    to the heights of your hope;
when we wandered to sin's edge
and dived in headfirst,
    he reached in to pull us
    to the safety of your love;
when we journey
to the center of death,
    we find him waiting
    to take us by the hand
    and lead us into life.

As we remember all his stories of how we are to live,
as we recall how he lived according to your Spirit,
we speak of that faith we can only call a mystery:

When Christ made his bed in Shē'ōl, God was there;
when Christ rose, God's hand took him into new life;
when Christ returns, God will lead us in the everlasting way.

You search for us,
finding us wherever we have run;
    you take us by the hand
    to lead us to this Table of reconciliation,
        where the bread and the cup
        have been prepared and blessed
        by the gift of your Spirit.
Fed by the Bread filled with grace,
may we dare go live
at the farthest edges of despair,
    to stand with those who have lost
    all hope and life.
When our arid souls have been
watered by the Cup of love,
may we dare to carry
the light of your joy and freedom
    to those living in the shadows
    of injustice and oppression.

And when those who have fled
to the edges of life to escape you,
and those who made their beds
in futility and foolishness
are gathered together in your heart,
to feast at the Table of the Lamb,
we will sing our praises to you
forever and ever and ever,
God in Community, Holy in One. Amen.

Pentecost 10/Trinity 9/Proper 12/Ordinary Time 17
Genesis 29:15-28; Psalm 105:1-11, 45b
Romans 8:26-39; Matthew 13:31-33, 44-52

Call to Worship
On this day of worship, we call on God's name,
and hear our own invitation to work for the good of all.
Gathered with neighbors and strangers, we call on God's hope,
and discover that a lifetime of service seems but a few days.
In this place of praise and prayer, we call on God's love,
and receive that grace which is as old as creation,
yet as fresh as each morning.

Prayer of the Day
You shape us in your image,
not so we would puff up with pride,
    but we might humbly serve others.
You have chosen us,
not because we are so special,
    but that we might become hope
    to a world bloated on despair.
Searcher of hearts,
we would tell of all your wonders.

You went and sold your life,
    so you could buy us back
    from sin and death.
You planted seeds of grace,
    so that the lost, the little,
    the least, the last, and even we
    could make our homes in you.
Bearer of God's Heart,
we would tell all your stories.

You offer sighs from the depths
of the very heart of God,
    when we cannot shape words.
With peace in your hands,
you step in to help resolve
    all of our broken relationships.
Heart of reconciliation,
we would listen to your hopes.

God in Community, Holy in One,
we would tell of your presence in us,
even as we pray as Jesus teaches us,
Our Father . . .

Call to Reconciliation
We spend so much time accusing ourselves, judging ourselves,
punishing ourselves for what we have done, or not done. But God
would draw us closer to the Heart of forgiveness, that we might be filled
with healing and grace. Join me, as we pray together,

Unison Prayer of Confession
    **What then are we to say about our lives, Searcher of our hearts?
We know how often we have duped others with our deceit. We**

remember how often we promise one thing, only to do the opposite. **We struggle to trust you, while we so easily listen to the promises of those who would pull us away from you.**

Forgive us, Heart overflowing with mercy. **Your grace is more powerful than any of our sins, your hope is more durable than our silly choices, your love will traverse anything, and everything, which separates us from you. In Jesus Christ, our Lord and Savior, we are forgiven!**

Silence is kept

Assurance of Pardon
Hear the good news: the One who could accuse us, saves us from sin and death. The One who could condemn us, cradles us in grace. The One who could punish us, prays for us.
Now we know, there is nothing, not a thing, that can separate us from God. Thanks be to the One who forgives us. Amen.

Great Prayer of Thanksgiving
May the Lord of the kingdom be with you!
And also with you!
Children of God, offer your hearts to the One
who calls us to serve the world.
We embrace the God of the loving heart.
God's people, sing praises forever and ever.
**We rejoice in the One who will not allow anything,
not a thing, to keep us apart.**

Hearts overflow with praise,
Good and Generous God,
for from you comes all that we need.
You gathered up all your dreams
and shaped them into the gift of creation:
    bright blue skies that flow forever,
    kittens chasing butterflies in backyards,
    children whose hopes know no end.
The seeds of grace and peace
blossomed into that garden
which could have been our home,
    but we chose to go out and buy
    the fallow fields of sin and death,
      to harvest the pearls of rebellion.
Prophets came, to tell us of hearing
the deep sighs of your broken heart,

but we thought their words
to be flights of foolish fantasy.
Your heart set so that nothing
might ever separate us from you again,
you sent Jesus to bring
your treasure of grace to us,
a treasure as old as the universe,
as new as your joy for each of us.

So, we join our voices with Jacob and Leah,
with Rachel, Laban, and all your children,
forever singing our praises to you,

Holy, holy, holy are you, word-keeping God.
All creation tells of your wonderful deeds.
Hosanna in the highest!

Blessed is the One who is the treasure of your kingdom.
Hosanna in the highest!

Holy are you, Covenant Rememberer,
and blessed is Jesus Christ,
the great Treasure of your heart.
He could have stayed at your side,
    but came to cast his net to gather
    sinners into your kingdom.
He could have shaken his head in silence
at all the foolish choices we make,
    but told us stories of the One
    whose heart overflows with mercy.
He could have left us on our own,
trying to make ourselves right,
    but gave himself up to death,
    to prove that nothing, nothing,
    can separate us from your love.

As we remember his life, his teachings,
his death, and his rising to new life,
we would speak of that mystery we call faith:

Christ died, with love more powerful than hate;
Christ rose, with life too strong for death;
Christ will come, with grace too deep for words.

Heart of goodness and joy,
send your Spirit upon us now,
that She might enliven this bread,
    so that fed, we might spend
    the rest of our lives
    in service to your children.
Immerse your Spirit
in the cup of mercy,
    so that as we drink from it,
    we may go forth to be poured out
    in lifetimes of compassion and caring
    to those who hunger for hope and healing.

And when that moment comes,
and you gather all your people
from every place and time,
to feast at the Table of grace,
we will lift our voices in praise to you,
God in Community, Holy in One. Amen.

Pentecost 11/Trinity 10/Proper 13/Ordinary Time 18
Genesis 32:22-31; Psalm 17:1-7, 15
Romans 9:1-5; Matthew 14:13-21

Call to Worship
We come to this place of worship,
to encounter the One who has called us here.
This Holy One - our God: is with us in every moment.
God is in our celebrations and joys,
God is in our darkest nights of loneliness.
This Holy God - our God: blesses us and calls us by name.
As night fades before the coming Light, we meet the One who saves us -
even from ourselves.
This God - our Holy God: touches us with the Spirit of hope.

Prayer of the Day
In the darkest moments
of our lives, Intriguing God,
    we have struggled with you,
    believing that if we were to defeat you,
    you would have to give us whatever we want,
not realizing you have already blessed us
with everything we need in life.

201

When our hunger for hope
overwhelms us, Gentle Jesus,
    you fill us with your presence;
when our need for more and more
would pull us further and further away from you,
    you heal us of our desires;
when we look away from those in need,
    your tears of compassion cleanse our hearts.

We would leave our pain behind us,
and run through your streams of
living waters, Spirit of God,
    that we might embrace
    our sisters and brothers in peace,
        knowing that our broken relationships
        have been made whole.

God in Community, Holy in One,
we lift our prayers to you,
in the name of Jesus Christ, our Lord and Savior,
Our Father . . .

Call to Reconciliation

We pick on sisters and brothers; we argue with our spouses; we fight
with friends and neighbors - we all live broken lives. We even end up
struggling with God, seeking to make God do our bidding. But it is God
who can heal our brokenness, God who can reconcile our differences,
God who can make us families once again. Let us confess our sin
together, seeking God's promised blessing for each of us, as we pray,
saying,

Unison Prayer of Confession

**Here at the river's edge, Healing God, we are hesitant to cross
over. For on the other side are all the people we have hurt. On that
far shore is everyone we have ridiculed, scorned, ignored. Across
the water stand the poor, the homeless, the lost - all those we have
looked down on, believing they are beneath us. On the other bank
stands the cross we must carry if we are to follow Jesus. Before
we can cross, Most Holy One, we must struggle with you. We
cannot meet the others, if we have not encountered you.**

**Forgive us and reconcile us, not only to them, but to yourself.
Bless us, that we would be a blessing to them. Rename us and
carry us across the river as faithful disciples of the One we are
blessed to call our Lord and Savior, Jesus Christ.**

Silence is kept

Assurance of Pardon
Here, face to face, God meets us. Here, face to face, we can speak
every longing in our heart. Here, face to face, God forgives us.
**Here, face to face, we meet the One who has great compassion for
us, and who forgives us of every sin. Thanks be to God. Amen.**

Great Prayer of Thanksgiving
The God of crossings and healings be with you.
And also with you.
People of God, lift your hearts to the One
who travels every journey with you.
We lift them to the God who gives us rest when we are weary.
People of God, offer your praise and thanks
to the God who feeds the hungry.
**It is our greatest joy to sing to the One
who fills our emptiness with grace and joy.**

Standing at the edge of chaos,
you took all the goodness in your heart,
and shaped it into the glory of creation,
God of Imagination.
Looking up, you placed
the moons, stars, and planets
    into the cradle of the sky.
You took the dust of the earth,
blessing it, and forming us
    into your image of hope and grace.
We were filled with the
abundance of your constant love,
    but we longed for the empty
    promises of sin and death,
        breaking your heart as
        we followed after them.
Prophets came to tell the truth
of your everlasting covenant,
    but we turned our backs on them.
So, to put an end to your great sorrow,
you sent Jesus to us,
bringing us all the gifts
you had stored up for us.

So, with those who stand at the edge of grace,
and with those who have crossed over to your peace,

we join our voices with all who forever sing to your glory:

Holy, holy, holy are you, God who listens to our prayers.
All creation beholds your face in righteousness.
Hosanna in the highest!

Blessed is the One who feeds us with grace and wonder.
Hosanna in the highest!

You are Holy, Redeemer of the lost,
and Jesus Christ, our Lord and Savior,
is your true blessing and hope for us.
When he could have deserted us,
as we continued to stumble through sin,
    he was filled with compassion,
      and came to be with us in our pain.
When he could have kept silent
in response to our fears and doubts,
    he told stories of your love and grace.
When he could have detoured
around our violence and anger,
    he walked straight into death,
so we might be saved.

As we remember all the gifts he shared with us,
as we tell of his healings and feedings for all,
we speak of that faith which is often a mystery:

Christ died, compassion for us in his heart;
Christ rose, blessing God forever;
Christ will come, so that we are never sent away.

As we gather at the edge of your kingdom,
coming once again to the Table,
we pray you would pour out
your Spirit of reconciliation upon us,
and on the gifts of the bread and the cup.
You feed us with this meal,
not that we might become gluttons,
    but so we might become servants
    in your kingdom of holiness.
Where we see only crumbs on the Table,
    you see enough leftovers for us
    to take to feed a hungry world.
Where we see only

the last few drops in the cup,
  you see enough grace for us
  to fill the empty hearts of your children
  forgotten and alone in the world.

And when we come to the edge of eternity,
all of our struggles over, all our pain left behind,
we will gather around your Table of grace,
joining with all who will forever sing of your love,
God in Community, Holy in One. Amen.

Pentecost 12/Trinity 11/Proper 14/Ordinary Time 19
Genesis 37:1-4, 12-28; Psalm 105:1-6, 16-22, 45b
Romans 10:5-15; Matthew 14:22-33

Call to Worship
Here, in this place, God welcomes all the dreamers,
as well as the doubters:
here, the worriers and wanderers
can call on God by name.
Here, in this time, we can remember
all the ways God has graced us:
here, in these moments, we are reminded
that God is with us, always!
Here are gathered those daring enough
to step out of comfort into the unknown:
here, in this faith space, we will find the courage
to cry out, 'God, save us!' in every situation.

Prayer of the Day
Making sandwiches and stirring the soup
for the hungry lined up at the door;
taking the night shift
at the homeless shelter;
talking with the prisoners
awaiting their trials:
you surround us with signs
of your hopes for all,
God of justice.

Bringing reconciliation
to strife-torn communities;
mending the broken promises
which have shattered lives;
holding your arms wide open

205

to embrace weary searchers:
everywhere we turn,
we hear people say,
'here comes that Dreamer!"

Inviting us to wander down
the streets of sacrifice;
hoping that every breath
will be filled with peace and hope;
gifting us with joy and grace,
so they can be freely given away:
you nudge us to get out
of our comfortable religion,
and to walk on those unfamiliar
waves of faith and hope,
Spirit of trust.

God in Community, Holy in One,
we give thanks to your name,
even as we pray as Jesus has taught us, saying,
Our Father . . .

Call to Reconciliation
Too often when life threatens us, we trust the world to save us, finding it easy to believe the empty promises of seduction and doubt. But our God offers us forgiveness and healing, if we will but trust and follow. Let us begin, by confessing our sins together,

Unison Prayer of Confession
It seems so easy to get into the boat and set sail on our journey, God of Promises. But when the winds of change begin to blow, we want to turn around and head back to the past's safe harbor. When sin's waves crash over the side, we try to wrap ourselves in the cloak of pride thinking we will not get wet. When Jesus calls to us to get out and follow in faith, we look around, hoping he is not speaking to us.

Swamped by our fears, and sinking in doubt, we long for someone to help us - so save us, Holy One, save us! Stretch out your hand, so we might be lifted from our despair to hope, from our worries to trust, from our foolishness to faithful living. Then, we will dare to follow Jesus Christ, our Lord and Savior, even if it means getting out of the sheltered lives we have built for ourselves.

Silence is kept

206

Assurance of Pardon
In confessing that Christ is Lord, we let go of the past, and turn to God's future. We step out of our fears, and walk into the light and life offered by our God.
In trusting Christ's resurrection, we trust all of God's promises, letting the Spirit work in and through us, healing and making us whole. Thanks be to God, we are forgiven! Amen.

Great Prayer of Thanksgiving
The Lord is with you!
And also with you!
People of God: lift up your hearts to the One
who invites you to daring discipleship.
We lift our hearts to the One
who calls us out of our comfort zones.
People of God: give thanks to the Lord our God.
We sing praises to the One who
enables us to walk the paths of pilgrimage.

To the one true and living God,
we can only bring our songs of glory and praise.
Through you, the light of creation
    dispelled the shadows of chaos;
from you came the imaginative Word,
        shaping the mountains that touch the sky,
        scooping out the hollows for the seas;
by you the Spirit of beginnings breathed,
        giving life to people created in your image.
In love, you embraced us as your own,
giving us the freedom to make our own choices.
Our foolishness led us to believe
that we were wiser than Wisdom herself,
and greater than the Creator of the stars.
        So we ran away from your glory
        and into the arms of sin and disobedience.
But as a mother tenderly nourishes her children,
as a father welcomes home the wayward,
        you would not abandon us to the powers of evil,
        but in your graciousness, you came to us,
speaking through the words of the prophets
and the witness of the faithful.
When we continued to turn away from you,
you sent Jesus Christ, your true Heart,
that we might see your love face to face.

And so, we join the faithful of every time and place,
who, beholding the glory of your presence,
sing with countless throngs of angels,
hymns of unending praise:

Holy, holy, holy is the Lord God Almighty,
who is, who was, and who is to come.
Let us praise and glorify God forever.

You are worthy, Lord our God,
to receive praise and glory,
honor and blessing.

How wonderful are the works of your hands, Holy God,
and how gracious is the gift of your Son,
Jesus Christ, our Lord and Savior.
When we were famished from eating
the empty promises of the world,
    he came, breaking the bread of fullness;
when we hungered from the vain feast of fame,
    he came, eating with the lost, the least, the little, the last;
when we found no nourishment in our disobedience,
    he came, breaking bread with sinners and outcasts;
when we chose to nibble on death,
    he came, to be broken on the cross of Calvary.

Giver of eternal life in Christ,
as we remember his life, his ministry, his gentleness,
his acceptance of all, his death, his resurrection,
we would speak of that mystery of faith
we claim as believers:

Worthy is the Lamb that was slain to receive
divine power, wisdom, and strength,
honor, glory and blessing.
Let us praise and glorify him forever.

Breathe on us, Breath of God,
and upon these gifts of the bread and the cup.
As we join Christ at this Table,
to be strengthened by your gifts of grace and hope,
    send us forth to be your faithful people.
Having tasted the Bread of Life,
    may we go forth to bring healing
      to every corner of our shattered world;

as we drink of the Cup of Salvation,
    may we be poured out
    in service to those who can find no life;
as you have broken yourself for us,
    so we will do so for everyone in your kingdom.

Then, when all creation is healed,
and all people are one family,
we will gather around the Feast of the Lamb,
singing our praise to you, Holy God:
through Christ, in Christ, with Christ,
and in the unity of the Holy Spirit,
one God, now and forever:

**Praise our God all you servants,
honor God, you who would be faithful,
small and great, young and old.
Let us praise and glorify God forever.
Let heaven and earth praise God's glory:
all creatures in heaven, on earth,
and under the earth,
the sea and everything in it.
Let us praise and glorify God forever. Amen.**

(The responses of the congregation in the Great Prayer of Thanksgiving
are adapted from a prayer by St. Francis of Assisi)

Pentecost 13/Trinity 12/Proper 15/Ordinary Time 20
Genesis 45:1-15; Psalm 133
Romans 11:1-2a, 29-32; Matthew 15:(10-20), 21-28

Call to Worship
Here we can come together,
people searching for healing and hope:
**here we are met by the One
who would bless us with abundant life.**
Here we are called to gather
as the family of God:
**we may find those who are strangers,
yet are sisters and brothers of ours.**
Here we discover the truth that God
makes no distinctions among us:
**here we are welcomed and embraced
by the One whose arms are open to all.**

Prayer of the Day
When we are alone,
you make us known
    to our sisters and brothers.
When we are lonely,
you whisper, 'come closer,'
    inviting us into your heart.
Great is your love for us,
Welcoming God.

When we wander lost and afraid,
you take us by the hand,
    so we may settle in your kingdom.
When we hunger
for the crumbs of hope
which the world offers to us,
you feed us with
    the fullness of your joy.
Great is your grace for us,
Accepting Christ.

When those around us
make clear they want nothing
to do with us, ever,
    you persist in being our friend.
When we stand on
despair's welfare line,
    you invite us to come
    to a sumptuous feast.
Great is your hope for us,
Embracing Spirit.

God in Community, Holy in One,
you weep openly as you welcome us
into your heart and your hopes,
even as we pray as Jesus teaches us,
Our Father . . .

Call to Reconciliation
Our words, our deeds, our lives build barriers between us and others,
between us and God. But God would shatter every distinction, God
would reshape us as new people. Let us come to the One who loves
us, and longs to forgive us. Join me as we confess our sins together,
saying,

Unison Prayer of Confession

We admit, Providing God, that we have difficulties living as your children. We could live in unity, but our words fracture relationships with family and friends. We have been shown the way to your kingdom, but turn into blind guides when asked for the directions by others. When we could offer others the precious oil of peace, we hand them the vinegar of despair and rejection.

Have mercy on us, Healing Heart, have mercy on us. When you call to us, may we listen with open ears, understand with embracing hearts, and share your grace with others, even as we have been graced by Jesus Christ, our Lord and Savior.

Silence is kept

Assurance of Pardon

Hear the good news for you: God has provided hope for you, filling you with joy, with mercy, with peace.

As mercy leads to mercy, we will take these gifts to share with the world. Thanks be to God. Amen.

Great Prayer of Thanksgiving

The welcoming God be with you!

And also with you!

It is not crumbs, but the fullness of grace given to you at this table.

We open our hearts to receive God's goodness.

Like precious oil to anoint us, God pours hope and love into our lives.

How good it is to lift our praises to our God!

When chaos threatened to control,
you spoke out of your own mouth,
crying, 'let there be light!'
and creation burst forth,
    rivers flowing like precious oil
        through the valleys of love,
    peace singing to all creatures,
        whispering of the gift of unity.
Shaping us in the divine image,
you whispered to us, 'come closer,'
inviting us to live with you
in Eden's joy-dewed garden.
    Sin and death, however,
    dazzled us with their lies,
        so we followed these blind guides
        into a world scarce on hope.
You did not reject us,

211

but continued to call us
through the mouths of prophets;
you continued to gift us
with your faithful presence.
Your dreams would
not be dismayed,
as you sent Jesus,
your mercy to beget mercy
for all your children.

With those overlooked by the world,
with those who have sought you in every time,
we lift our songs of joy and praise:

Holy, holy, holy are you, God of this day of wonder.
All creation would live in unity with you.
Hosanna in the highest!

Blessed is the One who is sent to all people.
Hosanna in the highest!

Holy are you, Joy of Creation,
and blessed is Jesus Christ, our Lord and Savior.
When he could have turned
a blind eye toward us,
    he came that we might
    be able to see our hope;
when he could have sent
us away from his side,
    he drew us closer
    to your mercy and love;
when he could have been
dismayed by our foolishness,
    he went into death's embrace,
    providing salvation for us.

As we remember his words of teaching,
as we remember his hopes for us,
we speak of that mystery we call faith:

Christ died, sent before us to preserve our life;
Christ rose, rejecting death's claim on him;
Christ will come, ordaining life forevermore for all.

Here in this moment and place,

we pray you would pour out
your Spirit of peace and joy
upon the gifts of the bread and the cup
and upon your children
who have gathered around the Table.
You do not give us crumbs,
but nourish us with compassion,
     so we might go to serve
     a world hungering for healing.
You do not touch our lips
with only a few drops,
but offer us great gulps of grace,
     so we might offer peace
     to a fractured and frightened world.

And when the famine of our despair is ended
and you gather all your children around you,
to be fed at the feast of the Lamb,
we will sing our thanksgiving songs to you,
as the precious tears of joy run down our cheeks,
praising you through all eternity,
God in Community, Holy in One. Amen.

Pentecost 14/Trinity 13/Proper 16/Ordinary Time 21
Exodus 1:8 - 2:10; Psalm 124
Romans 12:1-8; Matthew 16:13-20

Call to Worship
Our help is in the name of the Lord,
who made heaven and earth.
Our joy comes from the heart of God,
who transforms us into open-handed givers of hope.
Our grace comes from God's compassion,
who breaks the bonds which tie us to sin and death.
Blessed be the Lord our God!
Who reveals to us the One who brings us new life!

Prayer of the Day
When fear would enslave us,
     you set us free by your faith in us;
when the currents of hopelessness
would sweep us away,
     you cradle us in your promises;
when evil would exercise power,

you transform us into
members of the one Body,
    so we can overcome its efforts.
You are always on our side,
All Watchful God.

Through the mouths
of children and youth,
    you teach the foolish
    the wisdom of your grace;
through the gentle lives
of those harmed by hate,
    you open our locked hearts
    to embrace the broken.
You are always by our side,
Heart of Compassion.

Reluctant to let go
of all our gifts,
    you touch us with generosity's grace.
Hesitant as to what
we might do for others,
    you teach us the skill set
    of compassion and service.
Dwelling with loneliness,
    you nudge us to welcome
    the last and the least.
You are always at our side,
Spirit of Change.

God in Community, Holy in One,
we believe you are side-by-side with us,
even as we pray as Jesus has taught us,
Our Father . . .

Call to Reconciliation
While we may yearn to be like Jesus, we know that in our hotheaded
choices, our frantic lives, our impetuous words, we are too often like
Peter. But like him, we can confess Christ as our Lord, speaking of
our need for your saving presence in our lives.

Unison Prayer of Confession
    **We look for you in all the wrong places, God of the lost, and
wonder why we cannot find you. We wander the corridors of power,
while you are on the sidewalks, beside the homeless. We sit at the**

214

head tables of the world, while you are handing out soup to the hungry at the kitchen's backdoor. We applaud those who win the race, while you are cheering on those in last place.

In forgiving us, God of new life, you would transform our cold hearts into those melted in service to others. In granting us mercy, you challenge us to think of all those we have ignored. In gifting us with grace, you enable us to proclaim Jesus Christ, our Lord and Savior, as the hope, the joy, the peace the world seeks.

Silence is kept

Assurance of Pardon
It's not money, but our generosity with it; it is not power, but our willingness to humble ourselves; it is not our efforts, but Christ's gift, which transforms us into God's children.
It is more than just how we think. In mercy and grace, our hearts, our lives, our spirits are transfigured and made new. Thanks be to God. Amen.

Great Prayer of Thanksgiving
May the God of who watches over us be with you!
And also with you!
Children of God, open yourselves to the God of Moses and Miriam.
We raise our hearts to the One who changes the lives of all.
People of God, sing praises to the God of Jesus and Peter.
**We lift our glad songs of joy to the One who is with us,
in this time, and in this place.**

If you had not been on the side
of all that is good, perfect, and acceptable,
God of Joy,
chaos would have ruled.
But you swept it away
in your flood of creation,
which thundered through valleys
 carving majestic mountains,
which showered the soil
 with life, with hope, with love.
Transforming us from earth's floor
into people in your image and heart,
you gifted us to live with you.
 Sin and death begged us
 to follow in their footsteps,
 nursing our infantile foolishness
 with their seductions and desires.

215

You sent the prophets
to be midwives to us,
bringing words of new hope;
but our anger flared up
at their intrusion in our lives.
So, after we had ignored
Elijah and Jeremiah, Miriam and Hannah,
you sent Jesus to us, to open wide the gates
to the kingdom of your heart.

So, with those who remained faithful as slaves,
as well as with those who proclaim your Child,
we join our voices with folk from every time and place,
singing your praises forever:

Holy, holy, holy are you, God who keeps watch over us.
All creation is transformed by the wisdom of your Spirit.
Hosanna in the highest!

Blessed is the One who does not give up on us.
Hosanna in the highest!

Holy are you, God of Imagination,
and blessed is Jesus Christ, our Messiah, your Son.
If he had not been on our side,
    we would have continued
    to wander sin's pathways
    into death's oppression.
In compassion,
    he came to reveal your heart;
in generosity,
    he offered us the means
    to escape from sin;
conscious of his choice,
he took up the cross,
    where he was put to death,
    and swallowed up by the grave,
sweeping away death's power
when he was raised to new life
by your love and hope.

So, as we remember his willingness
to come and be by our side,
we sing of that mystery called faith:

216

Christ died, taking our side against sin;
Christ rose, taking God's side against death;
Christ will come, taking us to his side and into eternity.

Renew us, God of all joy,
by the gift of your Spirit
upon the bread and cup prepared for us.
If the Spirit were not with us,
we would become gluttons,
stuffing ourselves on your grace.
But She sends us out
    to empty ourselves for those
    forced into hunger and despair.
She nourishes us with your hope,
    so we might prevail
    against all those powers
which would oppress your children
with injustice and hopelessness.

And when all powers have been defeated,
when evil has gone the way of chaos,
we will stand side by side at your Table
in that kingdom of eternal joy,
singing our thanksgiving to you,
God in Community, Holy in One. Amen.

Pentecost 15/Trinity 14/Proper 17/Ordinary Time 22
Exodus 3:1-15; Psalm 105:1-6, 23-26, 45c
Romans 12:9-21; Matthew 16:21-28

Call to Worship
Gathered as God's people,
we come to worship together:
singing praises to the One who loves us,
opening our hearts to the One who calls us.
Called to be God's people,
we come to share our lives together:
to celebrate the joys of our hearts,
to mingle our tears with God's.
Challenged to follow Jesus to the end,
we come to learn how to be disciples:
offering our food to our enemies,
giving a drink of water to those
who have drained our souls.

Prayer of the Day
When we would rush
to get all our to-dos done,
you call to us to turn
    and notice your compassion
    burning (but not reduced to ashes)
        for those living in misery.
When we hesitate,
you ask us to remove
    all we think protects us from
    the fire of your justice,
        so we can draw closer
        to your heart's warmth.
YOU ARE the One we search for,
God of all held in bondage.

When we become
stumbling blocks to you,
you polish our stony resistance
    so we can become smooth pebbles
    on the path to your kingdom.
When we would tell you
how we think you should
bring about your hopes and dreams,
you show us your heart,
broken for the lost and the last,
    so we will look to their needs
    rather than thinking about our own.
YOU ARE the One
who leads us to freedom,
Servant of the poor.

When we believe we cannot speak
about your peace and hopes,
you give us words
    which spill out of our hearts.
When we put our palms
over our eyes, afraid to look
at the suffering around us,
you fill our hands with grace,
    sending us to serve your children.
YOU ARE the One who
teaches us new ways,
Impassioned Spirit.

God in Community, Holy in One,
YOU ARE WHO YOU ARE,
and we lift our prayer to you, saying,
Our Father . . .

Call to Reconciliation
In stories and in stores, in sandy deserts and on rocky roads, at school
events and Sunday worship, we encounter God. We meet the One who
fills every moment with the sacred. We confess our sins, in trust that we
can turn aside and notice God welcoming us with forgiveness and hope.

Unison Prayer of Confession
God of Moses and Mary,
we could live at peace with others,
> **but we choose to do wrong to them;**
we could welcome those we do not know,
> **but choose to close our hearts;**
we could make outsiders our best friends,
> **but choose the safety of our cliques.**

Forgive us, Genuine Love, for our foolish choices.
Hold on to our shaky lives,
until we learn to clasp your goodness to our hearts,
> **so we can give it away to those around us.**
Whisper your grace and hopes to us,
until we can stop cursing our enemies,
> **and bless them as our friends.**
Smooth the rough edges of our arrogance,
until we become polished enough
> **to win the gold in being honorable.**
Then, we would put aside our stumbling blocks to discipleship, so
we can follow Jesus Christ, our Lord and Savior, as he leads us to
your way of denial and life.

Silence is kept

Assurance of Pardon
In our love for others, we discover God's love for us. In our forgiving of
others, we learn once more how deeply God has forgiven us. Friends,
this is the good news offered to us!
We are God's children, called to be different, called to act
differently, called to live as new people. Thanks be to God.
We are forgiven. Amen.

Great Prayer of Thanksgiving

May the God of burning bushes be with you!

And also with you!

People of God, offer your hearts to God,

who calls to you from the mystery of grace.

**We turn aside from our worries to open ourselves
to the One who calls us to new life.**

Children of God, remember all the joy and wonder

which has been done for you.

**We will lift our voices in praise to the One who is
beyond all imagining.**

In a moment, creation began,

and from that time on, God of Freedom,

you began to pour out

your goodness and genuine love.

Earth laughed with flowers

and rejoiced with sunrises.

You shaped us in your image

and began to show us all

you wanted to give us.

But chasing after the temptations

and seductions of the world,

we tripped over the stumbling blocks

of sin and death, falling flat

on our fears and doubts.

Observing our misery in such living,

you sent the prophets

to call us back to you,

but we did not hear their cries.

Knowing we would continue

to suffer and lose our way,

you sent Jesus to come

and deliver us from our slavery.

Joining our voices with those

who have faithfully followed,

and with those who stumbled along the way,

we call on your name, singing praises to you:

**Holy, holy, holy are you, God of Wonder.
Watching our struggles,
    your heart breaks;
hearing our cries,
    you whisper our names;**

knowing our loneliness,
you came to deliver us.

Blessed is Jesus Christ, who comes in your name!
Hosanna in the highest!

Holy are you, Listener of cries in the night,
and blessed is Jesus Christ, your Child.
Hearing the pain of your heart,
    he came to speak of your hopes;
seeing the brokenness of our relationships,
    he came to make us whole;
knowing our fear of death,
    he came to defeat its power;
aware of what it would cost him,
    he journeyed to Jerusalem
    to embrace suffering and heartache;
hating evil so much
    he was willing to let it believe
    it had won the battle,
until he burst from the grave
bringing life for all
even as you raised him from the dead.

Remembering his wonderful works,
recalling his miracles, his words, his life,
we speak of that mystery we know as faith:

Christ rejoices with us,
Christ weeps with us,
Christ died for us,
Christ was raised for us.

As we prepare to gather around
your Table, God of Love,
pour out your Spirit upon us,
and on the gifts of the bread and cup.
Feed us on the rich food
of your forgiveness and grace,
    so we might go forth
    to feed all those we only know
    by the name 'enemy.'
Quench our thirst for power
with the sweet wine of your servanthood,

so we might choose
    honor over fame,
    humility over pride,
    forgiveness over vengeance,
and in so doing,
   lose ourselves in your life
    of denial and service,
giving ourselves to others,
thus returning your love for us.

And when all moments come to an end,
and the time has come to gather around
that great feast in heaven,
there will be no enemy, no them, no us -
just sisters and brothers joining
hearts and voices in singing your praise,
God in Community, Holy in One. Amen.

Pentecost 16/Trinity 15/Proper 18/Ordinary Time 23
Exodus 12:1-14; Psalm 149
Romans 13:8-14; Matthew 18:15-20

Call to Worship
When two or three gather, Christ lives in every moment,
where two or three gather, Christ is present with them.
Where two or three gather to worship God,
glad songs of praise are lifted, hearts are filled with hope.
When two or three gather to serve God's creation,
Christ is feeding the hungry, Christ is building shelters of peace.

Prayer of the Day
When we hold out our hands
to be cuffed by loneliness,
   you clasp our wrists
   to pull us into your heart.
When our lives are shattered
by the injustices done to those
passed over by the world,
   your love puts us back together,
   so we can serve them with your hope.
Emancipating God,
we praise you!

When we would build walls
between us and our neighbors,

you come to be the welcoming gate.
When we would curse someone
who has hurt us in our souls,
　　you sing us songs of blessing.
When we would focus only
on our needs and our desires,
　　you hand us the dinnerware
　　and ask us to set the Table.
Ever-near Salvation,
we would follow you!

When we would feed on
our bitter brokenness,
　　you would offer us
　　the Bread of reconciliation.
When we would grasp
the Cup of peace,
and drink it to the last drop,
　　you whisper, 'offer some
　　to those you don't like.'
Liberating Spirit,
we would be filled with you!

God in Community, Holy in One,
free us of all fears and doubts,
as we pray as Jesus has taught us,
Our Father . . .

Call to Reconciliation

All we are called to do is to love - everyone. Yet, as simple as it sounds,
by our actions and our words, we show how difficult a task it is. Let us
confess our failings as we pray together, saying,

Unison Prayer of Confession

**You do not ask much of us, Guardian of hope - to love, to serve,
to welcome. Yet too often, it is words of bitterness we speak to
friends and family. It is our stiff-with-judgment backs we offer to
those looking for help. It is our hardened hearts people find, when
they reach out, hoping to touch grace.**

**Love lived as Compassion, forgive us. We are broken, so make
us whole through the life of Christ. We are empty of peace, so fill us
with the reconciling Spirit of Christ. We are alone, so take us by the
hand and lead us into your kingdom of joy and grace, brought to us
through Jesus Christ, our Lord and Savior.**

Silence is kept

Assurance of Pardon
Gathered as God's people, we hear the good news: God has forgiven us,
God has made us whole, God sends us to serve.
**We will not wear jealousy or resentment, but put on the garments of
peace and hope. We are forgiven by our God. Amen.**

Great Prayer of Thanksgiving
May God be with you!
And also with you!
People of God, open your hearts.
We open them to the One who feeds us with freedom and hope.
Children of God, sing songs of thanksgiving
to the One who journeys with you!
**Graced with abundant life, we join our hearts
and voices in praise to our loving God!**

The moment you spoke
and liberated chaos, Holy God,
time marked the beginning
of created beauty and glory.
You watered earth with tears of joy,
planting those seeds of hope and peace
    so we might be fed by your heart.
But asked simply to be your children,
we could not obey that request,
    but wandered off to feast
    at the table groaning with lies and curses.
Your gracious word was sung
in new ways by the prophets,
    but we tuned them out,
    so we could listen to the seductive songs of sin.
You sent us your hope in Jesus Christ,
who came to set us free
and bring us home from
our exile in rebellion.

So, with those who longed for your coming,
packed and ready to journey into freedom,
we sing our praises in the company
of our sisters and brothers from every time:

**Holy! Holy! Holy! Living God of grace!
All creation echoes your praise:**

224

creatures roaming the fields,
dolphins splashing in the seas,
eagles soaring in the bright sky.
Glory to you forever and ever,
God of the captives!

You are righteousness, God our Deliverer,
and blessed is Jesus Christ, your Child, our Brother.
Because we break your heart
with our words and deeds,
    he came to shatter the chains
    of our arrogance and selfishness.
Because we have become gluttons,
feasting on bitterness and fear,
    he came to be the sweet Bread
    of healing and hope.
Because we become drunk
on sin's soured wine,
    he came to be salvation
    poured into our parched souls.
Because death smiles at us,
waiting with open arms,
    he came to gather us up
    in the embrace of grace and life,
carrying us out of the empty tomb
into your life of joy forever.

As you have prepared this Table for us,
gather us as your children, so we might remember
all the promises fulfilled to us in Christ our Lord:

When we eat of the Bread, Christ's life strengthens us;
when we drink from the Cup, Christ's Spirit nourishes us;
when we go to serve others, we proclaim Christ's death
    until he returns in glory.

As you bless the gifts
of the Bread and the Cup,
anoint us with your Spirit
which brings us together.
As your grace touches our lips
with hope and healing,
    may we reach out our hands
    to set free those captive to injustice.
As your peace is poured

into the empty corners of our hearts,
    may we go forth to love
    others as much as we love ourselves,
        and to serve them
        as we show our love for you.

And when time has marked the end of history,
and we gather with all our sisters and brothers,
    all division done away with,
    all brokenness healed,
    all barriers pulled down,
        and all your children set free from despair,
we will join our hands and hearts
around your Table of eternity,
singing praise through forever:

Glory to you, Liberating God!
Alleluia to you, Christ our Servant!
Thanks to you, Spirit of Peace!
Now and forever. Amen.

Pentecost 17/Trinity 16/Proper 19/Ordinary Time 24
Exodus 14:19-31; Psalm 114
Romans 14:1-12; Matthew 18:21-35

Call to Worship
In sacred times of word, wonder, and awe,
in ordinary days of work and play:
in every moment, God is with us.
Whether we are stuck in doubt's mud,
or standing on faith's shoreline:
in every place, God is with us.
In those who teach us
    and those who trouble us;
in those who surprise us,
    and those who forgive us:
in every person, God is with us.

Prayer of the Day
When we look over our shoulders
at fear shadowing us today,
you go before us into tomorrow,
    making a path through
    the sea of yesterday's doubts.
When our legs tremble

from the effort of standing up
for what you hope for all creation,
you are at our side,
    offering your heart's strength.
Cloud of Grace,
we offer our love to you.

When we turn our hearts
into deserts of stony bitterness,
you transform them
    into oases of joy.
When we come up
with all sorts of rules
for those who come to us
seeking to find you,
you tear up the list,
    stretching wide your arms
    in welcoming grace.
Servant of all,
we offer our lives to you.

When we would clasp
old worries to our hearts,
you open our eyes to that hope
    which paves the path ahead of us.
When we spend each day
consumed with doubts and fears,
you remind us that this day
    is the time to honor God,
    by serving God's children.
Mist of Mercy,
we offer our hearts to you.

God in Community, Holy in One,
as you are all to us,
so we would offer all we are to you,
even as we pray as Jesus taught us,
Our Father . . .

Call to Reconciliation
As we stand before God, we think of all the ways we bicker with others,
all those times we have not shown mercy and grace to those around us.
Let us bow our hearts and confess our sin to God, as we pray together,
saying,

Unison Prayer of Confession
It is never easy for us to confess
but deep down inside, we know that
    graced,
        we have trouble
        being grace-full to others;
    forgiven,
        we are eager to judge
        and punish all who hurt us;
    freed,
        we find ways to put restrictions
        on people we fear.

Forgive us, Servant God. You show mercy more often than we
deserve; you pardon us more times than we can count. And why?
Because we are the Lord's - sisters and brothers of Jesus Christ,
who died and lived again, so we might live beyond death with you.

Silence is kept

Assurance of Pardon
God's hand of mercy is stretched out to us, making a way through all that
threatens us, to touch us with grace and hope.
**We stand before our God, singing praise to the One who turns our
despair into joy, our fears into faith. Amen.**

Great Prayer of Thanksgiving
May the God of hope be with you!
And also with you!
God, our God, leads us through the flood of fears
into the future of wonder and hope.
**We open our hearts to the One who journeys
with us, in the past, in the present, into tomorrow.**
God goes before us, preparing the Table piled high
with grace and peace.
**We sing songs of glad thanksgiving to the One
who fills us with goodness and mercy.**

You stretched out your hand,
Cloud of Glory,
parting a way through chaos,
so your goodness might come forth.
You looked, and laughed out loud,
    as seas ran forth in joy,
    mountains played leapfrog,

228

and hills hopscotched with valleys.
Creation became a sanctuary
for those created in your image.
But we decided to live for ourselves,
    every day becoming one in which
        we could turn your dreams to ashes,
    your overflowing love into
        dust bowls of despair.
Out of pity, you sent the prophets,
those pillars of faithfulness,
    but we wrangled with their gentle words.
So, you sent Jesus,
to lead us through evil's deeps,
to that freedom found only
in your kingdom of life.

Therefore, on this day,
when we stand in your grace
around your Table of life,
we join our voices with all
who offer praise to the One who saves:

Living, we serve others in God's name;
serving, we die unto ourselves;
dying, we are given life eternal with God.

Blessed is the One who comes forgiving us
    more times than we can count.
Hosanna in the highest!

Holy are you, Cloud of Joy,
and blessed is Jesus Christ, your Son, our Servant.
When we were weak in faith,
    he came to strengthen us
    with your everlasting hope;
when we were slaves to sin,
    he came to lead us into
    the promised land of mercy;
when our hearts became like flint,
    he softened them with compassion;
when we could only focus on ourselves,
    he came to die for us.

As we gather at your Table,
we remember his love for us,

his patience with our failings,
his hope in our willingness to follow,
his trust in that mystery we call faith:

Baptized in Christ, we would live for him;
forgiven through Christ, we would emulate him;
putting on Christ, we wait for his return.
Alleluia! Amen!

Creator God,
send your Spirit in peace
upon us and these simple gifts
of the bread and of the cup.
As we share the bread,
we share the presence of Christ,
    strengthened to go out
    with forgiveness in our hearts.
As we pass the cup,
we share Christ's Spirit
with our neighbors,
    and are called to welcome all
    as our sisters and brothers,
        especially those held captive
        by the bitterness of the world.

As you gathered your children
to lead them to that promised land,
so you will bring all your children
from the very ends of time itself,
to seat us around your heart,
where we will feast on your grace,
lifting our hearts to praise you forever:
God our Maker,
Christ our Brother,
Spirit our Compassion,
one God, now and forever. Amen.

Pentecost 18/Trinity 17/Proper 20/Ordinary Time 25
Exodus 16:2-15; Psalm 105:1-6, 37-45
Philippians 1:21-30; Matthew 20:1-16

Call to Worship
In the prayers and the praise,
in the words and the wonder:
we are given enough joy to live each day.

230

In the justice for the oppressed,
in the unexpected generosity for the lost:
we are given enough compassion
to use in service each day.
In the promises made to all,
in the mercy offered to each:
we are given enough grace to share each day.

Prayer of the Day
Fresh as each morning
you come to us,
Crafter of manna.
    Your grace rests
    gently upon us,
        waiting to be gathered,
        to become the bread of life
we share throughout the day.

Fresh as compassion's justice,
you come to us,
Servant of the poor.
Choosing to give
as you desire,
you show us the last,
    so we can make them first
    in our hearts and hopes.
Doing no wrong,
    you make us right
    with God for all time.

Fresh as the water
which turns a desert
into a meadowland of flowers,
Spirit of uninterrupted grace,
you come to us.
When we would grumble,
    you give us the gospel to live out;
when we would protest,
    you teach us songs of praise;
when we would utter laments,
    you fill us with God's laughter.

God in Community, Holy in One,
refresh us with your presence

231

as we pray as Jesus taught, saying,
Our Father . . .

Call to Reconciliation
We continue to believe that we must earn our way into God's heart. But God's grace is given to each of us, for all of us, freely, unconditionally, always. Let us open our lives to this mercy as we pray saying,

Unison Prayer of Confession
It seems we cannot decide, Cloud of Glory. We say we will live to serve others, but end up meeting only our needs. We claim to live in a way that honors Christ, but we do not take him to work, school, home. We believe that the gospel can transform lives, (at least, for those who need it – but surely, not us).

Forgive us, Presence of Peace.
Instead of grumblers,
**   may we be ambassadors of grace.**
Instead of continual complaining,
**   may we carry compassion to the hurting.**
Instead of whiners,
**   may we be workers with Jesus Christ, our Lord and Savior,**
to reach out and bring the kingdom of God to everyone we meet.

Silence is kept

Assurance of Pardon
This is the good news: there is no ranking in God's kingdom. God graces everyone with the same gifts: mercy, restoration, new life.
God has kept the covenant. We have been forgiven, we have been made new people. Thanks be to God. Amen.

Great Prayer of Thanksgiving
May the God of all mornings be with you!
And also with you!
Children of God, welcome the One who shares
grace with childlike abandon.
We open our hearts so we might savor the
sweet taste of joy and wonder.
People of God, bring your emptiness to
this Table of hope and peace.
We sing praises to One who fills us with
Christ's presence for service to others.

On that first morning,
when chaos saw your glory,
you brought out creation,
 with stars and planets
  swimming in the skies,
 gazelles and giraffes dancing
  through the fields of goodness.
You shaped humankind in your mercy,
and fed us with grace, enough for each day.
Jealous that you were so gracious to all of creation,
 we grumbled that it wasn't enough,
 and went searching for sin and death.
Prophets came, telling the stories
of your wonder and presence,
 but for us, these were foolish words.
Finally, you sent Jesus
to come looking for us,
to show us your kingdom.

So, we join our voices with
wilderness wanderers and urban dwellers,
those who, in every time and place,
sing of your glory:

Holy! Holy! Holy! Glory to God's holy name!
Our hearts will seek God,
rejoicing in God's gentleness and grace.

Blessed is the One who comes looking for us.
Hosanna in the highest!

You are holy, Cloud of Compassion,
and blessed is Jesus Christ, your Joy, our Hope.
Child of glory and grace,
he chose to come to us,
 working in the fields of despair.
Hearing our complaints,
he came to speak
 of your dreams for us.
Firstborn of all creation,
he came to defeat
 that last enemy, death.

As we remember his life and death,
as we come to the Table he has prepared,

we sing of that mystery called faith:

This is the bread God gives us to eat.
This is the life Christ calls us to offer to others.
This is the journey the Spirit takes with us.

Pour out your Spirit
upon your children gathered,
and upon the bread and the cup
you have provided for us.
As you feed us with the bread,
so flood us with compassion,
    that we may go to serve
    all who are lost and broken.
As you open your heart
so that the cup of grace
might be filled with your hopes,
    send us out to bring the last
    home to your kingdom,
where they will be first in your joy.

And when all time has ended
and the whole family of God
is gathered around your Table,
we will join our voices together,
praising you forever:
God in Community, Holy in One. Amen.

Pentecost 19/Trinity 18/Proper 21/Ordinary Time 26
Exodus 17:1-7; Psalm 78:1-4, 12-16
Philippians 2:1-13; Matthew 21:23-32

Call to worship
Becoming a baby,
Christ transformed all of us into his sisters and brothers.
Telling us stories we had forgotten,
God helps us to walk the paths of discipleship.
Becoming foolish in the world's eyes,
the Spirit teaches us all we need to find our way into the kingdom.

Prayer of the Day
When we think your job
is to listen to our petty quarrels,
you lean over,
put your finger to our lips,

whispering,
'let me tell you a story.'
Rock Splitter,
we worship you.

When we want to ask you
all sorts of questions,
and demand to see
your background check,
you put your arms around us,
    gently saying,
    'i want you to meet
    some friends of mine.'
Self Emptier:
we follow you.

When we are burned out
by our chronic anger,
when our throats are parched
by our litany of laments,
you take us by the hand,
    inviting,
    'let's go get a cold drink
    down at Rock's cafe.'
Sharing Spirit,
we adore you.

God in Community, Holy in One,
you are God, to whom we pray, as Jesus teaches,
Our Father . . .

Call to Reconciliation
All too often, we tell God we will do better, and be better, and then just
go on living the same way we always have. Let this be the moment
when we tell our God of our failures and faithlessness, so we can go
forth to work in that kingdom of grace and hope. Join me as we pray,

Unison Prayer of Confession
   **We would want to be fountains of hope for others, God of glory,
but people find only hardened hearts. We would like to be
transformed people, but our stubborn pride prevents us from
bending a knee to you. We long to stand with those who are in
need, but our selfishness keeps our backs rigid with judgment.**
   **Forgive us, God who came down to us. Humble us, that we
might be true servants to the broken and lost. Split open our**

235

frozen hearts, that compassion might flow freely to those who are hurting. Fill our minds with the presence of your Spirit, that we might learn how to follow Jesus Christ, our Lord and Savior, into that kingdom of grace and hope.

Silence is kept

Assurance of Pardon
This is the good news: in Christ, God's plan for salvation was accomplished. You are forgiven, you are made new.
We will complete God's joy, by sharing compassion, forgiveness, hope, with everyone we meet. Thanks be to God. Amen.

Great Prayer of Thanksgiving
May the God who comes in humility be with you!
And also with you!
Beloved, lift your hardened hearts to God.
**We offer them to the One who will split them open
so grace can flow into the world.**
Children of God, sing to the One who turned the world upside down.
We open our mouths, praising God who shows us the way.

Streams of water flowed forth
when you split open chaos,
God of Wonder.
    Rivers divided to create valleys and hills,
    the sun became the beacon for each day,
    the moon and stars our night lights.
You breathed your children to life,
and longed to hold us in your lap,
    telling us stories of your goodness.
But while we told you
we would always do your will,
    we went running off to join
    with sin and death
    in their quarrels with you.
You sent the prophets
to remind us of all
we had known and heard,
    but we mocked them,
    not letting them sway us.
Then you sent Jesus
to be the One
to work out our salvation.

So, with those who sing your praise,
and those who complain bitterly,
with those who wandered in the wilderness,
and those who stand in places of worship,
we lift our voices in wonder to you:

Holy, holy, holy are you, Transforming God.
All creation flows toward your heart.
Hosanna in the highest!

Blessed is the One who stands with those who have nothing.
Hosanna in the highest!

Holy are you, God of Imagination,
and blessed is Jesus Christ, our Lord.
He put on humility's garb,
   so we might be clothed
   in the garments of grace;
he lowered himself
to walk the world with us,
   so we might be lifted
   from the depths of sin;
he suffered the death
of a common criminal,
   so we might receive
   the extraordinary gift of life
      forever with you.

As we remember his willingness to give up glory,
as we celebrate his resurrection giving us hope,
we tell of that mystery we call faith:

Christ emptied himself on the cross,
   that we might be filled with life;
Christ was called forth from the tomb,
   that we might confess him the Risen One;
Christ will come again, calling us by name,
   that God's joy be made complete.

Pour out your Spirit,
Nourishing God,
upon this Table of joy
and those who gather around it.
As you transform the simple gifts

of the bread and the cup
into grace beyond all imagining,
    may we be changed
    into fellow servants
    with Jesus Christ our Brother,
people willing to offer ourselves
in service and humility
    to those who have been
    defeated by the world.

And when all time has ended,
and we are at home with you forever,
we will gather around the Lamb's Table,
joining our hands, hearts, and voices
in never-ending praise to you,
God in Community, Holy in One. Amen.

Pentecost 20/Trinity 19/Proper 22/Ordinary Time 27
Exodus 20:1-4, 7-9, 12-20; Psalm 19
Philippians 3:4b-14; Matthew 21:33-46

Call to Worship
From north and south,
from east and west, we come:
God's people called to the Table
where simple grace nourishes us.
From down the street to across town,
from single households to apartment dwellers:
God's people are called to community,
where we live and serve one another.
From every class, every race, every status;
from little ones with sippy cups to elders with overflowing hearts:
God's people are called to witness to God's hope,
to offer peace to a shattered world.

Prayer of the Day
Seeing your children
in bondage and despair,
    you brought them to freedom
    by your compassion and hope.
Longing to create a people
who would care for one another,
    you spoke simple truths
    about integrity and justice.
Fill our worship

238

with sighs more precious than
all we value, Word Speaker.

You came,
not to build a grand scheme,
   but to be our foundation of faith.
You came,
not to choose sides like we do,
   but to be that peace
   which brings us together.
You came,
not worrying about what
lay ahead for you,
   so we could see
   your kingdom prepared for us.
Fill our worship
with your grace more precious
than our deepest fears, Word Bearer.

When we cling
to all which holds us back,
   you empty our arms,
   putting our past in a rummage sale.
When we hesitate
to stand with the lost,
   you nudge us forward
   with the wind of justice.
Fill our worship
with your peace more precious
than the brokenness we grasp, Word of Wisdom

God in Community, Holy in One,
hear the words of our hearts
as we pray as Jesus has taught us, saying,
Our Father . . .

Call to Reconciliation
We are good at rules: making them and then breaking them. Paul
reminds us that, when we gain Christ Jesus as our Lord and Savior, we
receive exactly what we need - forgiveness, grace, hope. Let us confess
our sins to God, that we might know God's healing love for us!

Unison Prayer of Confession
**If we were to name all the gods we have before you, Rock of
Redemption, we would be here a very long time. We elevate**

politicians into saviors, though they are as broken as we are. We misuse your name so much during the day, we have trouble speaking to you in prayer at night. We are so busy, we do not notice how creation witnesses to your goodness and grace.

Forgive us, God our Hope. Help us to let go of what we value most, so we may open our emptiness, our hearts, our lives to the healing and loving presence of Jesus Christ, our Lord and Savior.

Silence is kept

Assurance of Pardon
Persistently, patiently, lovingly, God pours out grace and joy into our lives, healing our brokenness, forgiving our sin.
Loved, we are sent to love;
forgiven, we are freed to forgive;
graced, we can offer our gifts to everyone we meet.
Thanks be to God. Amen.

Great Prayer of Thanksgiving
May the composer of heaven's music be with you!
And also with you!
Beloved, God has created you for faithful living.
We lift our hearts to the One who calls us to be Christ's Body.
People of God, sing to the One who cleanses us of our fears.
We will dance with joy to the Table of peace and hope.

Chaos trembled as you spoke,
not wanting to hear
your goodness breaking it apart,
Rock and Redeemer of all.
 Creation sang oratorios for you,
 while earth drummed out the rhythm.
Each day testified 'God is good';
 each night whispered 'Glory!'
All that was beautiful and true was created for us,
but wanting to know sin and death,
 we exchanged the best you gave to us,
 for the garbage they offered.
Using words and wonder,
silence and speech,
prophets came to call us back
into your covenantal love,
 but we continued to yearn
 for what we could not have.
Finally, you sent your Son,

240

in love, in hope, in peace,
that we would accept him
and the gift of new life.

So, with those who trembled at
the foot of your holy mountain,
and with those who press on to follow you,
we join our voices in praise to you:

Your Word opens our eyes to all creation;
your Word is the sweet taste of joy for hungry hearts;
your Word endures through every trial and triumph.

Blessed is your Word who comes in your name!
Hosanna in the highest!

Holy are you, God of all creation,
and blessed is Jesus Christ, your Son, our Lord.
Yearning for us to know you,
    he came to be your face
    of love and compassion for all.
Hungering for reconciliation
between you and your children,
    he became the broken Bread of Life.
Aching for our release
from the agony of sin and death,
    he suffered on the cross,
    so we might be made well.

As we remember his goodness and gentleness,
as we celebrate his life in us,
we would speak of that mystery we call faith:

Setting aside all he valued,
    Christ became our treasure;
setting aside his own life,
    Christ rescued us from sin;
setting aside our doubts and fears,
    we yearn for Christ's return in glory.

Here at your Table,
Redeemer of all creation,
pour out your Spirit
on the gifts of the bread and the cup,
and on our sisters and brothers in Christ.

241

Your Spirit gives us life,
    so we may go and serve others.
Your Spirit heals our brokenness,
    so we may bring healing to all.
Your Spirit graces us with peace,
    so we may be peacemakers
        for our communities.

And when we stand around your Table,
all hurtful words silenced,
all pain left behind,
with hope and grace our closest friends,
we will join our hearts and voices
with our sisters and brothers
who forever sing of your glory,
God in Community, Holy in One. Amen.

Pentecost 21/Trinity 20/Proper 23/Ordinary Time 28
Exodus 32:1-14; Psalm 106:1-6, 19-23
Philippians 4:1-9; Matthew 22:1-14

Call to Worship
Here in this place, with these people,
we come to worship the living God.
In you, O God, we hope;
in you, Creator of love, we live.
Here in this sacred space, in these very moments,
we are invited to the Table of Joy.
In you, Christ of the Way, we rejoice;
in you, dear Brother, grace is as near as your heart.
Here on this day of gentleness and beauty,
we are filled with the peace of God.
In you, O Spirit, we find our path;
in you, Teacher of hope, we learn to serve.

Prayer of the Day
When we realize how we are
blessed beyond every imagining,
    we can sing of your surprising grace
    and your steadfast presence
        to a world which has grown deaf
        from the noise of empty clichés.

When we remember your love
which has no beginning and no end,
when we stand in grace's sweet waters
swirling around our hearts,
    we can rejoice in your hope
    which sees every person,
        even those we would
        never invite into our circles,
            as your beloved child.

When we remember your call
to treat every single person
with dignity, justice, and hope,
    we can share your peace
    (even when we don't recognize it)
        with a society which believes
        violence is the solution
            to every single problem.

God in Community, Holy in One,
as you live in us,
so we will live for others,
even as we pray as taught by Jesus,
Our Father . . .

Call to Reconciliation
Called to have the same mind as Christ, we often spend too much time thinking about all those ways which then lead us astray. But, if we confess our sins, God will forgive us, and strengthen us to be Christ's sisters and brothers. Join me as we pray together, saying,

Unison Prayer of Confession
You would call us to your feast, Inviting God, but our busy lives keep us from responding. You remember every word we utter, every prayer we whisper, but we forget all the little ways you care for us. You would make your gentleness known through us, but we lash out in anger and fear towards others.

Forgive us, God of all hope, and remember your Servant, Jesus Christ. In him, we can live in your way. Through him, we can learn the dreams you have for us. With him, we can open our arms and embrace all the people we meet.

Silence is kept

243

Assurance of Pardon
As we are forgiven by God, we can begin to reflect on all those ways in which we can live justly, act honorably, love completely. This is indeed good news for us.
At the Wedding Feast, we are fed with grace, and nourished with joy, so we may go and bring hope and peace to everyone we meet. Thanks be to God. Amen.

Great Prayer of Thanksgiving
May the One who works wonders be with you!
And also with you!
People of God, listen to the One who teaches you life.
Unlock our hearts, O God, that we might hear you.
Children of God, you are called to servanthood.
We sing praises to the One who fills us with compassion, so we might know the deepest needs of those around us.

Silencing the noise of chaos,
God of wonder and might,
you created the heavens and earth,
    your steadfast love poured out
        into the oceans brimming with life,
    your joy flowing into every valley of hope.
Your heart melted with love
as you created us in your image,
    so we might live with you
    in that garden of peace.
But we exchanged your dreams
for the seductive lies of death,
    so we might graze in sin's fallow fields.
You longed to bring us back,
making your gentleness known
in prophets throughout the ages.
When we continued to refuse
your invitation to your heart,
you sent Jesus to us,
to round up all of your children
and lead them home to you.

So, with those who stood at the foot of mountains,
and those who continue on the journey,
we lift our hearts and voices,
praising your name forever.

Holy, holy, holy are you, God of peace and justice.
We have heard the good news of Jesus' grace;
    we have seen the service of his followers;
    we have received his hope from surprising people;
    we have learned to trust him in every moment.

Blessed is he who came to make us known to you.
Hosanna in the highest!

We praise your name, Catering God,
remembering your acts of grace.
Loving us with a passion beyond compare,
    Jesus came to fill us with compassion.
Aware of our hunger for hope,
    he feeds us with your steadfast grace.
Understanding death's grip on us,
    he came to defeat it's power,
    that we could live with you forever.

As we rejoice in the feast you provide,
as we remember the sacrifice, death and resurrection of our Lord,
we proclaim that mystery we call faith:

We celebrate the birth of the Babe of Bethlehem;
we remember the life which Jesus led;
we rejoice in Christ's coming to us in glory.

In your gentleness and wonder,
God of all joy,
pour out your Holy Spirit on us,
and the gifts of your Table.
As the bread of life
not only feeds us,
but makes us one as Christ's Body,
    may we bring healing
    to our broken world.
As the cup of grace
not only refreshes us
but unites us in the Spirit of service,
    may we go forth to be
    a river of righteousness
    flowing to those who live
        in oppression and hopelessness.

And when we gather at the Table
you prepare for us in glory,
when we feast with all
our sisters and brothers
from every time and place,
we will join our voices
and praise you forever,
God in Community, Holy in One. Amen.

Pentecost 22/Trinity 21/Proper 24/Ordinary Time 29
Exodus 33:12-23; Psalm 99
1 Thessalonians 1:1-10; Matthew 22:15-22

Call to Worship
Each morning, God's grace awakens us,
each evening, God's peace cradles us.
Compassion is our constant companion,
as we go through work, school, the day.
In every moment, God is present with us;
God whispers words which can change our lives.
Justice is our faithful teacher,
pointing to where we can carry out fairness.
When we find ourselves groping in the shadows,
God's light will provide a way home.
We turn the corner, and hope is waiting for us;
we return home, and find a feast prepared.

Prayer of the Day
Steadfast Hope:
when we want
to make all the rules
so we can win every game,
    you call us to your side,
    put your arm around us
        and whisper, 'play fair!'
When we tremble in fear,
worried that our lives
are about to crash to the bottom,
    you place us in
    the hollow of your heart,
        and give us safety.

Word of Joy:
when we would follow
those who pretend

246

to be our saviors
to achieve their own ends,
    you remind us that we have been chosen
    to be examples of faith to others.
When we would
fill our pockets with
the treasures of temptation,
    you ask us to empty them,
    so we can become
    servants of hope.

Crafter of Faith:
when others judge us on
our backgrounds, education, looks,
    you teach us how
    to treat all people as equal,
        to welcome each person
        as our sister or brother.
When we wonder how
our needs, our hopes, our lives
will be made known to God,
    you mention us, by name,
    in all your prayers.

God in Community, Holy in One,
we know you as
Glory, Grace, Goodness,
and lift our prayer to you, saying,
Our Father . . .

Call to Reconciliation
We know, despite our sincere efforts to live in God's way, that all too
easily we slip off the path to the kingdom. Trusting that God will answer
our prayers and forgive us, let us confess our sins, as we pray together,

Unison Prayer of Confession
Great Lover of Justice, hear our prayers:
called to treat all people equally,
    we take sides and pick favorites;
chosen to be your children,
    we arrogantly assume others are not so honored;
challenged to be examples of faith,
    we reveal our worst natures to our families and friends.

Forgive us, Giver of Rest. Enable us to stop putting you to the test, so we can open our hypocritical hearts to your healing touch of compassion and hope. As Jesus Christ, our Lord and Savior, has given all for us, may we give ourselves to you - confidently, completely, faithfully.

Silence is kept

Assurance of Pardon
Hear the good news: the One who created goodness and beauty is also the One who shows no partiality, but offers grace and peace to all.
God has heard our prayers and done the very thing we asked - forgiven us, healed us, restored us. Thanks be to God. Amen.

Great Prayer of Thanksgiving
May the exalted One be with you!
And also with you!
Open your hearts to the One who knows you by name.
We offer ourselves to the One who is always with us.
Give thanks to God, all of you, in prayer and song, in silence and service.
We sing to the One who calls us to worship.

Holy and Honest God:
in establishing all that is
beautiful and joyful,
    your glory banished chaos
    and your goodness became
        the shawl which warmed all creation.
You shaped humankind in your own image
and called us, each by name, favoring us with your love.
But we could not pass by sin and death
    huddled in the cracks of chaos,
    and turned towards them,
        offering a safe place in our hearts.
Because you would bring your people back to you,
you sent the prophets
to teach us your ways,
    but we thought they were hypocrites,
    speaking insincere words.
So then you sent Jesus
to show us your hope
and to reveal your dreams for us.

Therefore, we join our voices with all your people
in every age, time, and place,

248

who forever sing your praises:

Holy, holy, holy! Lover of Justice and Peace!
All creation sings of your hopes,
echoing your dreams for us.
Hosanna in the highest!

Blessed is the One who comes to reveal your gospel,
by word, by grace, by the Spirit.
Hosanna in the highest!

Great Giver of Joy:
you loved the world so much
that you sent your very heart to us.
We did not welcome him
as your beloved Child,
turning our backs as he approached us.
His faithfulness to your way
revealed our idolatry of the world.
His plain spoken truth showed the lies
we all too easily accepted.
He went to the cross,
defeating sin and death,
so he could claim what is yours
and give us back to you.

As we offer you the gift of our prayers and thanksgiving,
we remember Jesus, your Beloved,
who bequeathed to us that mystery we call faith:

We eat this bread,
remembering his brokenness;
we drink this cup,
to be filled with his grace;
we wait for Jesus to come again,
constantly proclaiming your love for us.

Holy Goodness:
pour out your Spirit of welcome
on the gifts of the cup and the bread.
Simple gifts made sacred by your presence,
may the grain which has
come to us from many fields
strengthen your people to go out
and serve in many neighborhoods.

249

May the cup which has been filled
by the fruit of many vines
    nourish us with faith and hope
    so our hearts will overflow with grace
    to those who thirst for your presence.

And when your people
have been gathered together
from every corner of creation,
we will know one another by name,
lifting our voices to you,
God in Community, Holy in One,
seated upon the praises of our hearts. Amen.

Pentecost 23/Trinity 22/Proper 25/Ordinary Time 30
Deuteronomy 34:1-12; Psalm 90:1-6, 13-17
1 Thessalonians 2:1-8; Matthew 22:34-46

Call to Worship
We are invited to share in Christ's ministry of compassion.
We will widen our hearts so we might cradle the lost.
We are challenged to learn more about God each day.
We will open our minds so we might discern God's dreams for us.
We are summoned to let the Spirit be planted within us.
We will deepen our souls so we might grow in love.

Prayer of the Day
Every generation has found
its home in you,
God our provider,
and discovered that every moment
spent in your holy presence
lasts beyond all imaginable time.
You watch over us in the night,
cradling us in your arms
as tenderly as a nurse
cares for her children,
and her neighbor's.

Full of wisdom,
Imagination of Creation,
you humbled yourself
that we might learn
to love those
who have been swept aside

by a callous and cruel world.
Witness to God's grace,
you call us to act
in ways of love of peace
to all we meet in this life.

In the fresh breeze
on a summer's day;
in the leaves dancing
across autumn's lawns;
in the crisp, new snowfall
crunching beneath our feet;
in the new life
flowering in the spring:
from everlasting to everlasting
you proclaim God's grace to us,
Spirit of Life.

God in Community, Holy in One,
continue to be the dwelling place
of our minds, our hearts, our souls,
even as we pray as we have been taught,
Our Father . . .

Call to Reconciliation

We have been entrusted with the message of the gospel, but all too often
act as if the memos from sin and death have more influence in our lives.
Let us confess our sins, so we might know God's great love for us.

Unison Prayer of Confession

**As you know, God our healer, we stand on the edge of your
promises and hopes, yet cannot seem to let ourselves cross over
into the life you intend for us. We seek praise from our families,
yet are unable to tell them how much we love them; we care more
about our needs and desires, than for the struggles of our
neighbors; we think more about the trash we read and see than
focusing on the Spirit of wisdom.**

**Forgive us, Everlasting God. Renew our lives with your grace;
restore our hopes with your vision of tomorrow; refresh our spirits
with your joy which comes to us new in each moment in the gift of
your Child, Jesus Christ, our Lord and Savior.**

Silence is kept.

251

Assurance of Pardon
This moment, this morning, this day, and in all the days to come, God's compassion and hope fill our lives. What joyous good news!
Our hope is not in vain. God forgives our sins, and is the dwelling place for all people. Thanks be to God. Amen.

Great Prayer of Thanksgiving
May the God of compassion be with you!
And also with you!
Each morning, God feeds us with steadfast love.
Each day, our hearts are filled with God's call to serve.
Children of God, sing your praises to God all our days.
We lift our joy to the One who is the dwelling place of all generations.

Refusing to let chaos
become our dwelling place,
God of the ages,
you called forth creation.
Whether in the blink of an eye,
or in moments spanning thousands of years,
deep valleys of hope were carved,
carpeted with grace renewed each morning.
You created humankind in your image,
knowing us face to face in love.
But we turned our gaze
towards that land of temptation,
chasing the false dreams offered by death.
Caring so deeply for us,
you sent prophets to call us home,
but their words withered in our hearts.
So you sent Jesus to bring
the message of good news,
and to lead us to
the promised land of eternal life.

Therefore, with those filled with the spirit of wisdom,
and those who were full of themselves,
with saints and sinners, prophets and pharisees,
we sing of your everlasting joy:

Holy, holy, holy, God our dwelling place.
You satisfy us with your love each morning,
you comfort us in your grace each night.

Blessed is the One who comes calling us to love:
   to love you without reservation,
   to love others without expectation,
   to love ourselves without self-condemnation.
Hosanna in the highest!

Holy are you, God our Peace,
and blessed is Jesus Christ, our Way of life.
Mindful of your hopes for us,
he came, so we might
discover you in our neighbor.
Soul of your soul,
he came, so we might
overflow with your grace.
Loving us more than himself,
he came, to defeat sin
and destroy death's grip on us,
so we might spend eternity
embraced in your life.

With remembrance of his life,
in the joy of the resurrection,
in anticipation of his return,
we proclaim that mystery we call faith:

Christ came, that we might know God's love;
Christ died, that our souls might be healed;
Christ will come again, that our hearts will be united with God's.

Pour out your Spirit of wisdom
on the gifts of this Table,
and on those who prepare to feast
on your bounty of grace.
As the bread fills us
with your love and hope,
we would go out to love
our neighbors with hearts
shaped by your joy.
As the cup refreshes
our minds and souls,
we would show our
everlasting love for you,
by serving the lost and forgotten
with lives molded by your compassion.

And when time, which was first wound at creation
has ticked its last moment,
when friends, neighbors, and strangers
are gathered around your Table,
we will join our voices singing your praises,
God in Community, Holy in One. Amen.

Charge
And now go forth,
to love God with all your heart, your mind, your soul:
with passion, with prayer, with intelligence;
to love your neighbor:
with forgiveness, with service, with love;
and to love yourself:
with hope, with joy, with peace.

Pentecost 24/Trinity 23/Proper 26/Ordinary Time 31
Joshua 3:7-17; Psalm 107:1-7, 33-37
1 Thessalonians 2:9-13; Matthew 23:1-12

Call to Worship
When we stand at the edge of fear and worry,
God invites us to step into the waters of faith and trust.
When we stand at the edge of the world's pain and need,
Jesus invites us to step into the land of humble service.
When we stand at the edge of our hunger and thirst:
the Spirit invites us to sit at the Table of grace.

Prayer of the Day
God-ever-with-us:
you draw us near to your heart,
so that, cradled in compassion,
    we might see the brokenness
    of all who are around us.

Teacher-beside-us:
you draw us near to yourself,
so that, by following you,
    we may discover the deep joy
    of serving the broken of the world.

Spirit-within-us:
you draw near to us with your peace,
so that, reconciled and restored to God,

254

we may be the healers
of a world shattered by despair.

God in Community, Holy in One,
as we draw near to you in this time,
we lift the prayer you have taught us, saying,
Our Father . . .

Call to Reconciliation

We know how easy it is to do exactly the opposite of what we learn from
our Teacher, Jesus. So, let us draw near to our God, for in confessing
our failures, we will discover the grace and mercy God has in store for
us. Join me as we pray, saying,

Unison Prayer of Confession

**When we come to the edge of your holiness, Constant Love, we
know how we have not lived as your children. We dam up for
ourselves your rivers of love, while the lives around us turn into
deserts of loneliness. All too quickly, we place our feet on the
quicksand of fear, not wanting to step across to your faith. We tie
up our angers and worries and burden our families and friends with
them.**

**Forgive us, Listener to our hearts. By your patient grace, give us
more time to practice our calling to discipleship, so we might learn
all we need to live as sisters and brothers of our Lord and Savior,
Jesus Christ.**

Silence is kept

Assurance of Pardon

This is the good news: God hears you, God forgives you, God is with you
as you journey into that land called Promise.
**Let the redeemed of God say: this is indeed great news! Accepting
God's word of joy and grace, we will live as God's children in all
the days to come. Amen.**

Great Prayer of Thanksgiving

May creation's Guide be with you!
And also with you!
Weary wanderers, offer your hearts to God;
who takes us by the heart to lead us back to faithfulness.
Do not hesitate, but step forward in joy into God's life.
We will do so, singing to the One who immerses us in hope.

Standing at the edge of chaos,
you cried out, Exalted Love,
    and all creation sprang forth
    from the goodness of your Word.
Grace overflowed from your heart,
    racing through the deep valleys of hope.
Creating us in your image,
breathing life and joy into us,
you drew us near to you,
so we could live in joy with you.
    But we chose to wander
    through the deserts of death,
    paving over Eden's promise with our sins.
Like a parent with her children,
you encouraged us to change,
sending the prophets to bring us back.
    But we would not listen,
    tying up the burdens of our lives
    and putting them on their backs.
Then you chose to send Jesus,
to be the Witness to your
never-ending love for us.

So, with wanderers and witnesses,
with those who cried out to you,
and those who followed your promises,
we lift our songs with our sisters and brothers
who forever sing your praises:

Holy, holy, holy Lord, God of steadfast love.
All creation overflows with your grace and mercy.
Hosanna in the highest!

Blessed is the One who calls us to humble service.
Hosanna in the highest!

You are holy, Creation's Guide,
and Jesus Christ, your Son, our Teacher,
is the One who comes to redeem us.
Seeing the barren lives we lead,
he came to till the rich soil
of your hopes and dreams,
    that it might bear life in us.
Watching us stumble
along sin's side streets,

256

he takes us by the hand,
　　to lead us to your feast.
When we would allow our pride
to become entangled with death,
he gently takes this burden
from off our shoulders,
　　carrying it to the cross,
　　and leaving it behind in the tomb,
as he strides forth into
the promised land of resurrection.

As we remember his words and witness,
as we would let his teachings shape our lives,
we speak of what we believe, great is the mystery of faith:

Christ was sent to be God's Witness.
Christ is our Teacher of the Way.
Christ will come to welcome us home.

Pour out your Holy Spirit
upon those gathered
from every corner of the world,
and upon the gifts of the bread and the cup.
As your grace fills us,
may we go forth,
in thanksgiving and humility,
　　to feed the hungry around us.
As the cup turns our parched souls
into fountains of hope,
may we overflow in service
　　to those who wander in our midst.

Then, when all time has ended,
when the truly humble find themselves
seated beside you at the Table in eternity,
we will join our voices in thanksgiving to
God in Community, Holy in One. Amen.

All Saints' Day
Revelation 7:9-17; Psalm 34:1-10, 22
1 John 3:1-3; Matthew 5:1-12

Call to Worship
At all times we are called
to bless God's name.

257

Our lips drench with praises,
our hearts exult in God.
The proud will bend knees in worship,
the humble will lift glad songs.
We are free from our fears,
we have searched for God and been found.
Our faces glow with thanksgiving,
our spirits overflow with grace.
God has wiped away our tears,
God has fed us from the storehouses of hope.

Prayer of the Day
They are gathered around you,
God of Forever and Ever.
Some are well known, like
Martin Luther,
Mother Theresa,
C. S. Lewis,
Helen Keller,
and so many more.
Some have been forgotten, like
Agnes and Cadoc,
Tuda, Mary of Egypt,
and Ebba,
while others have days named after them.

But many are ordinary folk,
such as the teacher from second grade
who guided our fingers under the words;
the nurse in the hospital
who held our hand while blood was taken;
the coach who trusted us with the ball,
not the end of the bench.

There is an old man who left retirement behind,
and a barren woman who laughed at your promise;
there are popes, princes, and power-brokers
who are taught heaven's hymns
by the paupers and pretenders;
there are those who moved mountains
and those who murmured in the wilderness;
there are those who founded the church,
and those who floundered on the waves of Galilee.

258

All saints,
just like us,
singing your praise forever and ever,
and we join in their anthem
even as we pray as Jesus has taught us, saying,
Our Father . . .

Call to Reconciliation
When God sets the table of the Lamb, all will be welcome – the young
and the old; those who were faithful, and those who failed; those who
followed Jesus, and those who lost their way. Let us confess to our God
our unsaintly ways, knowing how quick God is to forgive.

Unison Prayer of Confession
We did not listen, when the Teacher spoke, God of sinners.
Rich in pride and arrogance,
   our spirits have no need for a kingdom;
taught to not let anyone see us cry,
   we refuse your comforting arms;
seeing the greedy and self-indulgent have their way,
   we yearn to inherit their hardened hearts;
noticing the hungry standing by the side of the road,
   we make sure we get more than our share
   of the world's resources;
taking note of how the merciful are pushed aside,
   we develop calluses on our souls.

Forgive us, Saint Maker, that we follow the wrong examples and
listen to false teachings. It is the peacemakers who live into your
hope; it is those whose hearts are shaped by yours, who are able to
see you in the poor and broken; it is those who give themselves to
serve others who are your saints, following the example of Jesus
Christ, our Lord, our Savior, our Shepherd, guiding us to the
wellsprings of life.

Silence is kept

Assurance of Pardon
When we seek God, we are found;
when we cry out, we are heard;
when we confess, we are forgiven and made new.
We can taste the yeasty flavor of grace, we can drink the deep wine
of hope, we can find our home in God's heart, receiving mercy and
new life. Thanks be to God. Amen.

259

Great Prayer of Thanksgiving
May the God of saints and sinners be with you.
And also with you.
Join me in glorifying our God.
We offer our hearts as we praise our God.
Let us bless our God at all times.
Songs of thanksgiving will flow from our lips forever.

You stood before chaos, God of all time,
and cried out with a loud voice,
calling all that is good and beautiful into being:
    wiggly worms tilling the rich soil,
    owls watching over the gathering dusk,
    butterflies flittering through gardens.
You created humanity in your image,
the Spirit breathing life into our lungs,
all so we could live with you in creation's wonder.
    But we tasted the tempting goodies of sin,
    and saw all the promises death offered to us,
        and we placed our hopes in them.
Hearing our souls cry out to you,
you sent the prophets to us,
to remind us that we were your children.
    But we continued to fall on our faces,
    worshiping the false gods of hopelessness.
So you sent Jesus to us, to reveal you to us
as the One who will redeem us from ourselves.

We join our voices with those
of every time and place,
joyfully sing with loud voices:

Amen! Blessing and glory and wisdom
and thanksgiving and honor and power and might
be to our God forever and ever! Amen!

Holy are you, God who wipes away all tears,
and blessed is Jesus Christ, the Lamb who is our shepherd.
Rich in your glory and honor,
    he came to bless the poor in spirit;
Word by which creation's life came forth,
    he came to comfort all who stand at gravesides;
exalted by all the choirs of heaven,
    he came to give the meek their heritage;
emptying himself of all he might claim,

he came to feed us with your righteousness;
compassionate beyond all imagination,
    he came to offer mercy to all he encountered;
true Prince of Peace,
    he came to share that gift with God's children;
persecuted for being God's righteousness,
    he came, to bring God's kingdom into our midst;
reviled and crucified on the cross,
    he offers us that resurrection
    which is great in heaven.

Knowing that what we will be has not been revealed
but trusting that we will be like him,
we join all the saints in proclaiming our faith:

Christ died, so we might have life;
Christ arose, so we might have this hope of resurrection;
Christ will be our guide, leading us to the living waters.

See what love God has given us!
Here at the Table where the Feast of Joy
has been prepared for all of God's people,
the Spirit comes upon the gifts of the bread and the cup
and upon all who hunger and thirst for righteousness.
As we eat of this bread, we will taste God's goodness,
going out into the world as God's people,
    to offer shelter to those who sleep on the streets,
    to feed those whose hunger is palpable,
    to speak out for those who endure
        the great ordeal of oppression.
As we drink from the Cup, we will see God's hope,
committing ourselves to serve others
that they might see Christ as he is:
    Healer of the broken,
    Brother of the poor,
    Servant of all who are lost.

And when we gather with those from every nation,
those from all tribes and peoples and languages,
we will fall on our faces worshiping and praising you,
God in Community, Holy in One. Amen.

Pentecost 25/Trinity 24/Proper 27/Ordinary Time 32
Joshua 24:1-3a, 14-25; Psalm 78:1-7
1 Thessalonians 4:13-18; Matthew 25:1-13

Call to Worship
God has gathered us to this place,
where we hear those stories which show us
what the kingdom of God is like.
God summons us to this place,
where we can learn how to serve our God
without reservation, or hesitation.
God will send us from this place,
to tell others of God's hopes and dreams,
so they, too, can choose to follow God.

Prayer of the Day
You do not want us
to be ignorant of your
dreams and hopes for us,
God of holiness,
      so you speak to us in parables,
      hoping we might pay careful attention
            to your words;
you tell us stories about
our grandparents in the faith,
      so we might become mentors
      to our grandchildren, and theirs.
Filling us with the holy oil
of generosity and grace,
      you make us ready to welcome
      Jesus Christ into our lives,
and to open our hearts
to those who are in need.

On this day, we choose to serve you,
God in Community, Holy in One,
even as we pray as Jesus teaches us,
Our Father. . .

Call to Reconciliation
Throughout Scripture's stories and people, God is bluntly honest with us
about hopes, dreams, expectations. If we are to be as honest, we must
stand before God, confessing what we have done and said, as well as
our silences and inactions, so that we might be drenched in God's
healing tears of forgiveness.

Unison Prayer of Confession

262

We have so much trouble putting away our false gods, Patient Storyteller. When we could place our hope in you, we trust platitudes and shaky promises. When we could tell our friends about what you have done in our lives, we become forgetfully silent. When we could make ourselves ready to serve in your kingdom, we find other places to put our time and resources.

Forgive us, Holy Lover, and fill us with your tender mercy. As you whisper to us of your faith in us, may we listen to your transforming grace, so we can follow wholeheartedly Jesus Christ, our Lord and Savior, being faithful in our calling as disciples.

Silence is kept

Assurance of Pardon
Listen, my friends! The good news is that God is in our midst - moving, forgiving, renewing, restoring.
This day, we choose - to live with hope, to share God's grace, to tell of God's goodness in our lives. Thanks be to God. Amen.

Great Prayer of Thanksgiving
May the Lord be with you.
And also with you.
People of God, lift up your hearts.
We lift them to the One whose faithfulness never ends.
People of God, give thanks to the Lord.
We offer our praise and thanks to the One whose love is eternal.

How good and right it is to praise you,
God who gathers us around this Table!
You opened your mouth,
    and creation's glory sprang forth;
you appointed the stars
    to glitter in the night;
you established the waters
    to nourish the earth.
You shaped us in your image,
calling us to be your children,
to live with you in harmony and joy.
    But we chose to serve sin,
    crossing death's river back into chaos,
    our false gods clutched tight to our hearts.
Yet, you did not give up your hopes,
sending us the prophets
to get our attention with words
of challenge, as well as comfort.

When we steadfastly refused
    to let go of our reliance on idols,
you sent Jesus to us,
to die and rise again for us.

Therefore, we join our voices
with those who await in heaven,
as well as witnesses here on earth,
forever singing your joyous praise:

Holy, holy, holy Lord, God of parables and peace.
All creation sings of your glory.
Hosanna in the highest!

Blessed is he who leads us across the waters
    into the kingdom of God.
Hosanna in the highest!

You alone are holy, God of all time,
and blessed is Jesus Christ, our Lord, our Savior.
When we turned our backs on your love,
following the false gods of sin and death,
    you came to us in Jesus, to lead us home.
When we would no longer tilt our heads
in order to listen to your songs,
    your Word of hope walked among us,
    to be your love in our midst.
When we could not shake off
sin's grasp on our souls,
    Jesus reached out, taking our hands,
    showing us what the kingdom truly is.

As we remember his death and resurrection,
we would speak to others of that mystery
we know as faith:

Christ has died;
Christ rose again;
God will bring with him into the kingdom all who have died,
    that we will live forever.

It is at this Table of gentleness
that you pour out your Spirit
upon the cup and the bread,
and on your people you have gathered.

As we leave our false gods behind us,
we open our hands for that Bread
which, broken, can make us whole once more,
    that we might offer our lives for others.
As we would encourage others
who are searching for your presence in their lives,
we drink of the Spirit of Christ,
    that we might serve you
    in both the foolish and the wise.
Nurtured and refreshed,
we no longer can plead ignorance,
but with open eyes and embracing hearts,
we may welcome all you send our way,
    that we might listen to their souls
    even as we tell our stories.

And when we are gathered in your kingdom,
seated at the Table of the Bridegroom,
we will praise you forever and ever,
God in Community, Holy in One. Amen.

Pentecost 26/Trinity 25/Proper 28/Ordinary Time 33
Judges 4:1-7; Psalm 123
1 Thessalonians 5:1-11; Matthew 25:14-30

Call to Worship
This is the Lord's Day, the day of wonder and grace.
This is the day to worship the One who calls us here.
This is the Lord's Day, the day we are given joy and peace.
This is the day promised to us, the day of healing and renewal.
This is the Lord's Day, and it has come just in time!
This is the day we gather with hope, with faith, with love!

Prayer of the Day
Now,
in the silence,
when we struggle
to control our lives,
    may we, once again,
    empty ourselves of our pride and fears,
        to be filled with your hope.

Now,
in these moments,

when we cannot let go
of our worries and doubts,
　　　may we, once again,
　　　open our hands to hold your faith.

Now,
on this day
which is only and always
your gift to us,
　　　may we, once again,
　　　live into your kingdom.

Now, as we lift our hearts to you,
God in Community, Holy in One,
we once again pray as we have been taught saying,
Our Father . . .

Call to Reconciliation

When we remember all the mistakes we have made, all the careless words we have spoken, all the contempt we have given to those around us, we have trouble looking God in the eye. But God gazes at us with mercy and love, waiting to forgive us, even as we hesitate to speak of the brokenness of our hearts. Join me as we pray, saying,

Unison Prayer of Confession

Again we must confess, Master of the Universe, our struggles to be faithful disciples. Entrusted with all your gifts, we become fearful once again of misusing them, missing the chance to be a blessing to others. Invited to dance in the light of your love, we stand against the wall once again, keeping company with our old friend, sin. Called to be emptied for those who struggle in life, we fill ourselves once again, with scorn for the poor choices they make.

Have mercy, Journeying God, have mercy on us. Once again, open our eyes to your kingdom in our midst, so we might discover that your day of hope and grace has already come in Jesus Christ, our Lord and Savior.

Silence is kept

Assurance of Pardon

This is the good news: God intends for us to find life, to embrace hope, to receive forgiveness through Jesus Christ, our Servant.

The end of our journey is not rejection and emptiness, but the fullness of grace and hope in our God. Thanks be to God, we are forgiven. Amen.

Great Prayer of Thanksgiving
May the God of promises be with you!
And also with you!
Rejoice in the One who surprises us, people of God.
We lift our hearts to God who brings us salvation.
Children of God, join in glad song to the Giver of mercy.
Our voices join in praise to the God of love and hope.

When you had
had enough of chaos,
Covenant God,
you cried out in love
    and creation burst forth in joy.
You shaped us into images of you,
that we might be children of light,
    but we were drawn into
    the shadowy life of sin and death.
You sent people like Deborah
to call us back into your light,
    but we were scornful of their words.
Then you sent Jesus,
who came to fill us
with your love and hope.

So, with servants and sinners,
with judges and those who endure injustice,
we lift our voices, our hearts, our eyes
singing to the One enthroned on our hopes:

Holy, holy, holy, God enthroned in the heavens.
All creation looks to the hand of the Creator.
Hosanna in the highest!

Blessed is the One who walked the dusty paths of earth.
Hosanna in the highest!

Holy are you, God of Wonder,
And blessed is Jesus Christ, our Lord.
When the proud hurled
their contempt at him,
    he humbly knelt to serve them.

When friends urged him
to play it safe,
    he crawled out onto faith's limb,
    trusting it would hold him.
When death wrapped him
in its cold shadows,
    he burst forth into the light
    of resurrection joy,
that we might live
in the kingdom with you.

As we remember his mercy and hope,
as we celebrate the feast he has prepared,
we speak of that mystery we call faith:

Christ died on that day of shadowed hearts;
Christ rose on that day when death was surprised by love;
Christ will come to us on that day of light and love.

Your grace showers down
upon the seeds you have planted,
your hope warms the harvest
planted in our hearts.
As the Spirit gathers your gifts
and prepares them for your Table,
make us ready to receive them
with joy and gratitude.
As you send us forth
to serve your people,
    may our faith and love
        be transformed into winter coats,
        we can give to the homeless;
    may our hope become
        the meals we fix for the hungry.

And when that long-awaited Day comes,
when all times and seasons have ended,
we will gather at your Feast,
joining our voices with our sisters and brothers,
as we sing to you through all eternity,
God in Community, Holy in One. Amen.

Reign of Christ/Christ the King
Ezekiel 34:11-16, 20-24; Psalm 100
Ephesians 1:15-23; Matthew 25:31-46

Call to Worship
We come, for God gathers us here,
with that community called faith:
where the hungry are served first,
where the thirsty drink life's water.
We come, for God welcomes us here
into that home called grace:
where the naked are clothed in robes of hope;
where the stranger is embraced as the long-lost prodigal.
We come, for God reunites us here,
sisters and brothers in that family called love:
where the imprisoned model justice,
where the sick are cradled in God's peace.

Prayer of the Day
Searcher of the scattered:
where the bullies and biased
have gorged themselves
at cruelty's banquet,
    you will serve them justice
    for dessert.
Where the wounded
are turned away by indifference,
    you will bandage them
    in the swaddling clothes of hope.
Where the hungry
press their foreheads
against the windows
at Chez Plenty,
    you will open wide the doors,
    having made reservations
        for us all.

Bringer of justice:
when we would push
the outsiders further away,
    you pull them closer to your heart.
When we would shove
the next-to-nothings aside
to get to the front of the line,
    you pick them up
    to keep them next to you.

When we scatter our gifts,
throwing them away on foolishness,
 you gather them up
 and give them back to us
  saying, 'here, try again.'

Spirit of common sense:
as soon as
we wander into
the shadows of selfishness,
 you open the eyes
 of our hearts
  so we can see
  that place called home.
As soon as
we think we can find you
only in the rich and powerful,
 you humble us
 with the grace of Jesus.

God in Community, Holy in One,
gather us into your presence,
even as we pray as we are taught,
Our Father . . .

Call to Reconciliation

They are the promises stretching back into the dim recesses of time, yet
as new as this very moment. When we lose our way, God searches for
us until we are found. When we hurt others, God brings healing to all.
When we sin, God forgives us. Let us hold these promises close to our
hearts, as we confess those things we try to hide.

Unison Prayer of Confession

**We stock the food pantries, but brush aside those who hunger
for friendship. We give our hand-me-downs away, but overlook
those whose hopes have been stripped away. We glad-hand those
just like us, but turn a deaf ear to our neighbors who 'talk funny.'**

**Forgive us, Hope of the ages. You persistently search for us in
the side streets of the world, gathering us up and bringing us home,
so we may be drenched in the waters of your bottomless pool of
forgiveness, watched over by your Child, Jesus Christ, our Lord
and Savior.**

Silence is kept

270

Assurance of Pardon
God searches for the lost,
and finds us;
God invites the hungry to the table,
and feeds us;
God sends Jesus,
and frees us from death's prison;
God forgives all who sin,
and heals us with mercy and grace. Thanks be to God. Amen.

Great Prayer of Thanksgiving
May the Searching God be with you!
And also with you!
God gathers us up and brings us to this place.
We lift our hearts to the One who leads
us into the kingdom of peace and healing.
God collects us in the power of the Word,
whoever and wherever we are.
We will sing glad songs that remind us
that we are never, never! lost.

Out of the clouds and
thick darkness of chaos,
you spoke the creative Word,
God of wonder,
and creation burst forth in joy.
    Rivers and streams teemed with life,
    mountains were topped with snow,
    green pastures cradled all your creatures.
You shaped us in your image,
calling us to be your people,
living in your steadfast love.
    But your hopes for us
    were pushed aside by
    the seductions of sin and death,
        and we followed them into
        the uninhabited wastes of the world.
Because we were your priceless treasure,
you continued to search for us,
sending prophets in all the ages.
    When we continued to worship
    all the false powers,
you sent Jesus to gather us up
and lead us back to you.

271

So, with skeptics and scoffers,
with the faithful and the followers,
we join our voices together
singing our praise to you:

Holy, holy, holy, Shepherd of all creation.
Heaven and earth sing choruses of praise:
Hosanna in the highest!

Blessed is the One who comes to gather us back to you.
Hosanna in the highest!

Holy are you, Steadfast Love,
and blessed is Jesus Christ, your Child, our Savior.
Seeing us stripped naked by sin,
    he forages through glory's closets
    to clothe us in your joy and hope.
Setting aside his power,
    he would turn oppression inside-out,
    and injustice upside down
        to create the kingdom
        where the least are the most valued.
Searching for us,
    he left no stone unturned,
    even going through death and hell
    in order to find us
    and bring us back to you.

As we remember his service to all,
as we celebrate the promised resurrection,
we sing of that mystery we call faith:

Christ has died, bringing us your justice;
Christ is risen, offering us your love.
Christ will gather us up to lead us home.

In this sanctuary of your heart,
with sisters and brothers in the faith,
we pray that you pour out your Spirit
upon us and the gifts of the Table.
It is here all our scattered lives
are woven together in that tapestry
called the kingdom,
where we are strengthened
by the Bread of life,

272

so we may fortify all those
who have been exhausted by life;
where we are handed
the Cup of hope,
to quench the thirst
of all who wander through
the deserts of injustice.

And when you have gathered
all the nations into your joy,
when the losers and the lurkers,
the weak and the wise ones
are seated around your Table,
we will join our voices
with all of creation,
forever singing anthems of praise,
God in Community, Holy in One. Amen.

Thanksgiving Day
Deuteronomy 8:7-18; Psalm 65
2 Corinthians 9:6-15; Luke 17:11-19

Call to Worship
Our help is in the name of the Lord who made heaven and earth.
We glorify our God with songs of thanksgiving and joy.
God has done great things for us, filling us with grace.
God fed our ancestors in the wilderness, God clothes us with hope.
We will offer our hearts to God, always saying,
'Thank you!' to the One who loves us.
We will sing our praises, shouting of God's presence in our lives.

Prayer of the Day
Hot showers in the morning
and cool breezes in the evening;
work that provides for our families,
and abundance that makes us generous;
silly jokes told by third graders,
and the silent tears of a grandmother
lost in her childhood forever.
What blessings are ours, Creation's Joy!

Teachers who patiently help us with our math,
and mentors who keep us on the right paths;
friends who shovel snow off sidewalks before we waken,
and employers whose hearts are greater than their profits;

piano teachers who smile at our repeated mistakes,
    coaches who teach us (one more time)
    how to curl the ball into the goal.
What blessings are ours, Servant of Joy!

Dogs who bounce us awake early in the day
    and cats who lullaby us to sleep at night;
grandfathers who teach us how to whittle
    and sisters who give up a date to baby sit;
little boys who always forget to wipe their mouths
    and folks who always remember to say 'thank you.'
What blessings are ours, Joyous Spirit!

God in Community, Holy in One,
thanksgiving is in every word we speak,
even as we pray as Jesus taught us, saying,
Our Father . . .

Call to Reconciliation

We wonder what's for lunch, we worry about work tomorrow, we fret about the test that is coming up. So much worry, so much time wasted over things we cannot control. The One who showers earth with rain, who places the stars in the autumn sky, is the same One who wraps mercy tight around you, who feeds us on healing and hope. Let us confess how our worries keep us from trusting the God who hears us and restores us to new life. Please join me as we pray,

Unison Prayer of Confession

Because we live in this modern, tech-driven, twittering age, we often forget what you have done for us, God of every blessing. We pat ourselves on the back for our ability to learn new computer skills, but have forgotten that life is more than a machine. We have more than we could ever use yet, like squirrels, store up more and more. Our faith is often pushed to the back of the closet, to make room for all the fears we wear so easily.

Forgive us, Restorer of life. As you clothe us with your grace and mercy, may we share with those who have so little. As our hearts overflow with your love and wonder, may we offer them as gifts to everyone we meet. As you feed us with your joy and hope, may we welcome to the Table all those whose lives are filled with tears and pain. As we gather with family and friends during this season, may we continue to give thanks for the gift of Jesus Christ, our Lord and Savior.

Silence is kept

274

Assurance of Pardon
This is the good news: as God dresses creation in wonder, so you will be
clothed in grace; as God pours out abundance upon the earth, so you
will be blessed with peace and joy.
**We don't say it often enough, but thanks be to God for healing, for
life, for wonder, for mercy. We are blessed, for we are forgiven.
Amen.**

Great Prayer of Thanksgiving
The Lord of blessings be with you.
The Lord be with you, also.
Be glad and rejoice, God's people,
lifting your hearts to the Restorer of lives.
We offer them to the God who clothes us in grace.
People of God, come to the Table where you shall eat and be satisfied.
With shouts of joy, we gather to praise the name of God!

Your mouth was filled with laughter,
God of our every moment,
    as you sang creation into being.
The heavens rang with shouts of joy,
    as fruit-bearing trees sprang up,
    as green pastures rippled with wonder.
Crafted in your image, you would
satisfy us with the bounty of grace,
    but we chose the destroyer, death,
    hanging out with the life-cutter, sin.
Prophets and psalmists were sent by you,
longing to restore us to your side,
    but we put their words to shame.
So that everyone might be saved,
Jesus came to be with us,
herald of your grace,
bringer of your truth.

With those who lifted thanks by crossed rivers,
with those who offered gratitude for simple gifts,
we join our voice in praising your name:

**Holy, holy, holy! God of wonder and delight.
All creation is filled with your joy.
Hosanna in the highest!**

275

Blessed is the One who comes to clothe us in grace.
Hosanna in the highest!

Holy are you, Restorer of broken lives,
and blessed is Jesus Christ, Mediator of salvation.
Seeing the nightmare of our lives,
    he became one of us, so we
    might see the dreams you have for us.
Knowing how our hearts overflowed
with fear, bitterness, and worries,
    he came with peace and comfort.
Teaching that the body is more than sin,
that life is more than death,
    he became our ransom on the cross,
    our salvation by rising from the grave.

As we give thanks for his life and death,
as we shout with joy for his resurrection,
we speak of that mystery we call faith:

Christ died, the righteousness for all.
Christ rose, the resurrection for all.
Christ will return, the fulfillment for all.

Pour out your Spirit
doing great things with the bread and the cup.
Empty, we will be filled
with the plenty of your grace,
the broken bread strengthening us
    so we might bring healing to a world
    shattered by violence and despair.
Longing for hope, we shall be satisfied
with the cup of blessing and hope,
our lives overflowing
with your love and compassion,
    pouring ourselves out for the
    poor and marginalized of our time.

And when all our worrying hours have ended,
when we are clothed in your mercy forever,
we will gather with our sisters and brothers,
our mouths filled with laughter,
our hearts echoing glad songs of joy to you,
God in Community, Holy in One. Amen.

Reformation Sunday

Jeremiah 31:31-34; Psalm 46;
Romans 3:19-28; John 8:31-36

Call to Worship

Be still!
We come to quiet ourselves in this haven of holiness.
Be still and know . . .
we come to discern the Word that can set us free.
Be still and know that God is . . .
our Hope, our Help, our Refuge, and our Redeemer.

Prayer of the Day

You break the cycle of wars,
    so we may be enriched by your peace;
you shatter the grip of violence,
    so we may be freed from our fears;
you plant your words of hope deep within us,
carving on our hearts:
    'you are mine.'
You give us the word we need,
    so we might live in your grace,
God of Creation.

You freely become one of us,
    so we could be liberated
    from our addiction to sin;
you take us by the hand
    to lead us out of our doubts;
you give us the words we need,
    so we can continue to share
    your good news of life,
Friend of the needy.

You pull us to safety
    when sin's waters swirl around our feet;
you surround us with serenity
    when doubts rattle our souls;
you give us words we need,
    whenever we wander
    onto the paths of trouble,
Spirit of Holiness.

God in Community, Holy in One,
you give us the words we need
to pray as Jesus has taught us, saying,
Our Father . . .

Call to Reconciliation

We can no longer flatter ourselves about how good we are. We do not
need to make grandstand plays to get God's attention. We only need to
confess our lives, as God makes good on the promises of grace and
mercy. Join me as we ask God to reform us into God's children, praying
together,

Unison Prayer of Confession

**Heart of the Covenant: we have known your hopes for us, and
disappointed every one of them; we have heard your words of
faithfulness, and forgotten every one of them; we have seen your
dreams for us, and turned every one of them into ashes.**

**Forgive us, Hope's Heart. Silence every blustering word, so we
may hear your mercy; still every feeble attempt to justify ourselves,
so we may be made right with you; melt every frozen heart, so we
might be drenched in your river of joy. May Jesus Christ continue to
live in us, so we might be free to live forever with you.**

Silence is kept

Assurance of Pardon

Be still and know the good news: God has not forsaken nor forgotten us,
but redeems us.
**Why should we be afraid? God is in our midst - forgiving, restoring,
sending. Thanks be to God! Amen.**

Great Prayer of Thanksgiving

May God our refuge be with you!
And also with you!
People of God, lift your hearts to the One who created you.
We offer them to God, who writes words of hope upon our hearts.
God's children, come to the Table of grace.
We will feast on the wonders of the God who loves us.

You took creation by the hand,
leading it out of chaos,
   as the first morning dawned,
   mountains trembling in the mist,
   running rivers which gladdened your heart,

278

God of our lives.
You created all this for us,
giving us peace and righteousness
to be our playmates in the fields of grace.
    But when we beheld the works
    of temptation, sin, and death,
        we became their slaves,
            writing their lies on our hearts.
Longing to be our God,
you sent the prophets
to call us to be your people,
    but we refused to listen.
Finally, Jesus came, the bearer
of truth and freedom for all.

With those whose hearts are broken,
and those who long for your days of peace,
we sing our thanksgiving to you:

Holy, holy, holy are you, God who forms our hearts.
All creation finds refuge in your tender care.
Hosanna in the highest!

Blessed is the One who sets us free by your truth!
Hosanna in the highest!

You are our strength, God of holiness,
and Jesus Christ is your Son, our Savior.
When our lives are filled with despair,
    he is our Hope;
when we are lost and cannot find our way,
    he is our Help;
when the world closes its doors and heart to us,
    he is our Refuge;
when sin and death hunger for us,
    he is our Redeemer,
present with us in this life
and in the one to come.

As we remember his life, death, and resurrection,
as he continues to re-form us into your people,
we proclaim that mystery called faith:

Christ died, his heart broken for us;
Christ is risen, resurrection written upon his heart;
Christ is ever with us, in every moment, until your days come.

Pour out your Spirit
upon the gifts of this Table,
and upon the gathered people
who seek to be your faithful people.
The bread symbolizes that Life, though given,
which can reshape our brokenness into
the peace which a warring world needs,
the hope which can bring healing to others.
The cup which is filled with your grace
can strengthen us to be new people,
who go forth to speak truth to power,
who bring freedom to all the oppressed.

And when your days of eternity finally come,
when we gather as your children around
the Table of wonder and life,
we will sing your praises forever and ever,
God in Community, Holy in One. Amen.

Summertime liturgy
A liturgy centered around the idea of 'play'

Call to Worship
Give thanks to God!
We thank God for the joy of jumping rope,
and the laughter in playing leapfrog!
Give thanks to God at all times!
We thank God, for the cool waters of a pool
on a hot summer day, and the way the water
surprises us when we first jump in!
Give thanks to God at all times and for all things!
We thank God for fireflies
making our nights brighter,
and for butterflies
which tickle us awake after a nap!

Prayer of the Day
Every day is a day of wonder,
Imaginative God:
filled with empty refrigerator boxes
which can take us to the moon,

and long afternoon ball games
where the score is never kept.
You rub the sleep from our eyes
so we can see you at play,
in the children on the corner,
in the teenager balancing on a skateboard,
in the older couple waltzing the night away.

From the cereal which crackles us awake
to the cat stalking the sunbeam;
from the baby just discovering her toes
to the old man who puts sacks of tomatoes
on his neighbors' porches;
from the hummingbird drinking nectar
to the dog grabbing the hose out of our hand:
every day is a day of laughter,
Smiling Christ.

We hear the squeals of the children
jumping on the trampoline,
and the sweet sound of a ball
off the bat down at the playground.
We hope no one sees us
as we try out the chalk hopscotch
drawn on the sidewalk,
and we smile from our porch
at the father putting training wheels
on his daughter's bike.
We put yesterday out with the garbage
and wait for the delivery of tomorrow,
and we discover that
every day is a day of joy,
Spirit of Gladness.

Help us to play with you
each and every day,
God in Community, Holy in One,
even as we pray to you,
each and every day, saying,
Our Father . . .

Call to Reconciliation
In a world which teaches us to always be serious, God gives us children
who love to make silly faces. In a world which searches for perfection,
God hands us the platypus. Let us speak to God of our reluctance to be

281

playful, so we can be embraced by the One who was willing to put aside divine dignity to become one of us.

Unison Prayer of Confession

God of Wonder, you take mud, add a little water, and make mountains, while we worry about getting our clothes dirty playing with our kids. You nourish your creation with refreshing rain, and we grumble about having left our umbrellas at home. You grin at the sight of squirrels chasing one another up and down trees, and we can't remember the last time we laid on the grass, trying to guess what the clouds up in the sky look like.

Forgive us, Imagination behind Creation, for forgetting to enjoy, to laugh, to play. We take ourselves so seriously, that we lose sight of the wonder of your gifts. We think you want us to be so serious all the time, that we have forgotten the joy, the laughter, the delight which Jesus Christ, our Lord and Savior, brought into our lives.

Silence is kept

Assurance of Pardon

The good news is this: imagination and play go hand in hand with prayer, with service, with worship, with life.
God takes delight when we take the time to enjoy and play in the good creation offered to us. Amen.

Holy Humor Sunday

(Some churches follow the ancient practice of seeing the Sunday after Easter as a time to celebrate the great joke God played on sin and death by raising Jesus from the dead. Bright Sunday, Holy Humor/Hilarity Sunday are occasions for people to join in praise, laughter, and good humor in celebrating God's love for us, with the choir singing silly songs, the members dressing outlandishly, the preacher serving as a stand-up comic. Not for every congregation, but it does sometimes turn 'low Sunday' into a Sunday with a new glow. Feel free to adapt to meet your congregation's needs)

Suggested texts: Genesis 18:9-15; 21:1-6; Psalm 150
1st Corinthians 1:18-31; John 20:19-29

Call to Laughter

One: This is the time to rejoice!
All: **What better time than now!**

One: This is the day to laugh:
　　What did the cabbage pastor say to the people?
Pastor: *Lettuce pray!*
One: How many music directors does
it take to change a light bulb?
Choir: *No one knows, because no one ever watches the director!*
One: How many Presbyterians does it take to change a light bulb?
All: **Change? Presbyterians don't believe in change!**
One: What's the greatest joke ever?
All: **The one God played on death on Easter morning!**

Prayer of the Day
You smiled and the sun burst
through the shadows of chaos;
　　you chuckled,
　　and the platypus splashed
　　in creation's fountain;
you laughed,
　　and all that is good and beautiful
　　was given shape by you,
Imaginative God.

Snickering at the feeble attempts
of the evil one,
　　you showed us
　　how to resist temptation;
giggling at sin's desperate desire
to hold on to us,
　　you released us by your love;
howling with laughter
at death's foolish belief
that the tomb could hold you,
　　you burst forth into the kingdom
　　as the stars pealed with joy,
Laughing Jesus.

As you fill us with new life,
　　may we delight in sharing it with others;
as you tell us the good news
which can never be taken from us,
　　may we rejoice in offering it
　　to the broken, the sad, the lonely;
as you tickle us with grace,
　　may we give it away

with laughter on our lips
and joy in our hearts,
Spirit of Easter.

God in Community, Holy in One,
our hearts overflow with wonder
as we lift the prayer Jesus has taught us,
Our Father . . .

Call to Reconciliation
None of us likes to look foolish, but which is sillier? Chasing after the
world and all its gaudy trinkets which flatter our souls, or being a 'fool
for Christ', imitating him in service to others, offering ourselves in love
and joy to the world? Let us admit to God the foolish choices we
make each and every day, as we pray, saying,

Unison Prayer of Confession
**You know better than we do, Amused God, what important
people we believe we are. Believing we have to be serious all the
time, we miss out on the joy of your creation. Choosing to feast on
the pain of the world, we skip the picnic offered in paradise.
Clinging to the despair which is our best friend, we ignore Jesus.
who can bring us home to your heart.**

**Forgive us, Heart of Joy, and make us open to the startling, and
upside-down, ways in which you work. Fill us with Easter's
laughter; fill us with your healing joy; fill us with the love poured
into us through Jesus Christ, our Lord and Savior.**

Silence is kept

Assurance of Pardon:
The Gospels tell us over and over again of the joy which comes to us
through Christ. When Jesus was around, lives were changed, the sick
were healed, the sorrowful began to laugh with joy. The good news is
that this joy is now given to us.
**Through the Holy Spirit, we are gifted with joy. We are sent forth to
bring good news to the oppressed, to bring healing to the broken,
to anoint everyone with the oil of gladness. Thanks be to God, we
are forgiven. Amen.**

Great Prayer of Thanksgiving
May the God of love and ladybugs be with you.
And also with you.
Children of joy, open your hearts to God.
May God fill them with laughter, wonder, and joy.

284

Heirs of pleasure and grace, sing songs of thanksgiving.
**With banjos and bagpipes, with snare drums and saxophones,
we will praise the One who is filled with laughter.**

Into the face of cantankerous chaos, God of guffaws,
    you sprayed the waters of creation
    from the Spirit's seltzer bottle.
You laughed out loud as you shaped
    the platypus, ostrich, and catfish;
you whistled a merry tune for the songbirds
    to learn for that first Easter morning.
Your joy, your laughter, your heart-full spirit
overflowed in creating from your vibrant imagination,
    comets racing through the night skies,
    hummingbirds darting so fast we cannot see them.
All was created for those shaped in your image,
    but in our self-styled wisdom, we thought sin and death
    to contain all the knowledge we would ever need.
Prophets came, the greasepaint of judgment dabbed on,
willing to speak of your hopes with what
seemed to be foolish phrases,
    so we continued to learn from the sequels
    penned anew each day by sin.
Finally, when it seemed our lives were too barren,
you sent Jesus, to break into our midst
with laughter on his lips and joy in his heart.

So with those far-too-wise of every time,
with those who take themselves too seriously in every place,
we sing our glad songs to you:

**Holy, holy, holy, are you, Creator of dandelions
    and komodo dragons.
All creation joins in the laughter caused by the empty tomb.
Hosanna in the highest!**

**Blessed is the who comes carrying the joy of the Lord in his heart.
Hosanna in the highest!**

You are God, with a great sense of humor,
and your Son, Jesus Christ, blesses us with joy.
Taking off the resplendent robes of glory,
he put on the frizzy, rainbow hair,
the polka-dotted, baggy pants with the red suspenders,

willing to play the clown, tramping through our world
with that pair of shoes five times the size of his feet.
He was willing to look foolish,
    so we might wise up to our sinful ways;
he was willing to be laughed at,
    so we might hear your serious words;
he was willing to walk through death's wide open doors,
    so we might find the exit marked 'salvation.'

As we remember how foolish he seemed to be to many,
as we celebrate this joyous season of resurrection,
we join with those in the glad song of faith:

Christ died, foolish in the eyes of the world;
Christ was raised, wise enough to trust you;
Christ will return, gathering us up and taking us to you,
    laughing all the way.

Is there anything more foolish than to believe
we can be made whole by Jesus' brokenness?
Is there anything that looks more silly
than to think a common cup can hold grace?
Yet, in the wisdom of your foolish ways,
    the ordinary, the everyday become the sacred,
    the barren can bring forth new life,
we can reach out a finger and be grasped
by that love which will never let go.
So, as your Spirit is poured out
on the gifts of the Table,
as the bread and cup renew your foolish people,
send us forth to be bearers of joy to the broken,
    to be the bread of hope to all who hunger,
    to be laughter and light to all who live in shadows.

Then, when the evening of history comes,
and we awaken on the first day of eternity,
we will join our sisters and brothers around your Table,
celebrating your love, your salvation, your wonder
with clanging cymbals, steel drums, and didgeridoos,
a mighty chorus of praise to you,
God in Community, Holy in One. Amen.

Thom M. Shuman is a graduate of Eckerd College (St. Petersburg, FL) and Union Presbyterian Seminary (Richmond, VA). Currently active in transitional/interim ministry, he has served churches in Oklahoma, Virginia, and Ohio. His liturgies, poems, and prayers are used by congregations all over the world, and by individuals for personal devotions.

His Advent devotional books *The Jesse Tree* (2005) and *Gobsmacked* (2011) have been published by Wild Goose Publications/The Iona Community (www.ionabooks.com), as well as his wedding liturgy, *Now Come Two Hearts.* He is also a contributor to the Iona Community's Resource books *Candles & Conifers, Hay & Stardust, Fire and Bread, Bare Feet and Buttercups,* and *Acorns and Archangels,* as well as *Going Home Another Way: Daily Readings and Resources for Christmastide, Gathered and Scattered: Readings and Meditations from the Iona Community, 50 New Prayers From The Iona Community,* and *Like Leaves to the Sun, Prayers from the Iona Community.*

Piano Man, poems and prayers for RCL Year A is a companion book to *Playing Hopscotch in Heaven.*

Dusty the Church Dog and other sightings of the gospel has recently been published.

Bearers of Grace and Justice, Lectionary Liturgies for Year C as well as a companion book, *Pirate Jesus, Poems and Prayers for Lectionary Year C* were published in 2012 and available at www.amazon.com

He blogs at www.occasionalsightings.blogspot.com
www.prayersfortoday.blogspot.com
www.lectionaryliturgies.blogspot.com

Cover photo: Thom M. Shuman

Printed in Great Britain
by Amazon.co.uk, Ltd.,
Marston Gate.